Successful Strategies
for Computer-Assisted
Reporting   Cove

Successful Strategies for Computer-Assisted Reporting

Bruce Garrison
University of Miami

LEA **LAWRENCE ERLBAUM ASSOCIATES, PUBLISHERS**
1996 Mahwah, New Jersey

Lawrence Erlbaum Associates, Inc., Publishers
10 Industrial Avenue
Mahwah, NJ 07430

Cover design by Evelyn Amaya

Library of Congress Cataloging-in-Publication Data

Garrison, Bruce, 1950-
    Successful Strategies for Computer-Assisted Reporting
/ Bruce Garrison.
        p. cm.
    Includes bibliographical references and index.
    ISBN 0-8058-2224-0. — ISBN 0-8058-2225-9 (pbk.)
    1. Journalism—Data processing. 2. Reporters and reporting. I. Title.
    PN4784.E5G38 1996
    070.4'0285—dc20   96-16112
                                                 CIP

Books published by Lawrence Erlbaum Associates are printed on acid-free paper, and their bindings are chosen for strength and durability.

Printed in the United States of America
10 9 8 7 6 5 4 3 2 1

Contents

Preface

Nora Paul, one of the nation's leading authorities about how journalists use one major form of computer-assisted reporting—online information resources—to enhance their information-gathering role in society, has stated that computers have already had a long-term impact on journalism. "Computers have been changing the way journalists do their jobs ever since newsrooms threw out their old Royale typewriters and switched to cold type production systems" (Paul, 1994, p. 2).

Computers have truly changed the landscape of both gathering and disseminating information worldwide. As journalists move quickly toward the 21st century and, perhaps, a new era of electronic journalism, there need to be resources for these individuals and their news organizations to understand the newest and most successful computer-based strategies and applications of the newest tools of journalism. This book was written to serve that purpose. This book is designed to show both professional journalists and students which of the newest of personal computing tools are being used by the nation's leading news organizations and top individual journalists and how they are being used for some of the best recent computer-assisted reporting (CAR) projects. It also should serve as a reminder that CAR is not the end product, nor the sole basis for stories and projects. It is a relatively new and powerful tool to supplement other, more traditional forms of reporting.

"I consider the computer a tool for journalism, a tool to do better journalism. I think it starts us at a higher level and allows us to do better journalism, but it is no substitute for it," noted Brant Houston (Houston, 1995b), executive director of the National Institute for Computer-Assisted Reporting (NICAR).

Some news organizations have been slow to begin use of CAR and they have their reasons: money, newsgathering philosophy, skills, tools. The reasons take various forms of these primary barriers. The *Philadelphia Inquirer,* historically a leader in using computers in certain project-oriented newsgathering situations over the past 30 years, was one newspaper that did not move rapidly into CAR.

"Until a few years ago, *The Philadelphia Inquirer* was not a leader in the CAR field. As an institution, we had not decided to pursue it," noted *Inquirer* Editor Maxwell King (1995). "In 1992 and 1993, a core group of reporters and editors at the paper decided this was a foolish position, and the group convinced top management to make CAR a higher priority. Simply stated, making CAR a higher priority meant providing modest expense money for software and hardware, and providing some staff time at the reporting and editing levels to support computer-assisted projects. As a result, we have achieved a few visible successes and, much more importantly, built in capacity that informs and improves stories every week," King stated, pointing to his newspaper's assessments of the Philadelphia school system, public opinion surveys of residents' attitudes, and development of a newsroom database containing information about the city.

"The real value of CAR, once it is established in a news organization, is what it can contribute, day in and day out, to the depth, substance, and explanatory capacity of the newspaper," King added.

The title of this book reflects its orientation. Many journalists unfamiliar with CAR need guidance through presentation of successful models and approaches to using computers for more than writing and editing. Journalists—all communicators, in fact—are more wedded to their computing tools than ever before. Formerly, this "marriage" was a result of the requirements of production and distribution. Computers continue to be extremely important to typesetting and layout as well as circulation of the final product in printed or electronic formats. In recent years, in a movement paralleling the advent of power personal computing and advances in portable personal computing in the late 1980s and early 1990s, computers have taken on new and dominating roles in the process of news analysis, newsgathering, news processing, and more. Today's forward-thinking journalists often seek guidance about what they can do to strengthen their ability to be society's information processors and managers. Without them, as NICAR's Houston (1994) once said, journalists will be trying to play catch up with their readers.

My first book about computers and journalism, *Computer-Assisted Reporting* (Garrison, 1995), focused on the *computerization* of newsgathering. It serves as a solid introduction to the subject. That book described CAR at its development in 1994 and 1995 by presenting a description of online- and database-oriented reporting and newsgathering and, ultimately, a model for computer literacy in the newsroom. It demonstrated methods for reporters to get more from their computers—such as data retrieval, data analysis, information storage, and dissemination of that information in both processed and unprocessed forms.

This book is related, yet different. As a follow-up to *Computer-Assisted Reporting*, this book focuses on how *successful* journalists are using computers—their basic strategies—and the primary tools they are using in their daily and special projects journalism.

Two of the primary sources of the information for this book are major national CAR studies of daily newspapers conducted at the University of Miami in early 1994 and early 1995. Some of the data from 1994 are included in *Computer-Assisted Reporting*, but in a minor descriptive manner. These studies are part of a CAR research and training project directed by me at the University of Miami. This book describes the analysis and results of the two studies in more detail.

Another important source for the book was a series of interviews with many of the nation's leading CAR specialists. These individuals were asked to discuss their approaches to CAR, their views about CAR itself, and their concerns. Interviews were conducted in person and by telephone in many cases, but in the spirit of computer-assisted information gathering and new technology, an additional number of interviews were also conducted using exchanges of electronic mail on the Internet.

In describing CAR strategies, the book also provides several current examples of stories used for successful database- and online-oriented news assignments. These examples are part of a series of case studies incorporated throughout the book. It is believed that the additional depth of description and the presentation of portions of stories themselves in appendices will help readers to understand the complete process involving CAR-oriented journalism.

Compared to *Computer-Assisted Reporting*, this book uses more analytical detail to discuss the extent of computer use in newsrooms, computer training, CAR projects, CAR in daily reporting, the hardware and software most commonly used, levels and types of online services used in news research, and portable hardware and software. The book concludes with my assessment of the effects of personal computing in the newsroom and the future of personal computer applications in the newsroom.

The book is directed to working professionals. There are thousands of professional journalists actively seeking successful strategies to manage their changing workplace. This book can assist in their on-the-job education—retraining, perhaps—of the uses of computers in journalism. The book should also be valuable to academics and graduate students in the print and broadcast/cable industries and the news–editorial journalism and other mass communication academic fields, although there may be some general public interest in the subject as well.

This book will have value to undergraduate students and could perhaps be used as a supplement to advanced reporting classes focusing on such diverse topics as investigative reporting, online journalism, the Internet, or projects reporting. It can be used as a supplementary textbook in some seminars or research courses. This book assumes readers have successfully completed most newswriting and reporting courses, graduate communication courses, or have worked professionally as journalists. The need for books about new technology remains strong in the profession and in news–editorial journalism and mass communication education. As communication programs at many universities and colleges and professional continuing education opportunities continue to grow, demand for up-to-date information about technology and innovation remains.

Computer-based training is in high demand among communication professionals. Investigative Reporters and Editors (IRE) and NICAR have experienced growth in the numbers of journalists seeking training at their national conferences since 1993. The first three IRE and NICAR conferences in Raleigh in 1993, San Jose in 1994, and Cleveland in 1995, each had large numbers of participants. Some of the best-attended sessions at the three latest national conventions of the Association for Education in Journalism and Mass Communication in Washington, Atlanta, and Kansas City were devoted to research and teaching that involved computers and journalism.

As with *Computer-Assisted Reporting,* the focus of this book is mainly on print news media. However, individuals from broadcast/cable news reporting backgrounds and interests can find the information presented in this book useful as well. The use of CAR in nonprint news media is expanding each year.

It is necessary in a world of multiple platforms and operating systems to discuss the general approach of this book. The overwhelming majority of business and personal computer users in the United States are PC users. Thus, much of this book addresses use of personal computers operating with Windows 95 and its subsequent versions, Windows 3.x, and DOS. This is not to say that Macintosh and Macintosh operating systems are ignored. However, it is the intention of the book to focus mostly on the systems and tools in use by the large majority of news organizations, businesses in general, and individuals involved in computer-assisted reporting.

The approach to the book assumes a minimal familiarity with computers, but no advanced knowledge of operation of computers. Advanced applications or terminology are explained and defined for readers. The book is highly descriptive in nature. There is quantitative content in the form of tables and graphs to supplement the textual material.

For more information about CAR research at the University of Miami, visit the UM World Wide Web site at <http://www.miami.edu/com/car/index.html>.

Readers are encouraged to comment on the content of the book. The author may be reached at <bgarriso@umiami.ir.miami.edu> or at 73507,160 on CompuServe.

ACKNOWLEDGMENTS

It is impossible to produce a book, any book, without assistance. It is, like many activities in journalism, a collaborative effort. There was a group of individuals and organizations that assisted me in this project and I want to thank them.

I needed time and numerous resources to work on this project. For their contributions in providing these to me, I express gratitude to Edward Pfister, dean of the School of Communication, and to Paul Steinle, former director of the Journalism and Photography Program, at the University of Miami. Dean Pfister has been particularly helpful in funding the national CAR surveys and providing the many necessary computer hardware and software resources.

My colleagues at the University of Miami have been important in the completion of this project. I express thanks to my friend Raymonde Bilger once again. As a long-time administrator at the University of Miami, she understands the value of personal computers and she continues to share my passion for personal computing and for its benefits in the workplace as well as in the home.

The support of the leadership of the IRE and NICAR was necessary for the national newspaper surveys reported in this book. My special thanks go to my colleagues Rosemary Armao, executive director of IRE, and Brant Houston, managing director of NICAR, for their endorsements and encouragement.

Appreciation is also expressed to *World Communication*, which permitted use of parts of an essay review of Windows 95 I wrote.

There are a number of professional journalists that I would like to mention in gratitude for their time and assistance or their encouragement. Special thanks are extended to the following:

Whit Andrews, freelance reporter and formerly of *The Times* of Munster, Indiana; Neill Borowski, *Philadelphia Inquirer*; Alletta Bowers, *Philadelphia Inquirer*; Dan Browning, *Saint Paul Pioneer Press*; Bill Casey, *The Washington Post*; Rose Ciotta, *Buffalo News*; Jon Craig, Syracuse *Herald American/Herald-Journal*; James Derk,

Evansville Courier; Steve Doig, *The Miami Herald;* Elisabeth Donovan, *The Miami Herald;* Chris Feola, Waterbury, Connecticut, *Republican-American;* Barbara Hijek, Tampa bureau, *St. Petersburg Times;* Erik Kriss, Albany bureau, Syracuse *Herald American/Herald-Journal;* Sperry Krueger, Raleigh *News & Observer;* Jack Lail, *Knoxville News-Sentinel;* Jeff Leen, *The Miami Herald;* Mary Kate Leming, *Palm Beach Post;* Rick Linsk, *Asbury Park Press;* Penny Loeb, *U.S. News & World Report;* Beth Marchak, Washington bureau of the *Cleveland Plain Dealer;* Paul McElroy, Seattle *Post-Intelligencer;* Bill Miller, *Battle Creek Enquirer;* Carol Napolitano, *Omaha World-Herald;* Heather Newman, *Nashville Tennessean;* Paul Overberg, *USA Today;* Doug Podolsky, *U.S. News & World Report;* Neil Reisner, National Institute for Computer-Assisted Reporting and formerly of *The Bergen Record,* Hackensack, New Jersey; Ray Robinson, *The Press of Atlantic City;* Tom Torok, *Philadelphia Inquirer;* and Michael G. Walsh, *Muskegon Chronicle.*

In the academic world, I especially would like to extend my gratitude to Kathleen Hansen, University of Minnesota; Tom Johnson, San Francisco State University; Philip Meyer, University of North Carolina; Randy Reddick, Texas Tech University; and Michael Salwen, University of Miami. Their comments added depth and dimensions to the book that otherwise would be missing.

In the computer industry, I would also like to thank Bea McKinney, vice president of askSam Systems, for providing information about her company's database products. I also thank Tracy Van Hoof at Microsoft Corporation for providing information about her company's various products.

A special cheer of gratitude goes to Elizabeth Glenday, my research assistant for 3 years who graduated in 1996 to begin her own professional career. In addition to tolerating my many idiosyncrasies, she was an extremely reliable, productive, and thoughtful colleague. She did much to help the preparation of the manuscript and her help is acknowledged.

Finally, this book is dedicated to my parents, Melford L. and Gertrude C. Garrison, in gratitude for their lifetime of support and interest in my career. It really did make a difference . . . and it still does.

—*Bruce Garrison*

1

Successful Use of Computers in Newsgathering and Processing

Many journalists are just beginning to use computers as tools for newsgathering. How can it be done successfully? Many novices may not be quite sure how the process works. To get things going, let's consider the successful nature of these two case studies.

CASE STUDY: THE PHILADELPHIA PUBLIC SCHOOLS

Philadelphia's public schools had been judged by experts in 1994 to be failing their educational mission. But why? And how? Reporters and editors for *The Philadelphia Inquirer* sought to find answers and explanations. The newspaper's team of reporters began by collecting information about the performance of the schools in the School District of Philadelphia. Staff writers Thomas Ferrick, Jr., Craig R. McCoy, Neill A. Borowski, and Dale Mezzacappa found data and other forms of information in a variety of places. They obtained much of the data from the school district itself, but also found useful information from the Pennsylvania Department of Education, the University of Pittsburgh, the U.S. Department of Education, and a variety of other public sources. Led by Borowski, who is director of computer-assisted reporting (CAR) for his newspaper, the group worked with sociologists and other experts from Temple University to analyze data and uncover trends about the schools and their students.

Borowski (personal communication, November 17, 1995) explained:

Tom Ferrick has been with *The Inquirer* for years. In the early 1980s or late 1970s, he did, in essence, a project just like this with yellow sheets of legal paper and a calculator, books, and he did it by hand. This time, we did it with a computer. The other interesting thing is that the city school district, through the 1980s, would not release a lot of data. They did not want to have their successes or their failures measured in any way. Very, very little data trickled out. They got a new assistant superintendent who came down here with a different attitude. The old administration of the school district left. And they said, "We'll give you whatever you want. We can't give you student-level stuff, but we'll give you different groups and things like that."

The result of the investigation and analysis was an eight-page special section entitled, "A District in Distress," that told readers how the problems causing the district's poor performance in educating children were only becoming worse. It described how the city had two school systems: a mostly minority public system and a mostly White private and parochial school system. The reporters pointed to the facts: Students could not complete basic tasks, such as math and reading, and their academic performance was poor when compared to other schools on standardized tests. Other data showed that students did not attend school and that they did not graduate. The schools were unsafe and remained deeply segregated. The district, overall, was not doing well compared to nearby suburban districts. The project also demonstrated how the public school system was growing after a period of decline, but that funding was dropping. In the end, the team of reporters and editors found some cause for hope in a new superintendent, a court order to restructure the district, and a public focused on seeking change in the schools.

Most of the special section consisted of tables, color graphs, and charts of data gleaned from the vast collection of sources located by *The Inquirer* staff. These summaries were supplemented with short stories to explain data and photographs to illustrate points. The help the journalists got from experts paid off, Borowski stated:

We got all the data. We got someone from Temple University who was doing research. And we came out with the project. In a newspaper like *The Inquirer* that puts a premium on investigations and nailing the bad guys, it was embarrassing that the school district sent over its congratulations on this project and said they loved it. We wondered: "What did we do wrong?" We didn't do anything wrong. It was probably the best summary of school district statistics in a decade, something, I'm told, the school board can use as a reference.

The project won a National Education Writers award and other recognition from journalists.

CASE STUDY: ST. PETERSBURG/ TAMPA AREA TRAFFIC ACCIDENTS

Residents of Pinellas and Hillsborough counties in Florida know the safe and not-so-safe places to drive in their area. They have this information because a reporting team from the *St. Petersburg Times* analyzed the most dangerous intersections in the two most populated counties in the Tampa Bay area. The newspaper recently published a major Sunday edition project that outlined the most likely places that drivers would be involved in injury-causing traffic accidents on local and state roads. The newspaper placed the project's lead story on page 1 and included a location map displaying the most likely sites for serious accidents. Inside the front section, the report filled two additional open pages that contained:

- The main story jump from page 1.
- Three sidebars that focused on how to solve traffic problems.
- Sidebar describing a peculiar intersection of odd angles and blind spots.
- Two color aerial photographs of intersections with text labels to explain problem spots.
- Three informational graphics displaying how to improve intersections and how to change traffic signals.
- Project "How we did it" research methods box and an "About the reporter" background box.

Reporter Bill Adair, who covers the transportation beat for his newspaper, was assisted by researchers Simon Lau and Connie Humburg. The stories Adair produced were based on his review and computer-assisted analysis of more than 10,000 injury accidents in the two counties. Adair, 32, was a veteran of 5 years at *The Times* at the time he worked on the project. Adair and his research team acquired the data from the St. Petersburg and Tampa police departments. The statistics did not include expressways or interstate highways, nor did it include noninjury accidents because both types of accidents are reported differently by different law enforcement agencies.

Such a project is typical of how news organizations are using computers to enhance reporting in the last half of this decade. The project required some computing power combined with more traditional reporting such as interviews and public document searches and reviews. The result was a powerful and simple-to-understand report about traffic safety in the region. It demonstrates what contemporary news reporting should be—an effort taking advantage of all the best information gathering and analyzing tools at hand.

SUCCESS IN MERGING JOURNALISM WITH COMPUTING

The process of using computers for newsgathering is dynamic. Computers are now inescapable in newsrooms because of their widespread use in writing, editing, typesetting, page layout, graphics creation and editing, and picture editing. But computers are quickly becoming tools for information gathering as well and the discussion ahead focuses on ways to succeed in the endeavor. Computing is the new direction of newsgathering in the last half of the 1990s and in the decade to follow.

Computers have become a part of every journalist's professional life. Anyone regularly visiting one variation of the virtual newsroom of the late 1990s, also known as list serves on the Internet, knows the scenario: A new personal computer software product comes onto the market. Soon, the questions begin to appear about the product:

- "Is it a good upgrade? Is it better than . . .?"
- "How much is it? Should we buy it? Is the cost worthwhile?"
- "What new data massaging tricks can be done with it?"

A similar process occurs when significant new computer hardware appears. The questions are equally predictable:

- "Is the extra speed worth the cost?"
- "Is the additional storage (or memory) worth it?"

The exchanges and comments continue for days and even weeks on some of these more technically oriented lists. There is seldom early agreement among the list subscribers, but eventually some sort of consensus is reached. At some point in the evolution, individuals, as well as the journalists responsible for their news organization's CAR policies, make decisions about the requisite hardware and software and about the databases and online services needed for their work to succeed.

This is the highly informal and often casual nature of the serious computer-oriented journalist. This is how he or she builds the requisite toolbox for computer-assisted reporting, commonly known today as CAR. Most journalists, however, just use what is available to them. They are not that interested in the details of software and hardware, as long as they get the newsgathering job done.

More and more, it seems, journalists interested in CAR are required to use products someone else chose because of corporate decisions about hardware and software that relate more to what is happening in corporate America than in newsrooms. These journalists often must use what is provided, regardless of its suitability and the needs of the project. In some cases, journalists have had to acquire their own computing tools at their own expense.

The hardware and software selection process is highly influenced by the computer industry. Like many other businesses, the computer industry puts its products on retail store shelves and news organizations choose from them. Seldom, if ever, do news organizations create their own tools for CAR. When Microsoft, Computer Associates, Lotus, Packard Bell, Dell, Toshiba, IBM, U.S. Robotics, Hayes, or another computer company introduces a new product, it becomes a potential tool for journalists engaged in this relatively new form of newsgathering that uses computers to collect and often analyze the information. With few, if any, useful tools being developed in the news or information industries, there are not many alternatives. All of these decisions are helping to define success in CAR.

- What tools do journalists use for newsgathering today?
- How are these tools applied to news reporting?
- How do they learn to use them?
- What strategies work best?
- What stories have the most impact and public service?

These are some of the looming questions about uses of computers in journalism. In many ways, they are not very different from the questions asked about computer use in other professional environments. Newsgatherers are adapting the new technology of personal computers to their work. No longer do editors and reporters ask whether computers should be used in reporting. For most news organizations, the decision has been made. Computers do improve reporting and newsgathering. But the next generation of questions centers on different issues, such as those related to the most successful strategies for application of computers in newsgathering. What has the industry learned so far? The discussion in this and the following chapters provides an answer to that question.

Defining Computer-Assisted Reporting

Computer-assisted reporting is the use of computers to locate information and retrieve it from other computers and their databases as well as the use of computers to analyze original databases and databases obtained from other sources for news stories (Garrison, 1995). Simply put, CAR is gradually bringing the methodologies and strategies of the social sciences into the newsroom. CAR is sometimes also termed *computer-assisted journalism*, but regardless of its label, CAR is a process of newsgathering that employs the data processing power of both personal and mainframe computers. Thus, computer-assisted reporting is the term widely used to refer to the use of computers:

- To connect with other computers (online).
- To create databases or import existing databases, for analysis of data (databases).

"Computer-assisted reporting techniques allow you to take national datasets, localize them, or replicate stories that other people have done on similar topics with similar data across the country," observed Penny Loeb (1995), a CAR specialist for *U.S. News & World Report.* "Like social scientists, we can now build upon what has been done somewhere else and each time we will expand the knowledge . . . . The data are much easier to get now and the technology is much easier and cheaper, so we have a responsibility to our profession and to the public to always try to do our work better."

The Philadelphia Inquirer Editor Maxwell King (1995) believes CAR offers enhancement of existing strengths to newspaper newsrooms. "CAR is essentially the marriage of technical capacity with the sort of analysis and synthesis that marks strong enterprise and explanatory journalism. We should . . . aggressively pursue a strong position in this field. It is likely, if we are successful, to reward us with a special expertise, strength, and position in the markets we serve."

Rosemary Armao, IRE executive director, and Brant Houston, NICAR managing director (1995), have cautioned journalists about the limits of CAR: "[R]emember what computer-assisted reporting is not. It is not a different species of investigative reporting. It does not replace intelligence and good instincts. It does not end the need to develop sources or to coax people into revealing interviews. It does not reap award-winning stories out of raw numbers alone. But in the hands of careful and thoughtful reporters, computers can elevate their skills" (p. v).

Computers Have Changed Newsroom Work

The appearance of computers in newsrooms has forever changed the work of journalists just as computers have affected just about every other business and industry worldwide. With dedicated word-processing systems that were introduced to newsrooms in the early

1970s and uses of mainframe computers for polls and surveys and a few other unique investigative projects in the 1960s, journalists have had a generation of reporting, writing, and editing with computers available to them. Yet the finer applications of personal computers—introduced to the mass market in the early 1980s—have remained new to many newsrooms, even in the late 1990s, nearly two decades after the development of the first PCs. Today, the impact of computing is unmistakable and widely recognized.

"Journalism . . . has been transformed by computerization," Cole C. Campbell (1995, p. A2), editor of *The Virginian-Pilot* in Norfolk, recently wrote to his readers. "Computers now shape nearly every aspect of our work."

Utica College Journalism Professor Cecilia Friend feels the use of computers for news reporting is significant: "Computer access to government data and the technique of using a computer program to analyze them is a dramatic breakthrough for journalists—not only because it allows reporters to dig deeper and faster than before and find patterns not possible by traditional means, but because the tool can be value-neutral," Friend (1994, pp. 69–70) stated. "It can replace anecdotal tales or interpreted statistics with the record itself. By dealing directly with the unadorned numbers of a database, reporters can bypass the spin doctors and vested interests who previously not only supplied the information but selected and interpreted it as well."

The handful of journalists who have been working with computers for reporting spent the first half of this decade creating and fine-tuning strategies for use of their new tools in the newsroom. The process is still evolving. How can computer hardware and software be used to enhance news reporting? How can a news organization do a better job in covering its community empowered with CAR resources? These are some of the questions posed and, hopefully, answered in the following pages.

MAKING COMPUTERS WORK FOR JOURNALISTS

The whole point of CAR is to make computers work more efficiently for journalists. If computers did not make work faster, easier, better organized, more systematic, more thorough, or more analytical than that done by hand, there would be no need for computers as news reporting tools. There would be no need for CAR. But like their academic cousins, social scientists who have used computers to study human behavior since the machines were first developed,

> ## TWO APPROACHES FOR A CAR START-UP
>
> Philip Meyer, journalism professor at the University of North Carolina and the individual widely identified as the "father" of CAR, says there are two approaches to begin using CAR in newspaper, magazine, and broadcast newsrooms.
>
> "There are two basic models. One is the expert model where you assemble a team that will do all of the computer work. The other model is that every journalist should learn some minimal level of understanding. That's the Raleigh (*News & Observer*) model," Meyer (personal communication, September 23, 1995) explained.
>
> "Most people are adopting the first model because most journalists don't want to take the time, or don't have the aptitude, for learning it so they are leaving it for experts. I prefer the Raleigh model. But there are two problems with it. There aren't enough computer-smart people to go around. Or, if there are, newspapers don't pay enough to get them, especially with the cost pressures these days."

journalists know computers do make a difference in bringing new meaning to information.

Research that has focused on how computers are used in newsrooms has long documented that most journalists are painfully slow in adjusting to new technology. Early studies that looked at the newly appearing computers in newsrooms in the early and mid-1970s found reluctance among journalists to use computers for basic tasks such as writing stories and editing (Garrison, 1979, 1982, 1983). Almost a generation of journalists later, research continues to show reluctance on the part of many journalists to take computers beyond writing and editing functions. "So far, it seems, reporters use computers as new tools to do the same old journalism," concluded Carleton University researcher Catherine McKercher (1995, p. 228). "The fact that reporters are aware of the wider possibilities inherent in computer-assisted reporting but have not made significant steps toward upgrading their own skills suggests that training may be an issue. But it also suggests that many reporters feel they do their jobs well enough with their existing skills, or believe they have little incentive, time, or energy to spend on acquiring new ones."

CAR can be successful at any level. From college campuses, weekly newsrooms, and small-market television stations to the major dailies and news magazines to broadcast networks, CAR has been shown to be effective in improving how a community is covered. Most authorities argue, or preach, some critics say, that CAR works just as effectively and inexpensively for small news organizations as it does for the major dailies and networks (Feola, 1993).

The Philadelphia Inquirer, highlighted in one of the case studies at the beginning of this chapter, has a two-person team of CAR experts—reporters Neill Borowski and Tom Torok—who lead the newspaper's movement toward complete integration into the newsroom. The newspaper planned in 1995 and 1996 for a completely renovated newsroom with a PC network to replace an aging Atex editorial system, but it had to make the transition slowly until all reporters and editors are able to work with networked Pentium-grade PCs capable of running spreadsheets, Internet browsers, and other more common CAR tools. CAR is being brought into the newsroom in several ways, Borowski (personal communication, November 17, 1995) explained:

> Part of it is our Bit by Bit University where we teach spreadsheets, databases, basics of PCs, Windows, and Internet to reporters. It's one way to whet their appetites and get them interested. On the news side, actually applying CAR, it is a two-way process. Reporters will come to us with databases or reporters will come to us with data questions: "Here's a sheet of data. How do we analyze it?" Or, we are always trolling for data—looking for little gold mines within databases within government reports. Tom visits, every now and then, different county and state offices, engages people and finds out about databases. We then try to sell the concept to a reporter: This is a good story and so forth.

CAR Remains a "New Frontier"

Some of the most experienced CAR journalists in the United States still see their work as taking their colleagues to the new frontier in newsgathering. These individuals, in a sense, have been the explorers and have seen the new promised land, and now these individuals wish to tell others in the newsroom about this new place filled with opportunities. Rose Ciotta is one of them. Ciotta, who is computer-assisted CAR editor for The Buffalo News, has worked as an investigative specialist before beginning to direct her newspaper's CAR effort. She joined the newspaper in 1977 and has worked on business and finance stories, including award-winning projects about bank lending and home mortgages.

> I believe CAR is at a new frontier, in other words, facing the challenge of moving from the nerd in the corner to the middle of the newsroom. We all agree that we want this to happen. The biggest worry is that it won't happen or it won't happen fast enough or as completely as it should. Many people are working on different techniques, such as specialized training, to make this happen. I call it "just-in-time-train-

ing." Get people into classes for overview so that they can understand the tools and appreciate them. Give them an opportunity to really learn how to use them when they are working on a story or project. I did that recently with a reporter who did a story using census data on in and out county migration. By the end of it, he knew how to use the spreadsheet pretty well.

The other thing happening to insure that CAR moves out there is to use the software available to make it easier for reporters to use online information. Whether it's front-ends, Web sites, networks—anything that takes the computer-ese out of the hunt—will sell CAR. We in the CAR field also all agree that journalists must use these tools, so one of my fears is that not enough people will become believers soon enough. In just the eighteen months or so that I've been at this full-time, I've seen a dramatic change in software, World Wide Web publishing, online information, and so forth. The rate of change is amazing. The window is open a little still, but journalists can't think they can function in this business and stay out of the computer loop. I also fear that newspaper owners may not realize that they need to invest and continue to invest in skills training for everyone. There's certainly more training in newsrooms today than ever considering the demand being experienced by IRE/NICAR. We're just scratching the surface on what is needed, especially when you consider that most news organizations are moving to a PC-based operating system for their newsrooms. (Ciotta, personal communication, November 22, 1995)

Firsthand Views: Seeing CAR's Effectiveness

Some newsroom experts argue that reporters and editors will use the tools if they can see CAR's effectiveness firsthand. "Reporters and editors are very result-oriented. What they're interested in is getting good stories in the paper that have some impact and result in lots of 'well dones' from their bosses," noted Ray Robinson (personal communication, September 7, 1995), projects editor at *The Press of Atlantic City*, where he has worked on investigative and computer-assisted stories for 3 years:

As they start seeing more and more CAR stories that have those results, they'll start thinking more about how the computer can help them on their own stories. They'll realize that the copy of the budget they just got from the town they cover was probably prepared using a spreadsheet. And they'll understand that if they can get it on diskette instead of paper, they can pop it into a PC and do some pretty sophisticated analysis. With a little training and encouragement from management, I think CAR will take hold pretty much by itself.

CAR: Use It for Daily Stories and Projects

It is clear that CAR is most successful, newsroom managers and CAR experts both agree, if it is used for projects and for daily news reporting. Brad Weisenstein (personal communication, February 27, 1995), a bureau chief and CAR coordinator for the *Belleville News-Democrat* in Illinois, explained his newspaper's most effective approach:

> Our program has evolved from nine-track tapes and BIG projects only to lots of use on a weekly basis. We're much more spreadsheet oriented and quickly moving into online services. BBSs have been popular with us for some time, though. Our philosophy is to use technology to point out a story angle, but we then turn to very traditional methods—basic legwork—to make the story readable, relevant, and interesting.

Providing Adequate Access to CAR Tools

Another strategy is not to isolate the individuals using CAR, but to bring it to everyone in the newsroom by making the resources available on all computer workstations at all times. This is a form of empowerment through access. "The tools must be accessible," believes Paul McElroy (personal communication, October 13, 1995), systems editor at the *Seattle Post-Intelligencer* since 1991. McElroy serves as liaison between the newsroom and the Systems Department and handles most staff computer training.

> Here, CAR tools are not available on our mainframe Atex system. We have just had three PCs dedicated to CAR; one is in our library and the other two are in the newsroom. Some reporters are reluctant to use the PCs because it means leaving their desk and risking missed phone calls, among other inconveniences. For newspapers with PC-based systems, I'd hope that Internet access and a few other tools (spreadsheet, database, and so forth) are available from any desk. That will be our goal when we buy our next system.

Bill Casey (personal communication, September 22, 1995), director of CAR for *The Washington Post*, also feels access to CAR tools is important if CAR is to succeed:

> Doing CAR right for us is having more than a couple of people who are skilled with computers. That's pretty important. At the same time we do that, we recognize, like Pat Stith (an editor at the Raleigh *News & Observer*) does, that there is only a small percentage of people, fifteen or twenty years of this has shown us, have an aptitude for it or an interest in it. Achieving a balance between people understanding these tools and people realizing what they don't know is a big issue.

This is the position also held by Jack Lail, assistant managing editor of technology who assists reporters with CAR at the *Knoxville News-Sentinel.* He is also responsible for developing an online BBS service and Web site and is supervisor for the newspaper library. Lail argues that everyone in the newsroom should be taught the basic tools of CAR. "You have to get beat reporters to start doing at least the simple stuff themselves. It's a tool. They don't need to go off to the CAR department to figure out a spreadsheet. They ought to know that themselves and the challenge is to convince them of that and get their buy-in," Lail (personal communication, September 30, 1995) stated.

Need for Widespread Newsroom Involvement

Most individuals supervising or overseeing CAR in newsrooms believe there must be as many individuals as possible involved.

Dave Fallis (personal communication, January 28, 1995), assistant city editor for the *Tulsa World,* is one. He strongly supports the philosophy of widespread newsroom involvement. "It is very important to get as many people involved as possible. It has a domino effect. Relying on one person, unless it is a full-time job, is not enough. But start small."

PROVIDING TRAINING AND MOTIVATION

Another newspaper online expert believes success in CAR comes from training and encouragement. "I would like to see editors and reporters become more interested in using the technology available to them," observed *Modesto Bee* Librarian Kate Roberts (personal communication, February 28, 1995). "We have the talent to produce quality CAR stories, but I think that being on different computer skill levels and weak communication often blocks us from doing so."

The Washington Post's Casey agrees. Motivating individuals in a newsroom, large ones especially, is critical to succeeding with CAR. "This is a fragile process of cajoling and pushing and pulling, of showing people how it works and how it might apply to their beats. It is not any kind of simple thing. You just don't give classes and then people are all doing it."

Moving CAR fully into the newsroom is, perhaps, a classic case for study of adoption of technological innovation. There may be similarity, some experts feel, in what is happening in newsrooms of the 1990s with CAR and what happened in newsrooms in the 1970s when computers were first introduced for text processing and typesetting (Garrison, 1979). There is some difficulty on the part of some people to adjust to the new technological tools of newsgathering today. Will it, if the 1970s adjustment period is indicative, take a generation of journalists to adjust to using CAR on a regular basis?

"All technological revolutions in the workplace are adopted by a generation that is not present when it is originally introduced," Casey (personal communication, September 22, 1995), stated. "There's another generation of people, it might be five years back, or ten years or later, that represent the new technology and use it. And this is exactly what happens in newsrooms, with exceptions."

Use Patience and Understanding

Tom Torok, a member of the CAR team at *The Philadelphia Inquirer*, feels that bringing CAR into a newsroom requires patience and understanding about the individuals who will be using the new approach to their work:

> You have to realize that people view the world differently. Where somebody could think in database conceptual terms and others can't. To let those people know the potential, a conversation is not going to do it. You have to show it working, the whistles and bells going off, to sell it. Part of us has to be evangelical about this because—from what we have seen with what we thought was really powerful data, approaching people [on the newspaper's staff] and telling them what we could do—it didn't work. They just didn't get it. But once they saw it, we have more apostles and disciples. (personal communication, November 17, 1995)

Torok believes it doesn't really matter whether a new CAR user begins with a small project or a large project:

> The most important thing is to start, wherever the project is and to use CAR as a tool wherever CAR tools are. If you have a story that you're going to get into—whether you use a computer or not—and you can see that the computer would make a much better tool and you are going to have to do this project on a very large scale, I would just say start. Start big. If you don't have anybody with the expertise there, get it. One thing that I think is terrific about newspapers is that CAR has been a grass roots movement where everybody has had to push it uphill. Even if you are the fiercest competitors, there's always people at another paper willing to help with the strategy of getting it done.

Carol Napolitano (personal communication, September 29, 1995), a member of the public affairs reporting team of the *Omaha World-Herald* and former CAR coordinator for *The Times* in Munster,

Indiana, offered a networking strategy to get CAR off to a successful start in the newsroom:

> I found that starting out by working with individuals who are inter-ested to help them do CAR often resulted in their spreading the good word to others who had no idea CAR was out there, or were ambiva-lent, or were against it for whatever reason. Work with those individu-als and keep things simple at first. Don't take on huge projects. Have them surf the Internet, or make a ProfNet request, or try some simple spreadsheet work. Additionally, I often suggested to people that CAR might help their story and showed them how. And when I did a story involving CAR, I invited people to peek over my shoulder or sit down next to me and watch and ask questions. By doing that with several people, the word had spread and by the time I offered mass training two years after the first CAR story was done, 90 percent of the newsroom signed up voluntarily based on what they had seen others do and what they had heard. It worked, I think, because I tried to ease the concept into the newsroom, showing how it could be used on a daily basis. I didn't make it seem so huge and scary and sudden.

John Norton (personal communication, February 20, 1995), busi-ness editor of The *Pueblo Chieftan* in Colorado, agrees that journal-ists have to be persuaded that computers can make their reporting and editing work easier: "The biggest hurdle is getting the reporters to learn how to use computers. They are reluctant to take the time and don't see the value."

The managing editor of the 127,000-circulation *Knoxville News-Sentinel*, Vince Vawter (personal communication, April 18, 1995), offered a possible explanation: "It's funny," he stated, "that most reporters do not want to do CAR. Perhaps they do not feel confident in their analytical skills."

Creating Excitement and Commitment

Creating excitement is another key to success in using CAR. "The toughest job is teaching the staff and generating enthusiasm," stated Merritt Wallick (personal communication, March 3, 1995), assistant city/state editor at the 125,000-circulation *News Journal* in New Castle, Delaware. Wallick supervises training and database story preparation.

"The biggest requirement for being successful is having at least one person who really wants to do CAR and is willing to, unfortu-nately, invest personal time and probably personal money in the training," believes Steve Doig (personal communication, September 21, 1995), Arizona State University professor and former associate editor for research at *The Miami Herald*. "Most newsrooms are not going to nominate somebody out of the blue, send them to get enough training, and starting doing it. It's a thing that tends to be adopted by some enthusiast who then begins, on his or her own, to produce stuff that finally becomes valuable. The necessary condition is somebody who wants to do it."

Competition as a Motivating Force

Another editor feels that motivation may come from seeing how others have used CAR in a powerful and impressive manner. "Use examples of other reporters' work [in the newsroom]. Nothing gets the competitive juices going faster than showing another reporter an amazing piece of work that someone else did. I hear it all the time," stated James Derk, computer research editor at the *Evansville Courier* (personal communication, September 5, 1995). "How can a computer help me cover city government? The Water Board? Well, whip out three reprints from NICAR and say 'didja ever think of putting the city budget into a spreadsheet and seeing where the money really goes? Where is the city's money invested?'"

A Hurdle Too High to Jump?

On the other hand, success is hindered by a belief within some news organizations that the use of computers in newsgathering is a hurdle too high to clear. Problems such as not having the right tools, or the right people, or the expertise, or the ideas are often cited as barriers to proceed. "We have the technology. We understand the urgency," stated reporter Dana Nichols (personal communication, January 15, 1995), who works in CAR for *The Record*, a 53,000-circulation daily serving Stockton, California. "But we still feel overwhelmed. We need to have someone devoted to developing this."

Bill Kline (personal communication, February 18, 1995), managing editor for the *Pocono Record* in Pennsylvania, points to expertise as the central problem at his newspaper. "At small newspapers, CAR is a gray area. We don't understand it—consequently, we're shy to jump into it. We may have to hire someone who, on his or her own, can get us going."

Other small dailies, such as the 43,000-circulation *News & Advance* in Lynchburg, Virginia, must wait to begin using computer tools in their daily and project reporting because of the perceived cost. "We hope to begin in 1995," said Managing Editor Joe Stinnett (personal communication, January 16, 1995), "budget permitting." The financial concern among small dailies is echoed by reporter Clint Riley (personal communication, January 17, 1995). "Smaller dailies need to find more affordable ways to take advantage of computer research," said Riley, who is leading the *Citrus County Chronicle*, a 21,000-daily in Inverness, Florida, into computer-based newsgathering. "Affordable workshops to set up basic computer options at small newspapers would also be nice."

Amy Kerr (personal communication, February 19, 1995), an assistant editor for *The Herald-Dispatch* in Huntington, West Virginia, blames the problem on top managers in newsrooms. "Many upper-level editors who will say they see value in CAR are not interested in committing financial resources to its development."

However, a reporter who specializes in legislative and projects, Kendra Rosencrans (personal communication, March 28, 1995), feels most newspapers try to get past the financial pressures. Rosencrans, who works for the 20,000-daily circulation *Aberdeen American News* in South Dakota, explained: "It's a great tool, but it's a financial challenge to find the money to invest in the necessary software and hardware. We do what we can." Gene Tao (personal communication, January 30, 1995), editor of the 20,000-circulation *Hawaii Tribune-Herald* in Hilo, expanded: "We still don't have clear understanding about CAR. Cost is our concern even if the technology is available to us."

Robin Evans (personal communication, January 16, 1995), city editor of the *West County Times* in Richmond, California, says that making a transition to use of CAR poses a different set of problems. "We are at the very beginning stages of using computers. Most usage now is only for big projects," Evans explained. "I personally would like my staff to be able to use CAR for a wide range of reporting, from small beat projects to issue–trend stories to big projects."

GROWTH OF COMPUTERS AS NEWS REPORTING TOOLS

Computer-assisted reporting is the newsgathering tool of the decade in the United States, Canada, and, increasingly, elsewhere in the world. Online news research, reporting using online commercial services and the Internet, and news stories based on original database analysis by journalists are no longer ideas of future newsgathering. As many news librarians and news researchers have known for almost two decades, online tools are here to stay. For a decade or more, reporters and news researchers have not needed to be award-winning investigators at financially successful news companies to access and use online research tools. What has happened in recent years is a broadening base and growing awareness in the industry of the usefulness of these tools.

Similarly, growing use of originally developed databases and use of databases created by outside entities such as government agencies has also become an important part of CAR. Database specialists in circulation and marketing, advertising, and accounting departments of news companies have known the advantages of database tools for more than two decades as well. In newsrooms, only a handful of journalists used databases on mainframe computers before these powerful tools were introduced to the PC in the early 1980s with products such as dBase and Lotus 1-2-3.

However, some news organizations are still discovering these new tools. There are a growing number of newspapers and television stations and networks—especially larger ones—where CAR is a significant part of daily reporting and is not being reserved just for special projects (Johnson, 1995). For some news organizations, though, CAR is still perceived as a fancy topic for discussion at conferences or as a special projects tool used only by nerdy investigative reporters. "[T]hese keyed-in reporters find technology a tough sell, despite the fact that in the last six consecutive years, computer-assisted projects won Pulitzer Prizes. The movement occupies a newsroom niche, and its supporters struggle to wrest money from stretched budgets and to convince journalism professors and students that they need to get the religion," stated *Presstime* staff writer Rebecca Ross Albers (1994a, p. 34).

This situation is gradually changing. In the past 2 to 3 years, smaller dailies have begun to use these tools. More are going online each week, and more are beginning to use databases as part of news stories as they discover benefits such as improved reporting. Carleton University's McKercher (1995) studied both the *Montreal Gazette* and *Ottawa Citizen* to learn how computers enhanced newsgathering. She found two main uses: writing and checking electronic libraries, modernized versions of old-fashioned reporting tasks. McKercher identified computers as useful for communicating, conducting background research, conducting fact-finding research for stories, organizing information related to reporting, and writing.

Most journalists see CAR as a major growth area in newsgathering in the years ahead. In fact, it is hard to find anyone in a newsroom who feels otherwise. The problem may be that not everyone is doing something about it. "As computers become more common in the workplace and the home, growth can't help but happen. Already the new hires we are getting out of J-schools have had PCs in their dorm rooms. That's nothing new to them. The first thing they want is a parking space, the second is their free PPP account," stated the *Evansville Courier's* Derk (personal communication, September 5, 1995).

"No doubt about it," agreed Atlantic City's Robinson (personal communication, September 7, 1995), a veteran reporter who has also reported for the *State Journal* in Lansing, Michigan, and *The Daily Oklahoman* in Oklahoma City. "The use will grow as more reporters and editors become comfortable with computers. And that'll happen for two reasons: (a) more and more journalists these days have PCs at their desks, rather than the single purpose 'dumb' terminals they used to have, and (b) computers are penetrating an ever-growing share of the home market, and that includes journalists."

Kathleen A. Hansen, a professor at the University of Minnesota and co-author with Jean Ward of *Search Strategies in Mass Communication* (Ward & Hansen, 1996), expects continued growth of computers as reporting tools in the next decade:

> If only because news organizations will see themselves competing with other kinds of publications, information services, and highly skilled entrepreneurs who want to horn in on journalists' traditional bailiwick. In order to keep themselves relevant, informed, and capable of meeting society's needs for high-quality reportage, journalists will have to learn how to make the most of the power of computers as information tools. You see, unlike many others, I don't think any of this is really about computers (machines). I think all of this is about information (where it comes from, who manipulates it, how it is evaluated and communicated). There is my bias, but so be it. It just so happens that right now, computers are the information tools that are important—in some future scenario, it might be some other form of information device or strategy or process that takes center stage. It all comes down to how journalists manage and understand information, and communicate that understanding to an audience. (personal communication, September 19, 1995)

Some news organizations are excited about the new tools and their potential. Robert Long, an investigative reporter for the 50,000-circulation *Tribune-Democrat* in Johnstown, Pennsylvania, demonstrates the attitude: "We just purchased a PC for the newsroom dedicated to CAR in November [1994]," Long stated (personal communication, January 20, 1995). "We anticipate our use and capabilities will grow sharply in the next two years."

INCREASING ROLE OF PROFESSIONAL ORGANIZATIONS

There are a handful of professional organizations that have taken the lead in educating and training journalists and in setting the agenda for CAR in the United States and elsewhere in the world. Two of these organizations are headquartered in Columbia, Missouri, at the University of Missouri. Founded in 1975 at a meeting in Reston, Virginia, IRE has represented the professional interests of investigative journalism in North America. Originally begun as a separate entity, the Missouri Institute for Computer-Assisted Reporting was organized in 1989 as a focal point for the evolving specialization in reporting. Renamed in late 1993, funded by a substantial grant from the Freedom Forum, and armed with a new management and training team, NICAR joined with IRE and grew into its CAR leadership role at a national and international level by setting reporting and computing standards, testing new hardware and software products, offering annual conferences, providing training and workshops, giving free technical advice, and gathering public databases.

In 1995, NICAR also began to increase its service as a clearinghouse for government databases. The organization purchases federal and state databases and sells copies to news organizations at a lower price or sells partitions of the databases, such as regions or states, at a reduced cost. The revenue covers costs to acquire the databases. Among the national databases in the NICAR library are Federal Election Commission campaign contributions; Federal Aviation Administration airplane and pilot records; Home Mortgage Disclosure Act records; federal procurement data; Alcohol, Tobacco, and Firearms gun dealer records; National Bridge Inventory System data; Federal Bureau of Investigation Uniform Crime Reports; Social Security death records; Occupational Safety and Health Administration violations data; Department of Transportation truck accident and census data; several databases from the Small Business Administration; and Department of Education schools data (Houston, 1995a).

A different sort of organization that is making important contributions is the Transactional Records Access Clearinghouse (TRAC) at Syracuse University. Founded in 1989, this organization gathers and develops information about federal agencies. TRAC focuses on enforcement and regulatory activities of these agencies and serves news organizations by disseminating the information it assembles. One form of this information is data, but other information is distributed in reports, research studies, and a variety of services provided in offices in both Syracuse, New York, and in Washington, DC (Anonymous, 1995d).

Other nationally oriented professional groups have also begun to offer professional development opportunities in the area of CAR. Among them are the Society of Professional Journalists (SPJ) at Greencastle, Indiana, the National Institute for Advanced Reporting

(NIAR) at Indiana University at Indianapolis, and the Poynter Institute for Media Studies at St. Petersburg, Florida. The School of Communication at the University of Miami has also contributed to CAR development through its national research project on CAR uses and tools, described later.

"The organizations are extremely important. Look no further than the National Institute for Computer-Assisted Reporting at the University of Missouri," said Ray Robinson (personal communication, September 7, 1995). "The whole CAR movement would still be in its infancy if NICAR hadn't worked so hard to promote it and teach the required technical skills."

Evansville's Derk (personal communication, September 5, 1995) also underlined the value of what IRE and NICAR offer members and other professionals. "Groups like SPJ [Society of Professional Journalists] don't help me much. I read the *Quill*, but it takes hands-on groups like IRE and NICAR to help here. The week I spent at NICAR's boot camp for reporters, where twelve of us lived and ate CAR, and a conference like the one we had in Raleigh or at San Jose are much more helpful. You get your hands on a PC, you don't read about them."

Seattle's Paul McElroy (personal communication, October 13, 1995) feels organizations help facilitate information sharing and interaction among people who are doing the same things:

> Poynter, API, CAR Trek, CARR-L, and such are not absolutely critical for success, but they certainly help. The biggest benefit for me when I attended the annual CAR seminar at Indiana University in 1994, for example, was hearing about the many good projects done by other newspapers. As a journalist who has since become a "tekkie," I'm comfortable with computers, but I needed a dose of real-world CAR success stories to help inspire reporters at our shop. I have also found CARR-L to be extremely valuable for general CAR discussion and pointers to Internet sites that are helpful for journalists. One drawback is the periodically low signal-to-noise ratio when a flame war ensues.

Mary Kate Leming, assistant managing editor at the *Palm Beach Post*, is former head of the News Division of the Special Libraries Association, an international group of news researchers that has about 1,000 members in the division. Leming is one of a small handful of news librarians who have advanced to newsroom management at the managing editor level. She feel professional groups are important. "There is an educational role for organizations, to let people know CAR is available and how to use it. They need to work with other organizations, also. It is important to build those ties that help bring more education, more expertise, closer to your members,"

Leming stated (personal communication, September 15, 1995). "For example, we are working very closely with IRE and having joint sessions at our conventions."

What do participants gain from attending CAR conferences and training programs? *The Washington Post's* Casey (personal communication, September 22, 1995) understands the main benefits:

> People hear and see things that are going elsewhere. It's just like having mom and dad talk to them. It's not the same as seeing that your peers are doing things. It's exciting. It definitely has a catalytic effect. That effect is as true for a small or medium paper as it is *The Post*. People get galvanized to see and to hear ideas. That's the most important part. Skills development means nothing to me at these things. . . . These classes are consciousness-raising classes. You do not walk out of them thinking you know whatever you are learning. The idea is that you understand what these tools can do and maybe understand a little about how you can get into trouble, too. The skills part is not important to me. It is the other people and other papers part of the professional thing that helps people. We can handle the skills ourselves.

Participation in continuing education programs has made a difference for the *Champaign-Urbana News Gazette* in Illinois. "The newspaper has sent several people over the last twelve to eighteen months to seminars on CAR, specifically IRE and NICAR sessions," said Michael Howie (personal communication, March 11, 1995), a reporter and CAR advisor. "Lack of equipment in the newsroom has been our biggest holdup. Several Macs are for graphics first, reporters last. Attitudes about CAR vary widely on our staff, too."

A FORMULA FOR SUCCESSFUL APPROACHES AND STRATEGIES

There are a wide range of ways to succeed with CAR. Examples in the following chapters describe many of the best ideas. There is no sure way to be successful, but it seems that a formula may be evolving. The elements are rather simplistic:

- A solid story idea.
- Data or information in other forms to be gathered and analyzed.
- Willing and motivated journalists.
- Access to appropriate hardware and software tools.
- Proper training to use those tools.
- Newsroom management encouragement.
- Sufficient time.

Add these together, with that elusive element of a newsworthy story or project idea, and a successful project is *likely* to emerge. Likely. Nothing is guaranteed. Besides, what editors and journalists want from their stories will vary considerably depending on the side of the news organization and the original purpose of each story.

"So what makes a great computer-assisted journalism project? If you are a successful journalist, you already know: the same elements that make great stories done without a computer," observes Christopher Feola (1993, p. 28), news systems editor for the 60,000-circulation Waterbury, Connecticut, *Republican-American.* "In the end, readers don't care if you do a story on a multimillion dollar Cray or a $3.98 calculator—as long as it's interesting. Who wouldn't read a story comparing your school and city bus driver roster with your state's drunk driving conviction lists?"

WINNING STRATEGIES FOR SMALL NEWS ORGANIZATIONS

There are hundreds of small news organizations hoping to use CAR in their newsrooms. However, for one reason or another, they do not. Some of their editors think the costs are too high. Some editors feel there is none of the requisite expertise found in the newsroom. Others believe there are no hardware and software resources available for such work. These days, however, this is becoming more and more like saying the the telephone or fax machine costs too much and cannot be used. Ridiculous? Yes. Are phone bills too expensive? How long did it take individuals to learn to use the new phone system or the new fax machine? Do some people share telephones and desks? If answers to those questions were yes, then it is likely that CAR is a real possibility for even the smallest of newsrooms.

For the 26,000-circulation *Oshkosh Northwestern* in Wisconsin, the best place to begin CAR was with the newsroom staff, says editor Thomas P. Lee (1995):

> The most important part are the people. You have to make it work with people. Still, you have to have someone in charge of the newsroom who has to set the tone and say, "Folks this is the way we are going. Get on the CAR train, get on board, because this is where we are going." You have to get the message out to the troops.

> You can have two problems. I suspect the most common problem is editors who aren't excited about it, but the reporters are, and the editors are paranoid about having to spend money. Or, you may have the problem that I had where it was the reporters shying away from CAR. It takes a special approach in each instance.

Lee recommends that reporters that are not getting support from editors should start quietly on their own. He recommends looking around the building to find resources such as computers and software, even going to other departments. With some success in building resources, he then believes even a single reporter can begin CAR on his or her own:

> Talk it up quietly, and then start doing some stories. That will cause editors to develop an appetite for it. It will be a drug for them; they will become dependent on it. They will see how the average police story about crime in a neighborhood can be enhanced when you bring out nut graphs that say, "in this neighborhood, median income is $35,000, far below the $40,000 median income for the community." If you get into those types of demographic profiles in a regular story, then circle it and show it to the boss. Say, "I used our Mac to do this with census data." Then they will start working on their publishers. If all else fails, work on an editor's appetite to win awards.

When reporters resist, Lee believes, the best strategy is to sit down with each one—after training has been provided—and ask why he or she is not trying to integrate it into their work. Provide each resistant staff member with time to do the new type of work on a story, he also advises. When this fails, some people leave. Lee uses a vacancy as an opportunity to search for CAR-oriented replacements and advises other editors to do the same.

"Also go by your nearby universities. In some cases, the nearby university may have some people who will be way ahead of the newsroom in this kind of research," Lee (1995) stated.

John Kohlstrand (1995), a reporter at the 35,000-daily circulation *Chronicle-Telegram* in Elyria, Ohio, strongly feels that CAR can be a regular part of newsrooms the size of his newspaper. He recommends the following:

- Start small, but work up to higher levels in time.
- Build your own databases and use the graphics tools of the software.
- Brag a little about the "how-to" of CAR stories and projects to your editors.
- Work with government database managers for access and compromises.
- Find allies for projects such as "computer geeks."
- Use the resources of others (such as CD-ROM drives and CD-ROM databases at the local public library).
- Find and use cheap databases (such as the Toxic Release Inventory).

Omaha's Carol Napolitano advocates CAR in newsrooms of all sizes if journalists in smaller newsrooms are willing to make some trade-offs. "CAR can be for the journalistic masses," Napolitano (1995, p. 1) explained. "It takes a little bit of patience, a lot of knowledge about where to find the best buys, and lots of flexibility. Most importantly, though, it means understanding that computer-assisted reporting isn't always giant projects and flashy software."

Arizona State University Professor Ed Sylvester, who teaches CAR and who helped the *Oshkosh Northwestern* get its CAR program going in 1995, believes that small news organizations can find inexpensive ways to begin using CAR on a regular basis. In his view, locating existing hardware and software is the key to beginning with little or no expense in newsrooms with severely limited budgets. "My rule, basically, is that unless you are really rich in resources, unless you are the MIS person, here's what you've got: It's not only capital intensive to buy these tools, but it takes staff time," Sylvester (1995) stated. "There's a lot of virtue in running small and tight on software." Sylvester recommends that small news organizations should try to use software already in the building.

Sylvester also advises editors and reporters working together often on CAR stories. "The computer has allowed us, in some ways, to withdraw from the kinds of casual conversations we used to have more often. That's bad. But it doesn't have to. Editors and reporters need to keep in touch with each other, sort of a running conversation about what they are doing, what they need, what's working, what's not working," he advised.

Sylvester also recommends the U.S. Census databases as perhaps the most valuable database with which a small news organization can start a CAR program. A moderate investment as databases go, the widespread nature of census data, he says, has applications across the entire company, not just the newsroom. "I can't think of a single database that is more valuable to different departments on a newspaper than the census is," Sylvester stated. "An advertising director wants to know the demographics even more than the newsroom does. If you can get a number of departments interested, not only to split the costs, you have a unanimity of purpose that the publisher is more likely to go for." Even if a news organization cannot purchase census disks or CDs, Sylvester recommended using local libraries that may serve as repository libraries and have public copies of the census data for use there or for downloading to a diskette for later analysis on a portable or desktop PC. This does not cost the news organization any money at all, he noted.

THE MIAMI COMPUTER-ASSISTED REPORTING RESEARCH PROJECT

An ongoing national study of the development and use of CAR has been underway at the School of Communication of the University of Miami in Coral Gables, Florida, since 1993. Two years of data from this project, collected in 1994 and 1995, are reported in the following chapters. The foundation of the project is an annual nationwide survey. As this manuscript was prepared, the 1996 study was underway.

To begin in 1993, a national database of newspapers, managing editors, and CAR supervisors was built. From the database, an initial mailing of 514 cover letters, questionnaires, and stamped, self-addressed envelopes was sent to the nation's largest Sunday and daily newspapers in late December 1993. One follow-up mailing was sent in late January 1994. Using circulation figures from the latest editions of the *Editor & Publisher International Year Book* in 1994 and 1995, a minimum of 20,000 copies Sunday circulation was used as the cutoff point (Anderson, 1994, 1995). In late December 1994, the second data collection wave began with a mailing to 510 Sunday and daily newspapers. Again, a circulation of 20,000 on Sundays was the minimum for inclusion in the population. Two follow-up mailings were sent. The first follow-up was mailed in early February 1995 and the second follow-up was sent in mid-March 1995. In 1995, a total of 287 responses was received, a response rate of 56.3%. In 1994, a total of 208 responses were received, a response rate of 40.5%. Because the two waves of this study involved surveying entire populations, no significance statistics were computed.

Editors of the selected newspapers were asked either to complete the questionnaire themselves or to forward it to the person in charge of online news research and CAR. In some cases, as many as two or three persons completed various portions of the questionnaire related to their newsroom specializations.

Questionnaires used were developed from discussions and interviews during the IRE Conference on Computer-Assisted Reporting at Raleigh, North Carolina, in October 1993 and San Jose, California, in October 1994. The instruments consisted of four sets of questions including institutional and personal information, computer-assisted reporting, online news research, and field reporting use of computers. Respondents were also encouraged to include any additional comments on the subject. In some cases, follow-up interviews were conducted by telephone each year. The questionnaires are reprinted in Appendix A.

Earlier research on uses of computers in newsrooms has determined that significant differences in computer use exist between large and small newspapers. "[S]mall newspapers lag far behind large and medium-sized ones in newsroom computerization," Brooks and Yang (1993, p. 16) concluded. Because of the wide range of differences, most of the data reported in the 1995 phase of this study are reported by newspaper circulation size. The median circulation of the 287 newspapers was 52,800 copies. Therefore, small newspapers were categorized as those with circulations less than 52,800 and large newspapers were categorized as those with circulations higher than 52,800. In most cases, variables in the 1995 study phase are reported in contingency tables broken down by circulation size.

Data were processed using programs from the Statistical Package for the Social Sciences (SPSS) for Windows, Version 6.1.3 (Norusis, 1995) and the Microsoft Visual FoxPro relational database system for Windows, Version 3.0 (Microsoft Corporation, 1995).

NEWSROOM CAR USE
DEMOGRAPHICS

There was greater participation in 1995 than in 1994, perhaps a reflection of a growing number of newspapers getting involved in some form of CAR and willing to report that fact on a questionnaire. Of those responding, the largest proportion was from the South both years, as shown in Table 1.1. The mean daily circulation of responding newspapers was slightly over 100,000 both years. In 1994, it was just over 121,000 and it was 113,000 in 1995. The slight drop is likely a reflection of the growing number of smaller dailies becoming involved in one or more types of CAR.

The number of newsroom persons involved in CAR is increasing. In early 1994, the mean was 3.54 persons, and it grew 33.9% to 4.74 in only 1 year, reflecting a growing commitment of resources to CAR in each responding newsroom. Most respondents in the studies each year had CAR supervision (27.4% in 1995 and 26.5% in 1994) or overall supervision (19.5% and 19.6%) roles. Other involvement includes persons responsible for the newsroom computer systems, systems liaison, news projects supervision, training, production, and planning.

TABLE 1.1
Newspapers Participating in 1994–1995

	1995 Study		1994 Study	
Response *n*-size	287		208	
Population size	510		514	
Response rate	56.3%		40.5%	
Respondent newspaper region				
East	52	18.1%	38	18.3%
South	96	33.4	75	36.1
Midwest	77	26.8	59	28.4
West	62	21.6	36	17.3
Daily circulation mean	113,734.90		121,361.27	
CAR newspaper staff size mean	4.74		3.54	
CAR role or titles of newspaper respondents				
CAR supervisor	76	26.5%	57	27.4%
Assist, train, coach	12	4.2	28	13.5
Overall supervision	56	19.5	20	9.6
PC coordinator	13	4.5	19	9.1
Systems liaison	18	6.3	14	6.7
Planning	7	2.4	13	6.3
Projects	26	9.1	10	4.8
No CAR role	1	0.3	8	3.8
Online research	13	4.5	7	3.4
Setting up PCs	2	0.7	7	3.4
Production	13	4.5	5	2.4
Computer user	1	0.3	2	1.0
Word processing user	24	8.4	2	1.0
Publisher liaison	5	1.7	2	1.0
Graphics	3	1.0	2	1.0

2

Computers in the Newsroom

A small number of editors and reporters at *The Chronicle* in Muskegon, Michigan, use a range of computer tools and databases more often associated with larger news organizations in the Great Lakes region. However, small news organizations can also successfully use CAR. In recent years, the 55,000 evening circulation newspaper has developed local stories from information in numerous public databases obtained from state, county, and city government agencies through open records laws. Among them are the Michigan Department of Corrections Inmates database, bench warrants issued by area courts obtained from the sheriff's department, community service case tracking from the local courts, school district employee data, and Western Michigan firefighters data.

"I started building my own databases," *Chronicle* reporter Michael G. Walsh (1995), who has headed his newspaper's movement toward CAR, explained. Walsh said he would often approach individuals in the court system, such as bailiffs, who would provide him with copies of documents he needed for his databases. He entered cases as they occurred over a period of time and, of course, the databases grew into a usable form. He said his newspaper also bought public databases whenever possible. "We bought databases from the Department of Corrections, for example. . . . One lesson that I have learned from all this is that all data are cumulative. . . . I never throw anything out."

The Chronicle, a Newhouse newspaper, serves the Western Michigan area about 100 miles west of Lansing. The newsroom maintains a set of databases for regular use by reporters, librarians, and editors. Among the databases are drunken driving cases, sentencing data involving convicted criminals in local courts, and all published pending criminal complaints. *The Chronicle's* editors encourage staff members to take classes that focus on use of individual software products as well as to attend CAR seminars. However, in the beginning, because of limited resources, the CAR effort has been small.

"We are not there yet, but we now have four other people with laptop computers in the newsroom. But there are still a larger number of people in our newsroom who do reporting with the tools of the 1970s," Walsh (personal communication, September 29, 1995) stated. "I am pretty much the one person using CAR now. But those four others are hitting at it. We have much more administrative support now than we had a year ago. We have a lot of new hardware and software and it (CAR) is coming fast for us."

Walsh, who specializes in covering courts and conducting investigations, works with an editor on CAR-based projects. Walsh has used both a mainframe and PCs for his projects. In 1995, the newspaper was using a 486 desktop and Walsh used his own 486 notebook system. The computers were part of a network with a 1 GB server in the newsroom and a 500 MB drive on the desktop PC. Microsoft Works, a package of office-oriented products, provided a basic spreadsheet for simpler and smaller projects. Walsh also used Microsoft Office and Access for larger database reporting. Digital tape was the major storage medium used. Although these may not be the ideal configurations, these tools were more than enough for Walsh to work with local databases.

"Most of the circuit court records data was small enough for Works to accommodate my needs," Walsh (personal communication, September 29, 1995), explained. "All I needed was a flatfile program for the regular, routine projects."

The newspaper was spending about $2,000 a year in 1995 to make available such services as America Online, PACER, Data-Times, FedWorld, various government BBSs, and the Internet. The Internet and PACER, a federal courts database, were the most used services at *The Chronicle* in 1995. "Our ability to pull into deadline stories data that used to be days away, if reachable at all, has been our biggest success with online tools," Walsh (personal communication, February 20, 1995), his newsroom's spreadsheet expert, stated. "Spending too much as we learned how to use them is our biggest failure."

Chronicle reporters also use online services to report. Walsh likes to use the Internet and individual services aimed at journalists, such as ProfNet, for example, to find experts outside of the Western Michigan region. Walsh explained that, like many other journalists in the mid-1990s, he has begun to use the Internet extensively in his reporting. "My wife is an educator and, through a state network, I have my own Internet account which gives me unlimited access

---

SUCCEEDING IN A SMALL NEWSROOM

Muskegon *Chronicle* staff writer Michael G. Walsh (1995) recommends these nine useful ideas for success with CAR in a small newsroom:

- *Deliver, don't promise.* Get the job done. Don't just talk about it. At small newspapers, filling pages is critical.
- *Stay local and keep it simple.* Limit the initial efforts to a beat. Don't begin too big.
- *Get info-hungry.* Acquire as much data from government sources as you can.
- *Don't show off.* Don't overdo the details about how the work was done.
- *Think long-term and broaden your definition of CAR.* Work slowly and methodically with long-range goals.
- *Broaden the list of people you quote.* Use online sources to widen the range of experts beyond the usual local sources.
- *Steal ideas and adapt them to your requirements.* Check out what others are doing, especially larger regional news organizations and adapt their work to your situation.
- *Realize that a computer is only a tool.* Report beyond the numbers with human sources, too.
- *Verify everything that the computer tells you.* Check out the numbers.

---

for very little money each month," Walsh explained. "The paper will pay my expenses if I ask for it."

Walsh has completed numerous CAR stories since 1992. He has written about jail overcrowding and early releases to reduce the inmate population problem, drunken driving cases, drunken driving sentencing trends, and child abuser sentencing patterns. One example of Walsh's work, a routine story about jail crowding, is reprinted in Appendix B. In the story, Walsh used a locally obtained courts database and his spreadsheet software for the analysis and supplemented that work with some routine interviewing. "That story is an example of something you can do very quickly. It shows quick and dirty stories that you can do with very little time and money. Editors usually think that to do CAR stories, you need to take a long period of time. This shows how you can give a routine story more with some data and a spreadsheet," Walsh (personal communication, September 29, 1995) stated. "If you do these sorts of daily stories often enough, then editors start to expect it." Walsh has also used CAR for more lighthearted feature stories about popular pet names using pet license data and the most popular namesakes—such as celebrities, historically known individuals, and political figures—whose names are found on lists of individuals in trouble in the Muskegon County courts.

LOOKING AT THE POWERFUL PEOPLE OF TUCSON

Nashville *Tennessean* business reporter Heather Newman (1995) was a reporter for the *Tucson Citizen* when she examined the most powerful people in town for a project for the medium-sized Arizona daily newspaper. Newman described her work with desktop computers to complete the project:

> We had looked at the influential folks in Tucson five years ago in less depth, and decided that it was time to revisit the concept. We sent out hundreds of surveys to everyone we could think of and solicited reader comment to come up with some idea of who to include. In the end, we had profiles of the top five and one man who had burst onto the power scene; individual biographies of forty-six other powerful folks, including separate lists of ten women and ten minorities who did not appear elsewhere; stories on how women, minorities and public officials stacked up; a board game featuring the characteristics our powerful folks had in common; a "Where are They Now?" section for the people we listed five years ago; a main story on the nature of power; an issues story that pointed out areas of concern for the next five years and who might take the helm; a story about the lack of leadership training in town; and a list of everyone who was mentioned at least three times, including their titles and job descriptions. There may even have been a couple other stories—I've been trying to forget.
>
> The project took six months and had one reporter (me) and one photographer. It ran thirty-two pages. Here's the computer-assisted end of things: Before we even started the project, I sent out a general call on CompuServe and the Internet to other journalists around the country. In response, I got more than fifty usable suggestions on trends to watch for and places to look when putting the project together. I also got about a dozen copies of projects from other newspapers that had done similar analyses. That gave me a place to start when suggesting stories and gave our design person examples to look at for graphics and layout purposes.
>
> As a result of that contact, we also received a copy of askSam, a specialized database program, for one-third its retail price (still in the original shrink-wrap) from a database editor online who heard of our project. When we first decided to send out questionnaires, I created a database of names and addresses for who we would send them to using Paradox. I also used Paradox to retrieve addresses for people we wanted to mail to from my Rolodex, which was already set up as

a computerized database. Finally, Paradox enabled me to quickly select a variety of neighborhood representatives from neighborhood associations around town, ensuring that we had good coverage of the city for average folks.

Once we had mailed out the surveys and started getting some back in (including reader and staff comments), I set up another database. This one recorded every vote, what type of person the vote came from (based on codes written on the surveys) and what "position" the person was suggesting someone for (top ten, up and comers, etcetera). I also entered more than 1,000 names from nonprofit boards and committees around town into a separate Paradox database.

When everything had been entered, we ended up with about 5,000 lines of names and votes. I used Paradox to sort them by name, search for and replace any inconsistencies caused by using nicknames, and count them for us. We ended up with more than 950 individuals, many of whom were named once. I used Paradox to start ranking them in the orders you saw on your reports: who had the most mentions, who was mentioned the most for each category, who had the most "points" if we weighted what they were mentioned for, etcetera.

Once we decided who was going to be on our top lists, I put Paradox to work pulling out the names and phone numbers of people who served on groups or committees with the folks we had selected. When I began doing the actual interviews, I used a word processor (Word for Windows) to enter the notes. When I was ready to write a story, all I had to do was bring all my interview notes together with another database program—askSam—and ask it to select out the paragraphs that referred to a particular topic. For example, when I was writing the profile of Jim Click, all I had to do was tell askSam to get me every paragraph that mentioned his name. The program printed me out a list of all of my notes, paraphrases and quotes, along with who had said what. That enabled me to track more than a hundred interviews without having to flip through hundreds of sheets of note paper, and it took just seconds when I was ready to pull out notes on a particular topic. I used askSam in the same way for our issue and trend stories in the tab, asking it to give me every paragraph that mentioned "minorities" and so on. We used Paradox to alphabetize everyone that had been nominated for the project and cut out those people who had not gotten three votes, giving us our back page list. It also generated a list of everyone who had been mentioned three times that also had at least one nomination for a "women" or "minority" position, giving us a place to start on those lists.

For graphics, we used a spreadsheet program (1-2-3 for Windows) of mine to analyze affirmative action, city and board statistics to generate the numbers for the pie charts and bar graphs that appear next to the women and minorities stories. Once I did the legwork through our clips, that program also enabled us to generate the statistics on women in elections that we used in the story and in graphic form. And finally, I used a computerized project manager of mine (Lotus Organizer for Windows) to plot each part of the project and estimate the time to completion.

USING PERSONAL COMPUTERS IN NEWSROOMS

Computer users come in all "sizes" in terms of their expertise. Some are very experienced, whereas others are not at all experienced. Most users fall somewhere between the two extremes. Similarly, there is an equally wide range in the types of computers used by journalists in the newsroom. There are some news organizations that use mainframe computers for data analysis and others than use the tiniest of portable personal computers for their database-oriented reporting. In short, there is no single model for the types of hardware and software used for CAR.

Throughout the 1980s, a shift began to occur in computing. Not only did the use of mainframe computers slowly begin to be reduced because of the growth of other types of computing systems, such as more powerful minicomputers and desktop computers, but there was significant growth in access to online services as modems became faster and more locations with modems became available.

Furthermore, a shift from stand-alone computers on desktops to networked client-server systems began to occur in the workplace. Personal computers, originally used on their own, were gradually linked into local area networks and wide area networks for various group computing purposes, such as sharing software and database resources.

Neill Borowski, director of CAR for *The Philadelphia Inquirer*, began using computers in his business reporting in the early 1980s, but he began thinking about computer applications to his work even before PCs were developed. "My first job was covering city hall in 1975. I did a calculator and legal pad analysis of taxes and caused a taxpayer rebellion," recalled Borowski (personal communication, November 17, 1995):

> I have realized that you have to make a distinction between data and the computer. It was the data that were powerful, not the computer. The computer just gives us the ability to do more with the data. My first real CAR project was probably back in 1983–1984 when I was covering the break-up of AT&T. All the newspapers around the country were taking six or seven typical long distance phone calls,

giving them to AT&T, MCI, Sprint, and the others at that time, and asking 'What's the cost of this phone call?' and putting the cost in chart form. It dawned on me that there are data behind that to compute this, so I built a spreadsheet in DOS Lotus and put all the rate schedules in it. It enabled us to compute our own rates. We put out sections, one every quarter. We took a full page. People could sit down and figure out who would be the least expensive long distance carrier.

Changes in use of computers have come, but sometimes very slowly, to news companies in the 1980s and in the first half of this decade. However, these changes did not occur at all types of news organizations at the same time. In some cases, smaller newspapers and other news companies were able to make the change to PCs faster because of the lower costs involved. But in many cases, these applications were solely for production and did not, or rarely, involved CAR applications such as online services or database building and analysis. As shown in Table 2.1, size is clearly a distinction in general use of computers among daily newspapers in 1995. Large dailies, those with circulation over 52,800 in the University of Miami survey, clearly use computing tools for CAR more than small dailies. Overall, more than 70% of newspapers use computers in newsgathering, but larger newspapers (93%) nearly double the smaller ones (48%) in proportion of use. The comparison is similar in terms of use of mainframe systems.

Table 2.2 reveals a 3.4% growth in overall use of computers in newsgathering. In 1994, 66.3% of dailies used computers in reporting and the figure rose to 69.7% in 1995. Table 2.3 shows a much smaller number of newspapers (20%) in the U.S. using mainframes in newsgathering, but the larger dailies (26%) remain twice as likely as small newspapers (12%) to be the ones using them.

An often overlooked category of computers is the minicomputer. These systems were developed in the 1980s for heavy power and

TABLE 2.1
Use of Computers in Newsgathering, 1995

Computer Use of Some Type	Large Dailies[a]		Small Dailies[b]		Totals	
Yes	132	93.0%	68	7.9%	200	70.4%
No	10	7.0	74	52.1	84	29.6
Totals	142	50.0	142	50.0	284	100.0

Note. n = 287; missing observations = 3.
[a] Circulation over 52,800. [b] Circulation under 52,800.

TABLE 2.2
Use of Computers in Newsgathering, 1994-1995

Computer Use of Some Type	1994		1995		Percentage Change
Yes	138	66.3%	200	69.7%	+3.4%
No	67	32.2	84	29.3	–2.9
Missing	3	1.4	3	1.0	–0.4
Totals	208	100.0	287	100.0	

TABLE 2.3
Use of Mainframe Computers, 1995

Use of Mainframe Computers	Large Dailies[a]		Small Dailies[b]		Totals	
Yes	35	25.9%	12	12.4%	47	20.3%
No	99	73.3	83	85.6	182	78.4
Don't know	1	0.7	2	2.1	3	1.3
Totals	135	58.2	97	41.8	232	100.0

Note. n = 287; missing observations = 55.
[a]Circulation over 52,800. [b]Circulation under 52,800.

widespread use, but these systems did not have the size or power of mainframe systems. Still, they became popular at some newspapers as the workhorses of the production systems. Because of this, some newsrooms put these systems to work in the same manner as they might have used mainframes. A total of one quarter of the newspapers responding in the 1995 study reported used minicomputers in newsgathering. However, size is not a significant factor when discussing minicomputers, as shown in Table 2.4.

A NEED FOR CAR "DESKS"?

How does a news organization integrate CAR into its newsgathering? The idea was introduced in the first chapter that there are two main approaches to bringing CAR to newsrooms. One suggests the need to set up a special team of newsroom CAR experts. The other advocates bringing CAR to the entire newsroom. Because of the unique nature of CAR, some news organizations have set up desks

TABLE 2.4
Use of Minicomputers, 1995

Use of Minicomputers	Large Dailies[a]		Small Dailies[b]		Totals	
Yes	38	29.0%	18	19.8%	56	25.2%
No	88	67.2	70	76.9	158	71.2
Don't know	5	3.8	3	3.3	8	3.6
Totals	131	59.0	91	41.0	222	100.0

Note. n = 287; missing observations = 65.
[a] Circulation over 52,800. [b] Circulation under 52,800.

as a work center for reporters and editors using CAR in their daily stories and special projects. Yet, as noted, other news organizations have taken a different route by integrating CAR into the entire newsroom through comprehensive training and complete access to resources and tools needed for CAR.

Paul McElroy, systems editor for the Seattle *Post-Intelligencer,* feels CAR desks are not needed:

> This concept can give rise to the misconception that CAR projects must always be lengthy and complicated. In many, many cases, CAR is useful even when writing on deadline. Several of our reporters regularly dial into our state and federal court systems for online record searches. A few are also quick to turn to a spreadsheet to crunch numbers for budget or election stories. Having said all that, a formal CAR desk can be useful if the resources are available to create one. Reporters can concentrate on reporting while we systems editor types handle the technical infrastructure of getting data into usable forms. A CAR desk can also serve as a common meeting ground for discussing problems, techniques, ideas, and so on. (personal communication, October 13, 1995)

Neil Reisner, training director for NICAR and former database editor for *The Bergen Record,* also believes that existence of a CAR desk does not encourage widespread use of CAR tools in newsrooms:

> But that seems to cut against what much of the industry is doing. I believe that CAR is merely another arrow in the quiver of journalism's armaments. Everyone should use CAR techniques when appropriate, just as everyone uses the telephone or a newsroom writing terminal. There is no part of journalism to which CAR does not have some application, be it the municipal reporter analyzing a town budget, the feature writer analyzing census data for a lifestyle or trend story, or the sports writer using a spreadsheet to compile team statistics. I

believe concentrating the technology at a special CAR desk mitigates against these sorts of uses and promotes creation of a CAR elite. That's not the most effective use of the tool. (personal communication, October 30, 1995)

As shown in Table 2.5, a total of 44% of newspapers responding in 1995 used some form of a CAR desk to coordinate and conduct computer-assisted newsgathering. A total of 47% of the newspapers in the 1994 study had created CAR desks, and 21% reported plans to add a CAR desk or project team, as shown in Table 2.6. In the 1995 survey, the proportion of newsrooms with CAR desks dropped slightly to 43%. Of the 55% that did not have desks, 56% reported plans to add one within a year.

Newsroom individuals in charge of CAR have a wide range of titles and responsibilities. Many are called directors, supervisors, or coordinators. But their duties remain similar despite the variation in titles. The typical CAR manager coordinates use of the computing resources, acquires databases, often oversees use of online services, trains other reporters, and serves as a liaison with upper level newsroom management. At some larger newspapers, a CAR super-

TABLE 2.5
CAR Desks, 1995

CAR Desk of Some Type in Place	Large Dailies[a]		Small Dailies[b]		Totals	
Yes	93	66.4%	30	21.1%	123	43.6%
No	46	32.9	112	78.9	158	56.0
Don't know	1	0.7	0	0.0	1	0.4
Totals	140	49.6	142	50.4	282	100.0

Note. $n = 287$; missing observations = 5.
[a] Circulation over 52,800.   [b] Circulation under 52,800.

TABLE 2.6
CAR Desks, 1994–1995

Car Desk of Some Type in Place	1994		1995		Percentage Change
Yes	98	47.1%	123	42.9%	–4.2%
No	104	50.0	158	55.1	–5.1
Don't know/ missing	6	2.9	6	2.0	–0.9
Totals	208	100.0%	287	100.0%	

visor may be database oriented only, leaving supervision of online resources and research to the news research or news library director or editor.

The number of individuals involved in CAR in newsrooms is increasing even if the proportion of desks is decreasing. The mean number of persons involved in CAR in 1995 was reported to be 4.74 per newspaper, with numerous newspapers reporting none and one reporting as many as 75 persons. In 1994, the number involved in CAR was 3.54 persons. It makes sense to anticipate continued growth in the number of individuals involved in CAR in 1996 and beyond as more and more newsrooms take a full saturation approach.

EMPOWERMENT THROUGH NEWSROOM TRAINING

Most newsroom managers feel that computer-based analysis of public and private records in the form of electronic databases is important and will grow in importance for the rest of this decade (Friend, 1994; Garrison, 1995). That will require a lot of veteran journalists to learn a lot about computing in a very short amount of time. The training "gold rush" is on. The prize for the "prospectors" is computer literacy and full use of CAR's capabilities.

However, training is a sore spot for many working reporters and editors. It should be a major tool toward success in using computers in the newsroom, most computing experts believe. Many working professional journalists want training, professional development, or some sort of continuing education while they work because they simply cannot stop working, return to school, and earn a graduate degree or a second bachelor's degree. Many journalists feel it is part of their employer's responsibilities to employees to extend their education while working to permit personal career growth and improved overall performance.

Barbara Hijek, assistant library director in the Tampa bureau of the *St. Petersburg Times*, feels the need for training has modified the role of online news researchers:

> The role of the news librarian has changed. As reporters gain more access to databases (especially the lower-cost government access ones and the Internet as opposed to the more expensive boutique databases like Nexis), the news librarian is emerging more as an information coach—directing reporters to sources, guiding them through the maze of appropriate databases to use and cautioning them about the pitfalls of online information.

Many times I tell our reporters—consider this information as a good tip sheet—check it out and verify the info. Databases provide info-rich background on individuals. WDIA often lists an individual's employer. This is often valuable. For example, after the Oklahoma City bombing the media became obsessed about citizen militias. We decided to look into the activity level of our local militias. We found the leader of the 77th regiment of Pinellas County. The militias are united through their very basic belief that the federal government has gone haywire. They tend to have a deep distrust of the government. Well, our local militia leader would not disclose where he worked—only that he has a day job "enforcing contracts." Well, WDIA revealed that he worked for the local county in a permit office. Some anti-government minuteman! (personal communication, November 15, 1995)

A Critical Need for Continuing Education

Kathleen Hansen is an associate professor and online research expert in the School of Journalism and Mass Communication at the University of Minnesota. A former librarian at the University of Wisconsin–Milwaukee and at the University of Wisconsin–Madison, she feels that continuing education is the single most important way to succeed with CAR in the newsroom:

Training, training, training. Unfortunately, news organizations are among the most stingy groups on the planet when it comes to furthering the education of their workforce. But I have gone to meeting after workshop after conference with journalists who are *desperate* to upgrade their skills, including CAR skills. Some even go so far as to pay their own way during their vacation times to get to IRE workshops or special training sessions offered by some local or regional group. The obvious way to keep CAR going in the newsroom is to have a variety of types of folks who have "bought in" to the system and who understand how CAR can be useful in everyday reporting and editing. The worst strategy, in my view, is to designate some kind of CAR guru, the keeper of the secrets, the computer, and the database access codes. Spread it around, let everyone who's interested see how the skills and techniques can make their jobs easier, more interesting, more challenging, of better service to the community. This training should be done in-house as much as possible, with occasional "inspirational" visits by leading experts who come in to cheer on the crowd and keep interest high. (personal communication, September 19, 1995)

Newspapers have a variety of ways to bring training to newsrooms (see Fig. 2.1). At *The Philadelphia Inquirer,* for example, "Bit-by-Bit University" has been created to train reporters and editors how to use spreadsheets, World Wide Web browsers and Internet resources, and other CAR tools. The program consists of a series of classes held

- In-house classes
- Individual tutoring or coaching
- Local workshops or classes
- National or regional conferences and seminars
- Supplemental publications

FIG. 2.1. Popular approaches to CAR training.

in a small room just a few steps away from the newsroom. The classroom is equipped with personal computers, online connections, and software. It is used by news staffers, advertising staffers, and other employees of Philadelphia Newspapers, Inc., which also publishes the *Philadelphia Daily News.*

"Training is mandatory in my view. People must know the ins and outs of the software they are using, and the ups and downs of using numbers. Using computers to analyze data, for instance, opens up a whole new way to mess up our facts and maybe not even notice until it is too late," stated Carol Napolitano (personal communication, September 29, 1995), a member of the public affairs team of the *Omaha World-Herald* and a CAR specialist. She had been in charge of CAR training when she was on the staff of *The Times* in Munster, Indiana. "We began by individually working with the people most interested. Then we held training sessions, each three days long, nine hours a day. We covered the basics of personal computers, DOS, Windows, statistics and math, database managers, spreadsheets, graphing, mapping, and Internet use over those twenty-seven hours. Classes were small, three to five people per session. It was pretty successful."

Fighting Complacency in Newsrooms

Despite the interest to be trained and to offer training in some newsrooms, some editors report that their staff members are complacent and have no desire to grow beyond their current skills. CAR is one such area for improving reporting skills. Some editors say their staffs have no interest in learning CAR. They say they are quite perplexed by the seeming lack of interest in computing shown by younger reporters. One editor criticized colleges for not providing the computing background for graduates. "I am surprised by the lack of interest in CAR manifest in my reporting and editing staff of eighty-seven people. And these are young people!" exclaimed Managing Editor Paul Jagnow (personal communication, January 22, 1995), who selects, buys, supports, and develops CAR for the 95,000-circulation *Vindicator* in Youngstown, Ohio. "I'm not sure the 20- to 35-year-old group received enough computer training in college. They don't seem to be interested in, or committed to, computers, except to learn enough about them to input copy, write heads, and so forth."

Some small news organizations are using unique arrangements to bring CAR into their newsrooms and to facilitate CAR training. In Oshkosh, Wisconsin, for example, the 26,000-daily circulation *Oshkosh Northwestern* could not afford its own training program, so it became part of a program funded by a grant that brought an outside expert to the newspaper for part of a year. With funding from the Knight Institute for Journalism Excellence, the American Society of Newspaper Editors, and the Knight Foundation, Executive Editor Thomas P. Lee was able to invite Arizona State University Journalism Professor Ed Sylvester for a summer to help set up the equipment and facilities, within the newspaper's limited resources, and to teach CAR skills to staff members for 6 weeks on site (Lee, 1995; Sylvester, 1995).

The *Palm Beach Post's* Mary Kate Leming offered an argument for investing in training, whether staff members seek it or not: "A big problem with CAR is, since not enough training is done and reporters are not given time away from their daily beat, that it is often done sloppily. There's a real risk there. I've seen computer projects happen where you get to the day before publication and somebody goes, 'I don't know how I got that number. How did I get that number?' and they can't go back and replicate what they did. That's very scary."

Arkansas Democrat-Gazette CAR Editor Bob Dunn (personal communication January 25, 1995) agreed, saying CAR needs to be taught at journalism schools as well as on the job to working journalists: "Reporters need to learn how to use computers, databases, and spreadsheets. Journalism schools need to make that part of the curriculum."

Laura Frank is a former CAR team leader and reporter for Gannett's Rochester newspapers, the *Democrat and Chronicle* and *Times-Union*, who moved to the *Nashville Tennessean* in mid-1995. She emphasizes training in her role of "assisting reporters in using CAR for every-day stories." Frank explained the importance of learning CAR: "CAR is a powerful tool. Training is essential—any mistakes made with CAR are magnified by its power" (personal communication, March 27, 1995).

Nieman Fellow Brad Goldstein (personal communication, January 31, 1995), computer-assisted reporting editor for the *St. Petersburg Times*, was previously a reporter for *The Eagle Tribune* in Lawrence, Massachusetts. He supervises CAR for *The Times*. Goldstein was not satisfied with the Lawrence newspaper's approach to CAR: "Despite all of the successes, *The Eagle Tribune* staff does not see the light in terms of allocating resources, or even training, reporters to use their tools," he noted. "They (the managers) want it done on personal time, not company time. And they manage from editors down."

Many news organizations expect their staff members to learn CAR on their own. *Fresno Bee* reporter Russell Clemings (personal communication, February 5, 1995) explained: "Our management has historically failed to encourage or support computer use, other than for production (e.g., Leafdesk and remote filing of stories). Those who have developed those skills have mainly done so on their own."

Supplementing Training With Publications

The Hartford Courant is typical of many news organizations trying to supplement training with locally produced publications. *The Courant's* Computer Reporting Center publishes a monthly report for news staffers called *dataBasics*. Larry Roberts (personal communication, February 10, 1995), projects editor, organizes articles about databases, files, coverage ideas, analysis of data, new tools for staff, and plenty of how-to tips and ideas.

Similarly, Deborah Wolfe produces *Tech Talk* for newsroom staffers of the *St. Petersburg Times*. Wolfe, newsroom technology training coordinator, began the bimonthly in-house publication. Like *dataBasics*, Wolfe's newsletter runs 8 to 12 pages and covers a wide range of subjects such as newsroom information gathering technology, Internet ideas and tricks, upcoming in-house training classes, hardware and software advice, using the newsroom's Coyote system more effectively, accessing and using electronic public records, e-mail, and use of statistics (Wolfe, personal communication, August 11, 1995; Wolfe, 1995).

Prerequisite Skills for Employment?

Computer-assisted reporting skills are rapidly becoming the cutoff point in determining who makes the "employed list" or "preferred reporting team" and who does not in many newsrooms. At professional meetings, editors often discuss the need for employees to have CAR skills. Reporters know it. Students are beginning to seek them as an edge in the job application race.

"The candidates with computer-assisted reporting skills stay. All those without those skills are eliminated. The candidates with on-line searching experience stay. All those without that experience are eliminated," observed *Waterbury Republican-American* systems editor Christopher Feola and San Francisco State University Journalism Professor Tom Johnson (1995, p. 24). Feola and Johnson talked with consultants and newsroom managers. From their discussions, they concluded that reporters need CAR skills, particularly the ability to use spreadsheets, use data on nine-track tape, conduct online research, and the ability to manage new media such as electronic newspapers or the World Wide Web.

A New Role for News Researchers

Leading newsroom researchers agree that there needs to be more training and many argue that the individuals to do that training are news librarians. Some, such as the Poynter Institute's online authority, Nora Paul, believe that news librarians should become the trainers of newsroom personnel in the area of computer use, especially online services (Albers, 1994b).

In some newsrooms, training responsibilities have begun to fall into the news library's domain. At several newspapers, such as the Raleigh *News & Observer* and the *St. Petersburg Times,* news researchers have been tapped as full-time newsroom computer trainers. However, some news organizations depend on part-time in-house training provided by the existing CAR newsroom staff.

The types of training offered also vary. More and more, in-house classes are becoming common at larger newspapers. However, smaller news organizations must go outside for training, bring in temporary experts for special in-house classes, or send selected employees to workshops and seminars offered by outside experts, such as local computing companies or schools or journalism organizations such as the NICAR at the University of Missouri.

"I've taught some classes for our newsroom and I was encouraged by how much interest there was. The problem is that after the class, everybody goes back to their daily beat and very few make any use of it. Their skills atrophy and, by the time they're ready to do something CAR-related, they have to be taught all over again," observed Ray Robinson (personal communication, September 7, 1995), projects editor at *The Press of Atlantic City:*

I'm coming around to the idea that the best kind of training, at least in the beginning, is that which emphasizes possibilities rather than the nuts and bolts technical aspects. Instead of drowning them in how-to stuff that they're going to forget, dazzle them with what can be done using CAR. Then, when they're ready to tackle a project, you can teach the hard part to them on a more individualized basis.

Some papers are expecting all of their staffers to learn CAR and even tackle at least one CAR project. I don't like that approach. In any newsroom there are going to be some people who have a gift for this kind of work and some that don't. Those that don't should be allowed to use whatever other talents they have. Newsrooms are wonderfully diverse places, and we should encourage that, not try to turn every staffer into a database editor. Using a PC isn't such a vital skill that everyone should be required to learn it as a condition of their employment, at least not yet.

Neill Borowski, CAR director at *The Philadelphia Inquirer,* likes to use a "spider plant" model to teach CAR in his newsroom. He starts with his two-person CAR leadership team. "Like a spider plant, you have a CAR core. Like the plant, the core sends off chutes. And the chutes send off more chutes. There are generations of chutes and you eventually have a lush plant," Borowski (personal communication, November 17, 1995) explained.

Training Remains a Low Priority

Minnesota's Hansen (personal communication, September 19, 1995), a national authority in information technology, the sociology of news work, and related issues, sees in-house or localized computer services and databases training as much too low on the priority list in most newsrooms:

It is the rare newsroom or publishing hierarchy that sees fit to train their news workers. Therefore, the professional organizations are *crucial* for the educational function. I haven't thought much about their role for setting standards—I suppose they do that, but in a more informal way. My own knowledge and level of comfort with all of this has been greatly enhanced by my participation at IRE, Poynter, AP, and other types of professional workshops and conferences.

Lack of resources is one barrier to CAR training as well as CAR itself in many newsrooms, but training has been an even more severe problem for some news organizations wanting to begin CAR. If a desktop computer or several computers exist in a newsroom for part-time or full-time use for CAR, there may be such demand for use for the PC that training time takes a back seat. Because responsible and accurate use of computers in reporting requires considerable computer literacy, some sort of on-the-job training has become an important issue in almost all newsrooms. Although some recent entry-level journalists may be learning CAR in some colleges, most journalists must learn CAR while at work.

Dependence on External Training Programs

News organizations without their own CAR training programs are dependent on outside programs such as those offered by the IRE and NICAR. There are several journalism organizations that offer training on a regular basis. By far, the leader has been NICAR. Both IRE and NICAR have taken their CAR classes on the road since 1994, but learning opportunities are still rare for most journalists. The alternative, in-house training, is coming along slowly. However, the 1995 data, displayed in Table 2.7, show 44% reported some form of CAR-related training. Larger dailies (66%) use some type of training three times more frequently than smaller dailies (21%).

Table 2.8 shows a jump in growth in training. In 1995, 11% more newspapers offered some form of training than did in 1994. In 1994, only 30% of newspapers responding reported in-house CAR training

TABLE 2.7
CAR Training Programs, 1995

Training Programs of Some Type in Place	Large Dailies[a]		Small Dailies[b]		Totals	
Yes	90	66.2%	28	21.4%	118	44.2%
No	46	33.8	103	78.6	149	55.8
Totals	136	50.9	131	49.1	267	100.0

Note. n = 287; missing observations = 20.
[a] Circulation over 52,800. [b] Circulation under 52,800.

TABLE 2.8
CAR Training Programs, 1994–1995

CAR Desk of Some Type in Place	1994		1995		Percentage Change
Yes	62	29.8%	118	41.1%	+11.3%
No	117	56.3	149	51.9	−4.4
Missing	29	13.9	20	7.0	−6.9
Totals	208	100.0%	287	100.0%	

of any type (Garrison, 1995), but the figure was up to 41% of the responding newspapers in the 1995 study. This indicates more concern about training and investment in it by newsroom managers.

Without careful planning, training can go wrong. Editors who are unable to offer newsroom-wide training must make decisions about who to train and how to train the selected individuals. This is typical of the problems facing small newspapers with limited resources. "One thing you have to be careful about as an editor is training. You

---

HOW TO SUCCEED WITH CAR CLASSES

Computer-assisted reporting newsroom coordinators or newsroom trainers experienced in teaching journalists how to use their computers in a more effective manner know that certain things work and others do not. Here's a checklist of tips for successful teaching use of computers:

- *Syllabus.* Prepare an overall training program plan and individual class outlines. Like any teacher, preparation should be at least half of the total effort.
- *Schedules.* Schedule classes well enough in advance to permit planning and attendance, making sure supervisors approve of the schedule.
- *Handouts.* Prepare a class "textbook."A set of handouts will work if there is not enough time or resources to produce a text. (Tip: Consider using the latest workbook from the National Institute for Computer-Assisted Reporting. Copies can be purchased from NICAR.)
- *Coziness.* Have dedicated space for classes and keep each class small. This may be limited by the number of computers available, but each class member should have access to a computer for the most effective learning.
- *Pacing.* Don't try to go too fast or cover too much in a single class. Keep the classes focused.
- *Hands-on.* Provide ample time for hands-on practice no matter what subject is taught.
- *Examples.* Use plenty of examples with real exercises (e.g., related to current stories in progress, sample online searches, or real database analysis problems).
- *Discussion.* Encourage questions and answers during the class. Keep the session informal and casual.
- *Simplicity.* Avoid using too much software and hardware jargon unless class members understand the terms. If they do not, explain what each one means as each is introduced.
- *Interaction.* Seek feedback from class members to improve the effort next time around.
- *Accessibility.* Make certain that at least one newsroom computer is available between classes for student practice sessions.

have to figure out who you are going to send to seminars," stated Thomas P. Lee, executive editor of the *Northwestern* in Oshkosh, Wisconsin. "I wasted some money big time last year sending some people to seminars. They came back with nothing: The training, the encouragement—everything we could do and it just didn't happen. You send the right people and it's going to pay off. My advice is to make a list of the people who are going to do really well at a seminar and then throw in a couple of others and hope, through osmosis, it is going to happen."

A closer look at training at the newspapers in 1995, reported in Table 2.9, shows most training to be in-house classes or seminars (52% of those offering any training) or in-house tutoring (15%). Providing outside training opportunities, such as workshops and seminars, is also popular (15%). Another substantial number used ad hoc or informal training programs (9%). As with training in general, there are significant differences in large and small newspapers and the type of training they offer to staff members. Larger newspapers tend to offer more structured training programs than do smaller dailies. Larger newspaper programs are more often class oriented, whereas smaller newspapers use ad hoc or one-on-one training when it is available at all.

TABLE 2.9
Training Program Types, 1995

Type of Training Program	Large Dailies[a]		Small Dailies[b]		Totals	
In-house classes	52	58.4%	10	33.3%	62	52.1%
In-house tutoring	15	16.9	3	10.0	18	15.1
Outside workshops	13	14.6	5	16.7	18	15.1
Informal or ad hoc	7	7.9	4	13.3	11	9.2
Just beginning CAR	1	1.1	6	20.0	7	5.9
Newsletter or handouts	1	1.1	1	3.3	2	1.7
Committee work	0	0.0	1	3.3	1	0.8
Totals	89	74.8	30	25.2	119	100.0

Note. $n = 287$; missing observation = 168.
[a]Circulation over 52,800. [b]Ciculation under 52,800.

3

Projects and Daily Computer-Assisted Reporting

Often one news story leads to another. This was the case for *The Miami Herald* reporters Jeff Leen and Don Van Natta, Jr. Leen, an investigative reporter, teamed with Van Natta, a courts reporter, to begin checking into some impressions they had developed about crime in South Florida. Shortly after President Clinton selected a Miami resident, Dade County State Attorney Janet Reno, to be his new attorney general in early 1993, the newspaper began assessing at her overall record in South Florida to determine its successes and failures and, perhaps, to suggest her performance as the nation's top prosecutor (Carleton, 1995; Greene, Leen, & Van Natta, 1994).

"It was right after there had been several tourists murdered, especially one case involving some tourists from Germany, in summer 1993, that drew considerable international attention to Miami and its crime problem," Leen (personal communication, September 19, 1995) explained:

> The newsroom galvanized to look at crime. There were reporters writing daily stories and we were the long-range reporters on crime. Crime went to the top of the newsroom agenda that summer after it had been down the list for a period of time. We knew that Reno's office had a very aberrant record of sending people to prison, but we had not been able to investigate any of these problems we had heard about until then. Both Don and I had sources in the criminal justice system who had told us about problems with discovery, about various pressures on the legal system, and we suspected there was something there.

Leen and Van Natta began investigating the amount of crime and the degree of punishment in Dade County after the assessment of the Reno record led to the conclusion that there might be serious problems with conviction rates as well as sentencing for crimes of all types. The experienced court reporting team, working with Stephen K. Doig, *The Herald's* associate editor for research and CAR specialist, reporter Ronnie Greene, and a team of more than a dozen other journalists, began collecting data. The reporters searched court records for both Dade County and Broward County (Fort Lauderdale) on paper and on computer tapes acquired by the newspaper. They also checked crime statistics from major cities in the nation. They acquired and analyzed 10 criminal databases from federal, state, and county levels. The team also studied 14 years' worth of Federal Bureau of Investigation Uniform Crime Reports in electronic form and the traditional published form.

Leen and Van Natta enlisted Doig and Rich Gordon, another newsroom database editor and CAR specialist, to analyze the data while they conducted interviews and did other street reporting. Doig reanalyzed the data and found discrepancies in his findings and those from the county. He concluded that the county had been overcounting convictions; it was counting cases instead of people in compiling its statistics. He also found that one of the largest cities in the county had not reported any crimes or arrests for several years. Doig, a longtime user of the Statistical Analysis System on a mainframe computer, used SAS's OS/2 Ver. 6.10 installed on a 486/66 IBM clone PC in *The Herald's* newsroom to handle the analysis of the very large datasets. The PC was configured with a 1 GB hard drive with 16 MB of memory. The main county database used for the analysis contained about 200,000 counts that were transformed into about 40,000 defendants that had been processed over the period analyzed. The final file used was about 50 MB, Doig (personal communication, September 21, 1995) estimated. "It was very manageable in size for a PC with a decent-sized hard drive. It worked well."

The project took about 8 months from inception to publication. Doig (personal communication, September 21, 1995) explained:

> We, early on, started having weekly meetings of all the people that were involved in this project because it went on for eight months. That was a good idea because it helped us all understand the thing. My role in these kind of projects is not to spend the whole eight months focusing just on that. I was juggling half a dozen other things at the same time. So having these meetings would help me to understand the questions that the reporters wanted to answer. That's my job as CAR editor: to help reporters answer the questions that they have and to use tools that the reporters don't know how to use to ask questions of the data that they know is out there and to produce answers.

Doig said that Leen and Van Natta first checked for existing databases and other sources for answers to their questions about defendants and the rate of punishment they get. "They first looked at the easy ways of getting this, which would be reports by the criminal justice system and things like that. But they found they could not get good answers to their questions. The management information system for the criminal justice system has a different purpose than the purpose we wanted . . . to administer justice, not to measure it."

At some point in their work, the pair decided they needed Doig's help and he became a team member who sought the right databases, checked them, and then analyzed them. He quickly learned that the county's charge-based database was not what he needed. "I realized what we had to do was transform this charge-based database that the county had into a defendant-based database where each record represented an individual who got justice dispensed on a given day. It was a major programming task. I used SAS. Its real strength was that it allowed me to transform the data from one thing into another."

As the analysis proceeded, the answers started coming in. "It was bad, what we were finding out during the investigation. But we didn't realize how bad," Leen, who has worked at *The Herald* since 1982, recalled:

> We knew that things were worse than Broward County. But Steve's computer analyses at the state and national levels gave us context. We began to realize how out of whack we were in Dade County. We realized some things here were very different.

"CRIME & NO PUNISHMENT" DATABASES

Four main categories of databases were used in *The Miami Herald's* "Crime & No Punishment" series (Leen, Doig, & Van Natta, Jr., 1994, p. 1):

- Original research by *Herald* reporters to obtain conviction rates and prison incarceration data for 24 large cities in 13 states.
- *FBI Uniform Crime Report* data contained in 20 separate reports.
- Ten computer criminal justice databases purchased by *The Miami Herald* and analyzed on *The Herald's* mainframe computer.
- Eighty-seven reports on various criminal justice topics from the Bureau of Justice Statistics at the U.S. Department of Justice.

We were surprised. When we did our computer run we call "a day in the life" we did the ultimate analysis. It told us just how bad things were in a single day in Dade County. That part was 100 percent computer run.

Leen believes the computer work helped fill in the broader, more sweeping contours of the reporting that he and Van Natta completed. "We'd get the contours of the story from the statistics and reporting we did. But we filled in the contours and gave context to the stories with Steve's computer work. He was able to provide specifics. The computer data was able to tell us 'this is precisely what happens to career criminals as compared to regular criminals,' for example."

The project was ultimately divided into eight parts. The reporters and their editors decided on these major presentation packages:

1. *Crime & no punishment.* Miami has more crime and less punishment than any other big city in the United States. Criminal defendants go free for a wide range of reasons.
2. *Drug Court: A dumping ground for felons.* The Drug Court is getting attention, easing the court's load, but not getting much else done.
3. *Career criminals: Dade is not retiring its career crooks.* Most of the county's career criminals are not in jail, they are on the street.
4. *Discovery: Victims are getting mugged by the legal system.* The discovery system forces victims to defend themselves twice, once against the criminals and the second time against defense attorneys.
5. *The Herald poll: The consensus in the courts: Crime pays.* The people who work within the Dade legal system—judges, prosecutors, and public defenders—say there is plenty of chaos, leniency, and frustration.
6. *Soft punishment: The cost of leniency.* In Dade, criminals keep coming back to court and the court keeps letting them go.
7. *Sentencing: Miami judges are the most lenient in Florida.* Compared to other South Florida counties, judges were soft on felons. At times, the judges were found to be at fault; at other times, they were not.
8. *Solutions: How to reform Dade's criminal courts.* This portion of the series offered 21 ideas for changing the system, editorials, and columns.

The reporters determined that Dade County had a much lower rate of sending convicted felons to prison when compared to other counties in the state or to the national average. Billed as "Crime & No Punishment," the series was prominently displayed each day it ran. The opening story, introducing readers to the fact that hardened criminals get breaks from the court system to ease overcrowding, is reprinted in Appendix C. Leen and Van Natta, who left *The Herald* in mid-1995 for a position at *The New York Times*, also learned that the odds of being arrested were greater in Dade County when compared to the national average. The overburdened county court system simply could not handle its load, they explained, and the result was lighter conviction rates and shorter sentencing.

Leen and Van Natta got results. Only months after the project's eight-part series completed its run, the Dade Criminal Court experienced significant change. Attorneys volunteered to serve as deputized prosecutors for free. Sentencing toughened and a higher rate of imprisonment resulted. The newspaper also continued to monitor the criminal courts in the year after the series appeared.

"I was surprised with the impact the series had and the attention it got. I knew how entrenched the system was. The project opened the eyes of people who work within the system. They thought they were the same as everybody else," Leen observed. "We were able to examine beliefs that people who worked in the courts held, but never had been examined."

The reporters had expected some change in their relationships with sources within the Dade legal system. It did not happen the way they expected. "Things changed a lot. People in the system felt they had had a bomb dropped on it. They took it personally at first. But when the dust cleared, they saw the constructive element in the series. It hurt them in the beginning, but in the end, they were thankful for the changes it brought," Leen explained.

The reporters, their editors, and others supporting the project produced detailed summaries telling readers how the project was completed. The newspaper, according to Leen, spent about $200,000 in salaries and other expenses to complete the project. Databases, though, were a comparatively minor expense. Leen estimated the newspaper spent about $8,000 to $9,000 on purchases of crime database tapes from the state and other governmental bodies.

The "methods boxes" were published each of the 8 days and detailed the computer analysis and the databases used by the database editors, Doig and Gordon. Despite the details in the 15-paragraph box, readers were then encouraged to seek even more information the newspaper was making available by request. Readers were further offered a 20-page single-spaced technical annex/report for minimal cost (Leen, Doig, & Van Natta, 1994). The report remains available through NICAR or from the reporters themselves. By laying the types of databases and analytical procedures on the table such as this, the reporters and editors working on the project left no doubt as to how the findings were determined.

"If it had been up to me, the entire technical report would have been part of the project and it would have been a thirty-part series," Leen said. "I am a research junkie. I was only using the tip of the iceberg in the newspaper. I wish we could have used the entire technical guide." Leen said the guide was prepared as a matter of normal procedures. After the project was published, the reporters worked for several weeks on follow-ups and then went on a break. When they returned, they prepared the guide with the additional information in it. "We didn't hear any criticisms about our procedures or anything like that," he stated. "We had asked for their numbers and found them to be seriously flawed. We were never able to reconcile the differences, but Steve did it. He found that there were some coding problems."

Doig said such a guide is needed for several reasons:

> Producing a technical guide is at least a passing nod towards the social science tradition of trying to describe your results fully so that they can be replicated by somebody else and, therefore, tested, and so on. This project was so complex, in terms of what we had to do to the data to get it into a form to answer the questions we wanted, that I had to make a lot of arbitrary decisions about the ways we would do it. I wanted to be up front about what we had done. This was not an off-the-shelf database that we took and got a frequency count out of and there was the answer. This required a lot of very complex and, as I said, arbitrary decisions to be made. (personal communication, September 21, 1995)

A project such as "Crime & No Punishment" is not one done by two bylined reporters. It was truly a team effort. The support group for the project was rather massive, in fact. In addition to Leen and Van Natta as reporters, there was a third reporter on some parts of the series; two database editors; two photographers; three local section columnists; five graphic artists for illustrations, graphs, tables, and charts; an editorial cartoonist; a picture editor; a package design director; a page editor; a copy editor; and an overall project editor—or a total of 21 different persons.

The project not only got the attention of judges, attorneys, criminals, crime victims, and the South Florida public in general, it received peer acknowledgment in the form of national or regional awards in 1995 from the Society of Professional Journalists, Investigative Reporters and Editors, the American Bar Association, and the Florida Bar. It was also nominated for a Pulitzer Prize. "One of the lessons from a project such as this is that the computer runs are a starting point for a lot of intense reporting for what the trends mean," Leen, who was 37 when he worked on the project, emphasized. "This requires a lot of old-fashioned leg work—real people, real examples."

MORE SUCCESSFUL STORY AND PROJECT APPROACHES

News organizations that are beginning to use CAR techniques in their daily and project stories might want to consider the suggestion of Thomas P. Lee, executive editor of the *Oshkosh Northwestern*, a small daily in central Wisconsin. Lee recommends considering what makes a community unique and what makes it special to those who live in it. For Oshkosh, it is aviation. The city hosts an annual summer experimental airplane convention that attracts thousands of airplanes and aviators as well as tens of thousands of visitors to the air shows and exhibitions. Lee recommends using databases related to an area's special characteristics, such as Oshkosh's aviation orientation, to bring CAR into the newsroom and to use it successfully for readers. For his newspaper, a Macintosh 6100 with a 28.8-Kbps modem is the tool his news staff uses to access the current Federal Aviation Administration database. "Every market has some unique topic—maybe railroads, gambling, agriculture—in it. When you have the most important topic that makes a community unique, you need to buy some database that covers that particular topic," Lee (1995) suggested. "In our particular case in Oshkosh. . . we bought the aviation database, I think it cost us $300 or $400. There's always a crash at this event, with 10,000 airplanes there. We're guaranteed to have at least one crash. We gave reporters instructions to get the tail number when a plane goes down . . . radio it in, and we call it up on the database. . . . For our newspaper, we needed to make that expenditure."

In addition to choosing subjects unique to a region, what are the elements of successful story and project topics? What constitutes the formula for effective CAR? There are a wide range of perspectives in this ever-evolving form of journalism.

"When you strip away the diversity of topics, the locales and media, and the scope of the projects, the journalists who produced these [CAR] stories share much in common," observed IRE Executive Director Rosemary Armao and NICAR Managing Director Brant Houston (1995, p. v). "They sense something went awry. They saw an irregularity in a system. They possess an imagination for stories. They are indignant over public trust betrayed. And they use a computer."

WHICH WAY TO BEGIN?
BIG OR SMALL CAR STORY?

Penny Loeb, a CAR specialist for *U.S. News & World Report*, described the two major strategies for learning CAR on the job today. Loeb (1995) explained:

There are two schools of thought on computer stories. The first, which is probably less prevalent these days, is that your first project should really be fairly large. Struggling through the data problems and the software problems is the only way you can learn. Naturally, you want to give up at the beginning, in the middle, and, sometimes even at the end. But if you make it, you have learned some really valuable lessons.

The other school of thought, which I think is more prevalent these days, is that your first story should be quick and easy, probably patterned after one done somewhere else in the country. You'll get instant gratification and your editor won't grumble about why you are spending so much time in front of a computer screen.

Mary Kate Leming, assistant managing editor at the *Palm Beach Post*, feels that if CAR is done right, it improves the quality of journalism in a newsroom significantly. "It gives reporters information that they can use to write more informed stories. They have more facts than they ever had before. It can take them in different directions. They make less assumptions and have hard numbers to work with," Leming (personal communication, September 15, 1995) stated.

David Jensen (personal communication, March 30, 1995) is CAR editor for the *Sacramento Bee* in California. Jensen, who coordinates CAR and develops alternative information products for his newspaper, feels it is the small victories using CAR that will ultimately make it valuable to all journalists in newsrooms:

Some examples of the work we have done at *The Bee* illustrate the point that CAR has to be useful everyday to every reporter and editor. We wanted to do a profile of the most Hispanic neighborhood in the area. Sure, we knew many neighborhoods with lots of Hispanics. But which had the greatest percentage of Hispanics? We used census data off a CD-ROM, did a simple ranking and, boy, were we surprised. It turned out to be one of those forgotten little places that hadn't received anything but the slightest mention in the paper in years. The result was a fascinating and fresh story for readers.

Another example involved a new statewide achievement test. The state was not going to rank or compare schools. We took the electronic information, created our own ranking system and told a story about the best and worst schools and why they were that way. Of course, what readers wanted to know about was how their particular school performed. But the material was too voluminous to print in the paper. We took the electronic data, turned it into fax documents for each school that readers could get automatically, free, on demand. Readers without fax machines received the individual school reports from *The Bee* by mail. We faxed out more than 2,700 documents and mailed another 600.

Another example: The state compiles disciplinary records on all physicians but had refused to release the aggregate information electronically. After a successful suit to free the information, two reporters crunched the information and, with the help of eight others reporting, writing, and double-checking, produced a set of front page stories over three days. What it showed was a disciplinary system with serious flaws, one that left patients at risk.

Another example involved finding key sources on the Internet. The subject was domestic abuse and scuttlebutt about an underground railroad for threatened and abused women. Did such a thing really exist? We made some careful inquiries on the Internet and made contact with people who were involved. After interviewing them directly, not over the Internet, and checking their stories, the result was a series about this little-reported phenomena.

BIG AND LITTLE SUCCESSES WITH ONLINE RESOURCES

When asked, most editors, reporters, or news researchers involved in using online services or other online tools in their reporting will say that they have had some successes. Some are big victories, whereas others are little ones by comparison. When asked what their perceived "biggest successes" with online services were, responding newspapers in 1995 reported two categories of responses that stood out more than any others. As displayed in Table 3.1, the leading success was locating background information for news stories (20.4%). The second-leading success was in locating sources online (15.9%). Still, there were other newsgathering advantages or victories using online tools. A total of almost 9% of respondents reported that the simple fact that the resources were being used at all was a big success. Another 8% reported that online services meant extended government reporting through the Internet, Gopher, BBSs, and other government-database services. But the fact that 60.6% of the responding journalists could not report any success stands out as a statement that many newspapers have not

TABLE 3.1
Perceived Major Online Successes, 1995

Type of Success	Frequency	Percentage	Adjusted Percentage
Backgrounding stories	23	8.0	20.4
Finding sources	18	6.3	15.9
Now part of reporting	10	3.5	8.8
Extending government coverage	9	3.1	8.0
Only getting started	8	2.8	7.1
Handy on deadlines	7	2.4	6.2
Reporters getting experience	5	1.7	4.4
Finding hard-to-find information	5	1.7	4.4
Campaign finance news	3	1.0	2.7
Getting news faster	3	1.0	2.7
Making it available	3	1.0	2.7
Checking local records	3	1.0	2.7
Getting it used	3	1.0	2.7
Fully integrated in newsroom	2	0.7	1.8
Surveys and statistics	2	0.7	1.8
Internet coverage	2	0.7	1.8
Learning how to do it	2	0.7	1.8
Big database projects	1	0.3	0.9
Won an award	1	0.3	0.9
Added cyber beat reporter	1	0.3	0.9
9-track tape use	1	0.3	0.9
Better fact checking	1	0.3	0.9
Missing	174	60.6	Missing
Totals	287	100.0	100.0

Note. $n = 287$; missing observations = 174.

yet discovered the advantages of online journalism or, if they have, they are still a step away from using it successfully.

DEVELOPING SOLID CAR STORY IDEAS

The types of stories being produced from these computing tools cover a wide spectrum of subjects and approaches in both the 1994 and 1995 studies. From Pulitzer Prize winners involving agriculture in North Carolina in 1996, race relations in Akron in 1994, and hurricane damage in South Florida in 1993, to daily lifestyle and

---

EASY-TO-USE PUBLIC DATABASES FOR CAR BEGINNERS

Local Databases

- Traffic tickets and accident reports
- City and county government budgets
- Schools attendance and test scores
- Voter registration
- City and county election results
- Building permits

State Databases

- Professional regulation licenses
- Driver's licenses and motor vehicle registrations
- Traffic tickets and accident reports

Federal Databases

- FBI Uniform Crime Reports
- Federal Reserve Board Home Mortgage Disclosure Act records
- Federal Election Commission campaign contributors
- Social Security Administration death records
- Bureau of Census population reports
- Occupational Safety and Health Administration Workplace Safety Reports

---

pet features nationwide, the topics cover just about all aspects of publicly documented life. What are the most popular story and project topics? They didn't seem to change much over the year. Among the favorites, not reported in any order, offered by respondents in the 1995 University of Miami CAR survey of newspapers included:

- 1990 census stories.
- Political Action Committee political campaign contributors investigations.
- Long-distance or cellular telephone call records.
- Election results analysis.
- Local poll creating a database of public opinion.
- Crime statistics (such as homicides, incident reports, and drunken driving)
- Accident locations.
- State and local courts and their sentencing patterns.
- Public check registers.
- City budgets or other approaches to local government spending.
- Death records and medical examiner records.

- School system test scores.
- Environmental pollution or toxic waste data.
- Vehicle inspections.
- State or county personnel, payroll, and employment records.
- Alcohol, tobacco, and firearms licenses and records.

Most of the categories listed generated serious investigations and stories about problems in society. Something was wrong in a community, reporters identified it, and used CAR to document and analyze it. But there is a fun side to CAR stories as well. Some of the most popular feature ideas that have succeeded with readers or viewers include the analysis of pet license databases, marriage license databases, and winning (or losing) lottery numbers or ticket sales sites.

Extensive lists of such stories ideas are available from those who are deeply involved in CAR. Two such lists with even more ideas

---

SUCCESS AT A MEDIUM-SIZED DAILY

Ray Robinson (personal communication, September 7, 1995) , projects editor at *The Press of Atlantic City* in New Jersey, described how his newspaper has made effective use of CAR:

We've had several successes. The major one, I guess, would be a series we did on the charter bus industry. It was particularly important for this area, because about 1,000 buses per day come to Atlantic City. We got interested because a fatal bus accident in northern New Jersey, and the subsequent investigation, exposed some real flaws in the regulatory apparatus for the bus industry. We found out that the state conducts thousands of surprise, roadside inspections of buses bound for Atlantic City every year.

But because of New Jersey's 19th century attitudes to public information, we were unable to get the data. We did some more digging, however, and found out that the inspections are conducted under a grant from the U.S. Department of Transportation. And the results of the state inspections are uploaded to the feds.

Using the federal FOIA, we were able to get the inspection data for the entire country. Our analysis showed that about 10 percent of the buses are found to be too dangerous to be on the highway under federal standards. We also found that the same companies get caught again and again, but choose to pay the incredibly small fines as a cost of business, rather than fixing their buses. The series prompted New Jersey to pass a new, tougher bus safety law, which was signed into law this year.

than those already listed have been compiled by Carol Napolitano (1995), a public affairs reporter and CAR specialist at the *Omaha World-Herald*, and 1996 Pulitzer Prize winner Pat Stith (1995), a database editor at the *News & Observer* in Raleigh. Another excellent source is the IRE's annual collection of CAR projects (Barnett, 1995).

CAR IN TELEVISION AND RADIO NEWSROOMS

Although CAR got its start at larger newspapers and news magazines, it is also catching on in medium and small dailies. Gradually, some broadcast newsrooms are adopting the tools, but they have been much slower than their print counterparts. For the most part, more local market television newsrooms are using online CAR tools than database tools. However, the network television and radio organizations are using CAR more than local broadcast journalists and using it for both its online and database advantages. This is slowly changing at the local level. Network television and radio news have been longtime users of surveys and polls, one of many CAR database-oriented tools, but other applications of computers to newsgathering have been adapted in recent years. Both local television and radio news organizations are beginning to use online tools with regularity in their newsgathering and some are also beginning to use database tools.

Mike Wendland, an investigative reporter for WDIV-TV in Detroit, is one of the local market television journalists using CAR tools in his on-air work. "We are the minority, those of us who are in television news. More and more are, though. A couple of years ago, there were two or three television journalists at these conferences," Wendland (1995b) told a group at a NICAR conference in Cleveland. "Now we've got well over a dozen."

Although he may have been joking slightly, the fact is that television and radio are not the best formats for CAR stories. Not yet anyway. Bringing quantitative information to television, or any video format for that matter, is a difficult task. Television stations have been trying to find the best ways to do this since the 1960s and 1970s, even with today's advanced computer technology and graphics tools.

Paul Adrian (1995), a reporter for WAVE-TV in Louisville, believes it can be done in an effective manner:

> Some folks say computers produce numbers and numbers don't work well on television. Well, too many numbers don't work well in print

either. We must do the same thing in television that print journalists do in their database stories. Use numbers as a foundation only. Wrap real people around every statistic. . . . [H]ere's the difference between a database piece and the typical consultant-driven TV story: After doing a data analysis story, we have the best foundation for a story we've probably ever had. So, if it's well told, I believe that will make your story rise above all the others in the newscast. I use everything at my disposal to make a data piece interesting. That includes music, graphics, and fancy video. I also boil down the stats to the bare essentials, because I know having too much information is no better than having none at all. (p. 2)

Wendland is a bit unusual in that he began his career as a newspaper reporter. He worked for 10 years at *The Detroit News.* This may explain part of his interest in more sophisticated reporting tools, but it probably simply shows a different orientation to the newsgathering process than most reporters in television have. Wendland gathers information first and then finds a way to make it visually attractive. Most television journalists work in reverse; that is, finding the video and writing the story to it. Although this may not be true of all broadcast news stories, it is certainly a factor for many of them, and this contributes to the difficulty many television and radio journalists have in bringing database-oriented CAR to their newsrooms.

The situation may not be true for online services. Many television stations in 1995 and 1996 began to use online tools to communicate with audiences, but not as much in a newsgathering capacity. This is changing, also. Just as Wendland noted that few television journalists are going to the extreme of attending conferences devoted to CAR techniques, the number is growing slowly. Just as happened with newspapers and some news magazines in the early 1990s, the process is beginning with one or two computer-savvy individuals in the newsroom and gradually spreading to others.

Rich Robertson (1995), an investigative reporter for KPHO in Phoenix and a former *Arizona Republic* reporter, believes that setting up CAR for a TV newsroom is no different than for a newspaper. "I came from a newspaper which was the 16th largest newspaper in the country and was barely getting into computers. In the last three or four years, we managed to build a program (at his newspaper) from scratch in a way that we can do in television as well. We have now got a fairly sophisticated set-up at our station."

Wendland (1995b) recommends broadcast newsrooms start slowly, beginning with one or two online services, such as America Online, CompuServe, or the Microsoft Network (MSN). Each have easy use for beginners, but also provide strong news content, Internet access, and significant television and broadcast components such as MSN's access to MSN News, or NBC's SuperNet, he explained, that are valuable in TV newsrooms. He also recommends investment in several basic reference CD-ROM discs as well as the more common inexpensive federal agency databases available on disc:

> We became a quick expert on the Michigan militia when the Oklahoma bombing occurred and when the raids occurred in Michigan. Between going online and using the data we were already able to pull up from directories, we were able to be on the air for three solid hours constantly using the laptop and computer in our newsroom and bringing information back to the set. Some of it was stuff the wires were behind on, but it was able to keep us talking and reporting.

Going online has another advantage for television journalists as well, both Wendland and Robertson agreed. "One of the things you need to do to get CAR going in your newsrooms keep in touch, to do a lot more networking using e-mail, for example," Wendland stated.

"A few years ago, developing a document mentality was always beaten into investigative reporters. There's a document for everything," Robertson (1995) said:

> That is slowly changing now to suggest we have to develop a database mentality. Everything out there that you are looking for is probably in some form of data or database. That might be the budgets for the city council on through to some of the federal transportation safety board records. . . . When you go out and start thinking about applications for computer-assisted reporting, there's almost nothing that you get involved in—I can't think of a story that I have done in the last six or eight years—that hasn't involved a computer in some way in processing the information, storing it, gathering it, or whatever.

David Bartlett, president of the Radio-Television News Directors Association in 1994–1995, has observed a steady growth of online usage by broadcast journalists. In fact, Bartlett believes electronic journalism itself is changing and use of online tools is part of this metamorphosis. Bartlett (1995) stated:

> The definition of electronic journalism is going to be broader; it will not be just radio and television any more. It will be graphics, the Internet, text, data. Great libraries of information all will become integral parts of electronic journalism. . . . So far, I'm not aware of anybody making routine use of the Internet to retrieve audio and

video. Some of them are putting it onto the network, but nobody's making a business out of it. For retrieval, it's being used by other print and electronic media for gathering information and data (in print form). This is becoming an adjunct to the well-established technique of computer-assisted reporting.

A recent national survey of television and radio news directors underlines Bartlett's predictions. The study reported that 76% of news directors questioned either had or planned to add an Internet World Wide Web site (Cahners Publishing Research Department, 1995).

A NEWS MAGAZINE CAR PROJECT

Perhaps much of the attention thrust on CAR in the past 5 or 6 years has been caused by a few award competitions. The awards might not have caused the flurry of attention, but these honors certainly have not hurt the cause for CAR. It is widely known among CAR believers that these tools can lead to major recognition for projects of significance. From 1989 through 1994 and again in 1996, for example, Pulitzer Prizes were awarded to major projects by newspapers in Raleigh, Atlanta, Minneapolis, Indianapolis, Kansas City, Miami, and Akron (Garrison, 1995, p. 11).

However, major CAR projects are not limited to daily newspapers. *U.S. News & World Report*, the weekly news magazine based in Washington, DC, has built a reputation in recent years for its projects as well. For example, in 1994, the magazine published a 5-month project that investigated the safety of blood and risks involved in transfusions at hospitals and other medical centers. The project investigated specific cases involving patients who had died or experienced additional medical problems because of blood that was contaminated in one way or another. Reporters Richard J. Newman, Doug Podolsky, and Penny Loeb worked on the project, completing approximately 150 interviews with sources, reviewing U.S. Food and Drug Administration records, and analyzing additional FDA databases for their 10-page special report.

"For 'How Safe is Our Blood,' we got six different databases and built three of our own. We made sixteen Freedom of Information Act requests, 150 interviews. This was a huge project and we were able to say some very precise things about what was going on about our blood supply," said Podolsky (1995), a health and medicine reporter for the magazine since 1990. "Basically, it is not as safe as most people think. There are lots of problems with the way blood is being handled. There are lots of mistakes made and there are even mistakes made by donors."

The reporting team used the Freedom of Information Act (FOIA) to access a total of nine government databases that contained information about blood safety that were analyzed. In addition, the reporting team created new databases from information contained in Food and Drug Administration (FDA) records. One new database combined more than 1,000 FDA recall records with data manually taken from almost 3,000 pages of FDA reports. Two other databases drew from more than 10,500 visually scanned microfiche documents concerning FDA actions taken. The fourth database was developed from a survey of 15 blood banks taken during the project.

Podolsky (1995) explained one of the important databases for the project:

> The FDA keeps a database of errors and accidents reported by blood banks and plasma. It shows whether the blood bank involved was licensed or unlicensed, whether it was an American Red Cross blood bank or non-ARC blood bank, state, name of blood bank, when the error occurred, when it was discovered, when it was reported to the FDA, when the FDA received the report, the type of error involved, type of blood product involved, and the actual unit numbers that identify the blood bags involved. Error codes help you to analyze whether errors were made in routine testing for blood type and compatibility, viral testing, collection, labeling, donor screening, deferral, product quarantining, storage, and shipping. It also shows whether the error was due to a computer malfunction, instrument malfunction, or data entry mistake.

Databases made a major difference in the project, Podolsky stated. "Getting the data enabled us to summarize—during every step of the way in the blood line through screening potential donors to the actual transfusion—the different types of problems that arise and how many per year that occur."

The project was published with full-color graphics, such as one that depicted how blood is handled from donor to recipient. Other informational graphics included a summary of the most frequent error and accident reports involving blood banks and the most frequent blood center blood recall repeaters. There were also three sidebars and three smaller profiles of patients who suffered additional medical problems caused by bad blood.

"A lot of the data we put on one page, in chart and graph form. The package was very precise, but told a very compelling story," Podolsky noted. "There was a lot of data, but you cannot lose sight of the fact that there were people. We used a lot of anecdotal illustrations of real people, real stories, and real names of people who had problems with blood . . . HIV problems, hepatitis, and blood borne bacterial disease."

DAILY REPORTING INVOLVING ONLINE SERVICES

One of the biggest selling points about CAR is the ease of access to information through online connections to the Internet, commercial services, and other networked databases. The advantages and purposes of online research are well documented (Garrison, 1995; Paul, 1994), but more journalists each year are learning how to integrate online CAR into their daily newsgathering. Identifying and locating sources are two of the main routine uses of online CAR for reporters.

"I hate having PR people choose what I should write about, much less shape, spin or subtly slant my stories. So I scout out my own experts and story sources on-line," stated California freelance reporter Joel Grossman (1994). "Cyberspace is teeming with virgin sources and experts overlooked and unquoted by the media masses. It's just a matter of hanging out at the best virtual watering holes. I can locate virgin experts on my computer, make a quick call and have fresh quotes several hours or days before PR people can choose the 'appropriate' expert for me to publicize" (p. 10).

CAR PROJECTS INVOLVING PUBLIC DATABASES

Building an original database is one of the steps toward computer literacy in a newsroom. Whereas some stories and projects will require use of databases obtained from government agencies or other sources, many databases needed for stories and projects are not available in electronic form. Faced with paper records, the choice often becomes whether to use the data by building an original database or to bypass it. More and more journalists are making their own databases from paper or from parts or combinations of existing databases. Veteran CAR journalists Shawn McIntosh of the *Dallas Morning News*, Barbara Pearson of *USA Today*, and Christopher H. Schmitt of the *San Jose Mercury News* (1995) advise that:

> Not all information is stored neatly on nine-track tapes or floppy diskettes. . . . To fully exploit information like this, you may have to build your own database in order to apply the capabilities of computer-assisted reporting. Generally, to create your own database, you'll either manipulate information already electronic form—but not yet in a format suitable for analysis—or you'll input data from paper records. . . . Today, many news organizations doing computer-assisted journalism are breaking news with databases they create from scratch. Though not entirely painless, stories or projects that involve creating your own database are more rewarding than you might think.

They are the very best way to show off the computer's analytic potential without getting bogged down in the technical stuff. They are a great way to sell your editors on letting you do more computer-assisted stories. And usually, if you're forced to create a database yourself, chances are no one else has done the good story you're pursuing. (p. 2)

Houston Chronicle Looks at Ticket Injustice

In 1995, *Houston Chronicle* reporter Dianna Hunt (1995) prepared an exhaustive report based on her newspaper's study of traffic law enforcement injustice. The articles were published under the project name, "Ticket to Trouble." *Chronicle* computer programmers, working with Hunt and her project editor, Don Mason, were able to analyze driving records for the entire state of Texas after a year-long battle with the Texas Department of Public Safety to obtain the database of the state's drivers and their driving records. At first, the state wanted $60 million for the database of 16 million records, but with intervention of the state legislature, the newspaper got its data.

The battle was apparently worth it, because Hunt's analysis and her package of stories revealed numerous patterns of injustice toward minorities. In one story, Hunt described how minority drivers were much more likely to be ticketed in certain areas than nonminority drivers. For example, she noted that one mostly White Houston suburb, Bellaire, ticketed Blacks 43 times more often than Whites.

Hunt also analyzed cities outside of the Houston area because she was using a statewide database. She found the state's leading speed trap, a community that issued 99% of its traffic tickets for speeding. Although she found that statewide statistics mostly mirrored population proportions, there were extremes that put minorities at a distinct disadvantage. Hunt discussed the trouble spot findings with state and local leaders, including those in the Black and Hispanic communities, and she discussed the findings with local police department representatives, who often disputed the findings because they felt the population demographics of their community might not reflect the demographics of the drivers using the community's roads.

The Chronicle's analysis included 16.2 million individual driving records and almost 3.7 million driving citations for a 3-year period between 1991 and 1994. The database, to say the least, was massive in that it required 48 nine-track tapes, or 7.5 gigabytes of data. If printed, the database would fill 2 million pages, single-spaced. *Chronicle* computing experts said it was the largest database the newspaper had ever reviewed and, at first, it could not be loaded into the newspaper's IBM mainframe system. After several months of effort by a *Chronicle* programmer, the database was analyzed for Hunt. The large database was split into more manageable smaller ones that Hunt further analyzed using Paradox and Quattro Pro on her Compaq portable PC.

A total of 633 cities with at least 100 citations during the period were analyzed. Hunt and *The Chronicle* used two outside statisticians from the Houston area to assure standardization and correct approaches to their analysis. Both are experts in government statistics. The stories were supplemented with locator maps, enforcement trouble spot maps, several ticket–population demographics proportion bar graph charts, ticket–overall population bar graph charts of the state's major urban areas, a "speed trap" table containing cities in which 90% or more of the tickets issued were for speeding, a "hot tickets" table of the most frequent offenses cited, and assorted other photographs and informational graphics. Hunt's package contained seven stories that she prepared and one highly detailed methodology story prepared by Mason, Hunt's editor.

Newsday Reviews the New York Bail System

Newsday editors and reporters for the newspaper's now-closed New York edition's investigating team were concerned about New York City's bail system. They suspected numerous inequities in the system and, to confirm their suspicions and anecdotal information, the newspaper acquired and combined two major databases that required nearly a year to obtain through FOIA requests.

- First, the newspaper analyzed data from the city Department of Correction that described all defendants awaiting trial in city facilities on a given date in 1992.
- Second, the newspaper obtained a database from the state Office of Court Administration that contained data for the same date on all defendants awaiting trial out of jail on bail.

Database Editor Russ Buettner, who moved to the *New York Daily News* in 1995, analyzed the data for the investigative team. There were a total of 27,810 criminal cases pending on the chosen date in the databases. The city paid millions, the analysis showed, for holding accused individuals unable to post bail for nonviolent crimes. Reporter Kathleen Kerr wrote the major stories for the project called "Jail or Bail: Unequal Justice." The project debuted as a Sunday cover story for the tabloid newspaper, proclaiming bluntly that if a defendant had no money, he or she had no freedom. The city's bail system is beyond the reach of the poor and minorities, Kerr concluded in the opening story of the series. The stories were supplemented with photographs, several case study sidebars, an explanatory methods box, a short history of the city's bail system, a table containing the status—by crime type broken down by race and ethnicity—of suspects accused of felonies on the date used for the analysis, and a bar graph chart displaying cases involving individuals released on recognizance by crime type, broken down by race and ethnicity.

Kerr also told readers that money and family ties rank high in the bail system. She supplemented her data with anecdotal reports that focused on individual cases that illustrated the general findings in her data. For instance, in the Sunday installment, she focused on a man who spent 4 months in jail awaiting trial for an attempted house break-in. The homeless man had been beaten and detained by the homeowner and was arrested and taken to jail to be held for arraignment. When he was brought into court, he could not pay his bail and was sent to jail to wait 4 months for his day in court. After a number of administrative mistakes, the case was eventually dismissed after a jail stay that cost taxpayers more than $20,000.

St. Petersburg Times Analyzes Gun Regulation

Florida's *St. Petersburg Times* produced a five-part series in 1993 that used a federal database to assist in an analysis of regulation, or lack of it, of federally licensed gun dealers in Florida. Making the point that it is easier to get a license to sell guns than to get a license to drive in Florida, the newspaper's two reporters assigned to the project studied the federal data collected on gun dealers in Florida in conjunction with several other state and local databases. Reporter David Olinger worked with the *Times'* database editor, Bob Port, to produce the package of stories and graphics that was supplemented with photographs. Public records researcher Connie Humburg also made contributions to the package.

Port, who left *The Times* after 12 years in 1995 to join The Associated Press CAR team in New York, checked the Bureau of Alcohol, Tobacco, and Firearms (ATF) database of 285,000 gun dealers in the United States for Florida links. He found 8,000 dealers in central and northern Florida alone. Using the ATF database to begin, the reporters took the project further with relational database power to:

- Determine whether criminals were licensed to deal guns, so they compared the data in the ATF database to criminal databases from their newspaper's area counties.

- Determine whether law enforcement officers were legally dealing guns by relating the ATF database to Florida Department of Law Enforcement records.
- Determine whether gun dealers were active and whether they complied with the criminal background check requirement by analyzing state computer records of criminal background checks requested by dealers.

The project's five major focal points, each one a day's installment of the project, emphasized (a) problems with federal and state regulation, (b) illegal and unregulated gun sales at shows, (c) law enforcement officers who sell guns as a second income, (d) gun dealers who sell weapons without registration or licenses, and (e) potential solutions to the regulation and enforcement problems outlined in the project.

Olinger and Port also conducted interviews with dealers, police officers, and victims of crimes committed with guns. The project started on page 1 for each of the 5 days it ran and totaled 14 stories by Olinger and Port. The stories included several sidebars focusing on specific dealers and gun shows. There were also two accompanying editorials published on the editorial page.

The Philadelphia Inquirer Measures City's Vital Signs

In fall 1995, prior to the beginning of the 1995 political campaigns, *The Philadelphia Inquirer* conducted a poll of 824 city residents to determine their thinking about major local issues such as crime, the city's schools, quality of life, the city's financial condition, the direction of the city, and a variety of neighborhood issues. It became part of a major local reporting project entitled "Vital Signs: Campaign '95."

Polls, one of the original uses of computers for newsgathering, remain as valuable projects for newsrooms in political and nonpolitical contexts. Once polls are designed and conducted, the database that is developed can be a rich and productive source for news stories. *The Inquirer's* project, one example of dozens conducted by newspapers in 1995 and 1996 at the local, state, and national levels, led to the 5-day series of articles, tables, graphs, and charts that explained the "state of mind" of the city's residents.

Written and supervised by reporters Craig McCoy, Lea Sitton, and Thomas Ferrick, the poll-based CAR project was designed to be a background study for readers leading to the fall mayoral elections. The project was started in April, the fieldwork of the survey conducted in June, and the results compiled, analyzed, and reported in September. The reporters worked with the Eagleton Institute of Politics at Rutgers University.

"The poll allowed us to break down into racial groups and things like that. We tried to identify what the issues were. The campaign was pretty boring. It was pretty clear that Rendell would sweep the election. But we wondered what can we do as a newspaper? We can write about the campaign, but why don't we try to identify what the issues should be?" explained *Inquirer* CAR Director Neill Borowski (personal communication, November 17, 1995). "We used the survey as our guiding light and put a lot of economic and demographic data in. We didn't report a lot about the survey. It was really there to tell us what to concentrate on."

In addition to the poll, reporters worked with data from other sources. They also used census data, individual research, and review of decades of city records. The resulting databases covered a dozen different subdivisions of topics. Ferrick and McCoy directed the project, Borowski handled analysis and data processing, and Sitton reported from the city's neighborhoods. Photographers, page designers, and graphic artists also made contributions.

DAILY REPORTING INVOLVING DATABASE CAR

Reporters who are using databases in their daily reporting often wonder how they managed without them. It may be the beginning of a trend, but more and more reporters seem to be using CAR tools in their daily information gathering. There's room for CAR for both beat reporters and general assignment reporters, not to mention projects reporters.

For example, David Bloom, a reporter for the *Los Angeles Daily News*, uses spreadsheets to build databases of ordinary government information that he uses on a variety of subjects. Bloom recommends working on databases a little at a time, bit by bit, eventually giving the user a useful compilation of information. Bloom (1994) stated:

> Much of what I do involves incremental projects, collecting the paper that government generates each week, then punching in highlights from a few contracts or commission appointments or whatever as it comes in. I let the data build up over six months or a year, then check to see what it all means. The spreadsheet tools are handy for this sort of work, because they are so simple to set up and flexible to move around. The overhead of data entry from week to week is low, too, when you use an incremental approach. When you have enough

---

DOING COMMUNITY-ORIENTED PROJECTS

Community-oriented projects that include computer tools require five distinct steps, advises *Wisconsin State Journal* investigative reporter Andy Hall (1995). Hall feels the steps flow from one another in this model:

- *Think.* "Don't start out by thinking about databases and computers. Think about other big issues confronting your community. Think about the stories that ought to be told. The best stories focus on people, neighborhoods and specific addresses," he argues (p. 1).
- *Pick topics.* "After discussions with residents, your sources, public officials, your colleagues and neighbors, identify some topics you'd like to explore. Don't try to plan a whole project at this point. Let it emerge naturally from your reporting."
- *Identify techniques.* "Identify the reporting techniques you'll use. These might include traditional interviews, unusually large amounts of time spent in particular neighborhoods, investigative reporting, computer-assisted reporting, public-opinion polling and civic journalism methods such as townhall meetings and pre-publication discussions with key figures."
- *Boot up.* "This is the point at which computers may begin playing a role in your reporting. In no case should use of a computer replace any of the other techniques."
- *Take a balanced approach.* "Let each technique influence the others."

---

information to begin analyzing, you often have a resource that just isn't available in electronic form otherwise. (p. 10)

However, handling data can be tricky, especially for beginners. There are ways to succeed with database-oriented reporting required for some large investigative projects. David Migoya (1995, p. 11), a reporter for the *Detroit Free Press* who specializes in CAR, offers these tips:

- *Segregate data.* Use simple and easy-to-remember file names in your computer.
- *Export and import data.* Learn how to move data files from database programs to spreadsheets and vice versa.
- *Shop for the right software.* There is often specialized software that differs from the more common spreadsheets or database managers that do specific things with data better than the old favorites.
- *Use statistics and statistics experts.* "If you have a problem with [mathematics], consult a math professor at the local university."

- *Overcompute.* "If you're on a roll, as we often were, go with it. You never know what numbers will add perspective later."
- *Use all data that fit.* "In other words, don't squeeze something in that's incomplete or exhaust yourself trying to obtain everything."
- *Check for data cleanliness.* Names and addresses are often wrong and must be cleaned up.

ONLINE PUBLIC ACCESS TO NEWSROOM DATABASES

When a database is built or otherwise manipulated for use in a news project or story, usually it is used for the original purpose and then put on a shelf. However, a number of more creative and innovative newsrooms are attempting to give these databases new life. Many of these databases were not cheap to originate. Either they were purchased from a government agency for a few hundred dollars or created from scratch for more money than that—if time and other resources are computed in dollars. So it seems to make sense to "recycle" databases.

Some news organizations have begun to place recycled databases in newsroom data libraries for reuse by other reporters for other stories or projects. This not only makes sense, it is an excellent means of sharing resources across departments and beats and this, of course, encourages teamwork. Taking this approach one step further is the idea of placing these databases on servers for public access through the World Wide Web, an electronic news product, a bulletin board system (BBS), or other form of online access.

One newspaper that has used this approach effectively in the past several years is the Raleigh *News & Observer* in North Carolina. Originally, editors and reporters recycled databases with front ends designed with Visual Basic to make access to acquired or original databases easier for newsroom staffers. But as the *NandO Times* online grew, its editors began to create and make databases available for public access also. One example of this is the Wake Schools Reassignments Project database (Seese, 1995). Wake County, where Raleigh is located, reassigned many of its students. To serve residents in a way not possible in the newspaper itself, the electronic edition editors created a database that permitted users to type in a street address in the county and determine which schools at each of the three levels serve that address.

Innovative? Perhaps the database itself was not, but it certainly is if the use of computer tools to better serve readers is considered. The look-up program utilizes a database from the school system updated by editors. The project included online maps that are linked to school information pages that are linked to attendance area maps. Users simply click, in the manner of the World Wide Web, to jump around. To do such a project requires sophisticated understanding of the Web, mapping software, database software, and hypertext markup language (HTML). But with the right combination of expertise, it can be another successful application of computing in journalism.

PUBLISHING DATABASES WITHOUT STORIES?

A few years ago, editors and most reporters would have never considered using databases without narrative or explanation in their newspapers, on their television screens, or, more recently, even in electronic publications available online. The early users of databases believed that these listings, compilations, and raw information in its different formats, styles, and shapes, were not the sort of thing readers, viewers, and other audiences wanted. Things have changed.

With the growth in demand for information, particularly information that may be customized, editors, producers, and reporters are looking for new ways to serve their audiences. One way that is evolving in the last half of this decade is presentation of raw, minimally edited, databases for public consumption. A news organization that is succeeding at this is the *Dayton Daily News*. In fall 1994, the Ohio newspaper began publishing weekday infoPLUS pages for readers (see examples in Figs. 3.1 and 3.2). The news feature evolved out of an effort to increase circulation. These almost full, open pages combine more traditional reporting with CAR and contemporary news graphics. Each day, the page focuses on a standard topic such as the workplace, traffic and travel, crime and public safety, education, and government and the community. The packages are produced by two reporters, a database editor, and a graphic artist. The newspaper uses mostly national databases, but local information is taken from these databases and emphasized for readers. Local data are also used from the usual public sources. Managing editor Steve Sidlo (1995b) feels "infoPLUS is an excellent way to use computer-assisted reporting to provide information in a non-threatening and unbiased fashion to our readers" (p. 1).

"We tie these into the Metro or other pages when we can. . . . We are into massive data crunching on a daily basis," explained Sidlo (1995). "We grab databases where ever we can find them and milk them for whatever we can get out of them to fill these pages" (p. 1).

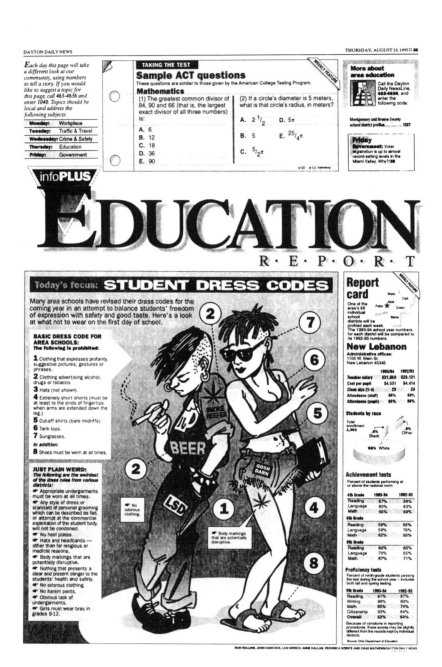

FIG. 3.1. Sample of the Dayton Daily News weekday infoPLUS page about education and dress code.

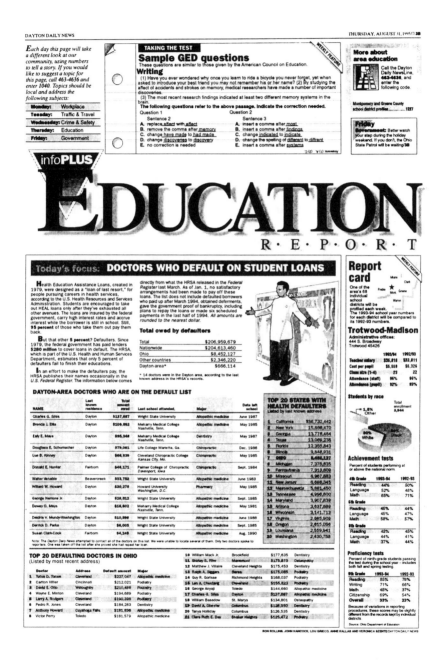

FIG. 3.2. Sample of the Dayton Daily News weekday infoPLUS page about education and student loans.

Readers in Dayton seem to be attracted to listed, tabled, graphed, or charted data presented with little or no narrative. "This is very successful with readers. We do readership surveys every three or four months. We test new things. And we found out that this one is really well read and readers like it," he added.

STRATEGIES FOR EDITORS
SUPERVISING CAR REPORTERS

There is growing interest, both on the part of reporters and editors, in successful strategies for managing CAR programs. This includes several levels of concern. First, there is the general management of a program involving computers and newsgathering from the personnel, budget, and the equipment resources perspectives. Second, there is the relationship of CAR journalists and their editors. Traditionally, investigative reporters and teams of journalists working on special projects went off, did their work, and reemerged days, weeks, or months later with a draft of the final product. In some newsrooms, this is how CAR operates. But in others, there is a different model developing. Some editors are working more closely with reporters involved in investigations or projects. One of the barriers to this working successfully is the level of computing literacy of both middle-level editors and, especially, higher level editors.

Philip Meyer, a journalism professor at the University of North Carolina and author of *The New Precision Journalism* (1991), believes how managers work with their CAR reporters is an important newsroom concern. Perhaps the old model, where investigative reporters disappear for long periods of time, Meyer wonders, cannot work with CAR: "Evidently, this is a problem for computer-assisted reporters who are so different from the usual mold that they don't think that they are managed well. I've heard some editors say, one in particular, that the badger goes into the hole and disappears and after a while you have to pull him out. People who manage news on a daily cycle get understandably anxious when the badger disappears for a long time," Meyer (personal communication, September 23, 1995), a former projects reporter for several Knight-Ridder newspapers, explained. "At Knight-Ridder, I had it easy because I was the only one doing this and nobody understood what I was doing. Management was very permissive and relaxed about it."

Some journalists involved in CAR feel that their editors need certain understanding and even an advanced knowledge of CAR to be successful supervisors. "When editors know how the elements of CAR work they are most helpful," said Whit Andrews (personal communication, October 6, 1995), a free-lance environmental journalist and former newsroom Internet trainer for *The Times* of Munster, Indiana. "An editor who can suggest a sage approach to a story is invaluable; an editor who can point out when an approach is likely to be fruitless may be even more valuable."

Several forward-thinking newsroom managers have tried to cope with the changing skills and reporting tools of their more technologically advanced journalists. Steve Sidlo, managing editor of the *Dayton Daily News*, is one of them. A Cox newspaper, the *Daily News* has used CAR tools since 1989, and recently, under the guidance of Cox editor and CAR founding father Elliot Jaspin, has been conducting a number of collaborative projects with other Cox newspapers.

Sidlo (1995a) stated:

> What we are talking about here is managing a program much like you would manage any other program in the newsroom. To be successful (with CAR), you have to have good management. A lot of this means you have to sell this to your bosses and to your staff. We have worked real hard at that in Dayton. . . . When you are buying a lot of equipment, you have to sell this stuff. Even if you have bosses, who are in theory in support of it, you have to demonstrate value. One way is to demonstrate that this is more than just big investigative projects that win awards but builds circulation as well. We have been able to demonstrate that some of the things that we are doing on a daily basis with computer-assisted reporting is actually building readers.

Sidlo strongly believes that it is important to find allies in other managers in the company, but not limited to those in the newsroom:

> We worked very hard at explaining our program to the publisher, but not only the publisher. This includes the other non-news executives in the building, the people who decide about capital purchases, equipment purchases. We brought them down to the newsroom, showed them what we could do, let them ask questions, worked very, very hard at explaining exactly what we were doing and why. And it took a while. It is a lot easier to motivate *some* of your staff. What we did when we started was grab some people out of the newsroom who I knew were interested in a general sort of way. None of them had any strong computer background and they were mostly reporters, a couple of copy editors and our library director. . . . I told them to find out what kinds of databases are available, at what cost, and how we could use them to do stories. They broke into committees and worked and came up with a plan. It was my advice and *their* plan. Because it was their plan, they had an almost fanatical interest. That group I

didn't have to sell at all. What we have struggled with in Dayton is broadening the circle of people who do this.

Sidlo (1995a) recognizes the unique problems in this situation facing a manager. He offers 11 valuable tips for editors and reporters hoping to build a better relationship:

- Send signals to the staff that editors value CAR.
- Consider creating a CAR group that oversees needs, issues, and story ideas.
- Sell the publisher on the idea and need for CAR investment.
- Don't underestimate the importance of a continuing training program.

SUPERVISING CAR REPORTERS

"Editors or the person responsible for the data analysis must ask the tough questions at the front end of a project or even an individual story. Before anyone gets really excited about data, everyone should be aware of the margin of error and whether there are any red flags in what is on the screen," says Rose Ciotta (personal communication, November 22, 1995), CAR editor at *The Buffalo News.*

As for generating stories, I find that several approaches work. First, the best stories are the ones that start with the reporters. If they can be encouraged to come to you (the CAR editor) with a hunch or story tip, you are likely to end up with a good story. I had that happen recently with a business reporter who had heard about problems with business exemptions. We ended up with a page one story that showed that one-third of the businesses that got the tax breaks were commercial entities like pizza parlors and hotel chains—certainly not the type of places intended to get help when the law was passed.

The other approach that seems to work is what I call the "planting of seeds approach." Let a reporter know what is possible, talk to them about a story idea. I find it's always best to get the reporter excited or at least interested in a story before I talk to his editor. The last thing you want is to force someone into a story. Yes, that may be necessary at times, but I prefer working with people who see the tools as opportunities.

A lot of little things add up. In other words, getting a reporter to use a CD-ROM to look up a phone number one time leads the next time to checking on-line property records and then using a spreadsheet. As a supervisor type you want to communicate that everything counts and nudge the reporter into the next level.

- Don't rely on just one or two people for the entire CAR effort.
- If projects get into heavy duty databases and number crunching, consider bringing in outside computer experts to help.
- Do a detailed inventory of staff member computer skills.
- Develop a sophisticated staff understanding of what public records and databases are available and how to use them for stories.
- Milk databases for as many stories as possible.
- Use computers in the newsroom that were acquired for pagination or other purposes for CAR whenever possible.
- Look to collaborate with other newspapers in your group or chain.

"The most important thing, if you are an editor, is to send signals to the staff that you value this, that it is important to the paper, that you expect them to get it done," said Sidlo (1995a).

Jonathan Krim (1995), assistant managing editor of the *San Jose Mercury News*, is responsible for supervising the investigative teams and the conversion of his newsroom to a PC-based system, among his duties. Krim feels that the model used by many newspapers, starting with a few specialists in the newsroom does not work well any longer. He prefers teaching CAR throughout the newsroom and recommends a completely digital newsroom that includes CAR with pagination and other production-oriented tasks.

"All of your staff has to be computer literate," Krim (1995) argued. "If they are not, they are not going to survive as we move forward."

This CAR management attitude led to a different problem: His newspaper had to finance and acquire enough computer equipment for everyone in a large newsroom. For *The Mercury News*, with a circulation of about 280,000 daily and 340,000 on Sundays, this meant a considerable effort and investment during the PC conversion. "There really is no longer any substitute for a PC-based newsroom," Krim stated. "Essentially what's on your desktop is a PC that is both your publishing system and your data analysis and Internet system."

Krim also believes there needs to be regular editor–reporter contact when CAR is involved in a story or project:

What you want to get to is a situation where, either on a daily or a weekly basis, you're analyzing the areas of coverage that your beat reporters are doing . . . computer analysis on a regular basis. With our project team, we're fairly long-term oriented and we give some time for a fishing expedition as it were. I am also a little reluctant to have somebody come and say, "Why don't we buy this database and take a look at it." I'm more apt to get excited about that if we've seen some cases where we think there is a problem and it's worthwhile as a long-term project.

Still, Krim believes, the leadership in the newsroom has to keep a distance when CAR is involved in a project or daily story. "I think it is really important that top editors be willing to walk away even if there is an investment of time. . . . If the story doesn't pan out, it doesn't pan out."

In Dayton, Sidlo says the only way to develop an editor–reporter relationship involving computers is bottom up:

> We tried to get away from real top-down management where you have an editor dictating to reporters what they are supposed to be doing. But you still have to have to have some control. We have tried to set up a system where you have teams of people. Each team will have a team leader or an editor working with the team. We expect them to talk to each other and, if they are going to get into something that is messy and takes longer than expected, I want to hear about it. I don't want to find out, two months into a project, that we are floundering around on something. If I find out, I'll put more strict controls on that particular person to make sure that doesn't happen. You want to give support to people so they don't get into trouble like that.

At another Cox newspaper, *Palm Beach Post* Assistant Managing Editor Mary Kate Leming (personal communication, September, 15, 1995) works with online news researchers on a regular basis as head of the news research department, and she agrees that everyone needs to have CAR tools and skills. "We want to empower every reporter to have CAR, not necessarily have a reporter who is also a 'chiphead' who is just off working on things. We've done projects like that, and sometimes they are so data-intensive, that that's bound to happen. But, in general, what we would like to see is to have this information used continuously, in every day reporting," she stated.

Editors have to learn more about CAR to supervise their CAR reporters, some newsroom managers feel. Said Leming:

> I'd like for editors to know a lot more than they are willing to know. It is real easy for editors to say, "yes, my reporters ought to be using spreadsheets," but if they don't really know what it takes to set up a spreadsheet, then it may be an unrealistic expectation that they may be overseeing the amount of training required to do it. The main thing you should not do is tell the CAR reporter or news researcher that they shouldn't do too many things. You really need to let them go and explore. I think there is a point where, if you manage a department like that, that is going to be spending a lot of money, you have got to realize they're going to be spending a lot of money. That's how they

are learning and you have got to figure that into your budget. If you are trying to nickel and dime it too much, they are going to be afraid to take the kind of risks they need to take to really do good research and to learn. Get a budget and let them go.

Some reporters feel that editors need to be more connected to the work being done by their staff members. "Editors must be more involved in supervision of CAR projects. They must ask more pointed questions. 'Why are we doing it this way? Have you consulted a statistician?' Too many CAR reporters are winging it, and it's going to come back to haunt the profession at some point. You can go wrong with a story. You can go way wrong with a CAR story," said Dan Browning (personal communication, October 16, 1995), CAR specialist for the *Saint Paul Pioneer Press*. "On the other hand, editors absolutely must give CAR reporters time to do the project properly, and time again to check and recheck the results of the analysis. CAR done quickly is a disaster waiting to happen.

"In my experience, some editors balk at CAR because they don't understand it, they're of a generation that is fearful or suspicious of computers, or they can't get around the notion that we're creating news. Editors don't like to look uninformed. They often pretend to understand what CAR reporters are doing when they don't have a clue. These editors must take some basic spreadsheet and database program classes."

ADEQUATE SUPPORT FROM NEWSROOM MANAGERS?

If there is a wide range of management attitudes toward CAR from news organization to news organization, it seems there may also be considerable variation in attitudes within individual organizations, especially the larger ones. Some former distinct and separate news organizations are linking together to share resources at the group or chain level. Most often, this occurs within a news corporation. Gannett, Knight-Ridder, and Cox have demonstrated this in recent years. "CAR-pooling," as it could be called, is done to stretch resources to their maximum benefit, of course, and to permit smaller organizations to become involved. Said San Jose's Krim (1995):

> What you are beginning to see is chain-wide sharing of these kinds of resources. Obviously now, all kinds of technological opportunities are opening up where papers can be on their own wide area network. They can share data files via private mailing lists or file servers or whatever. . . . Some are using a buddy system where larger papers are helping other papers in their region that are smaller. We're doing

a tremendous amount of cooperative projects. The neat thing about this is that it is not being driven by the corporate executives. This has grown out of the people who are working at these newspapers who recognize the value of doing a lot of sharing.

Sidlo (1995a) described a recent project involving all Cox Newspapers that got mixed reactions from the independent-thinking editors of the chain:

> We have been working our way toward more and more collaborative projects. We just did one on Medicare that involved analysis of more than 100 million records—a record of every payment made to Medicare doctors in one year. We analyzed it nationally and analyzed it for each of the states that had Cox newspapers. We got a good series of stories out of it. But it was painful. We have a lot of cultural differences among our different newspapers. Some editors were resistant to being asked to run something. They're used to being very independent . . . but we overcame that. We got it published and there's a lot of excitement now. . . . I think you are going to see a lot more of that.

If conflicts such as those within Cox about a major chainwide CAR project can be overcome, why is there continuing resistance to CAR in newsrooms? A number of reporters have ideas. Some think it is generational. Some think it is technophobia. Some think it is a management attitude. Whatever the reason, there is resistance to CAR in some newsrooms at middle- and upper level management positions.

The 1.9 million-circulation *USA Today* may be a prime example. Paul Overberg is database editor for the newspaper, a position he has held since 1992. Working as a reporter, copy editor, and database editor, he has observed numerous reasons for the differing points of view. "Our newsroom managers run the gamut in their attitudes to CAR. Some get it and know how to use it, others don't get it, others are downright hostile," Overberg (personal communication, September 19, 1995), stated. Overberg used his experience to offer some general observations on editors and CAR:

- "Most journalists, managers or not, aren't big on quantitative thinking. Being told that they should understand, foster and absorb it into newsgathering isn't easy, either intellectually or emotionally. Some word people see numbers as the other side of a Manichean duality."
- "Many are pre-PC folk, older baby boomers or even older. They spent formative professional years on typewriters. Learning CAR means learning a whole suite of PC skills first."

- "Many are already overwhelmed coping with the digital revolution's effects in graphics, design, photography, etcetera. My personal experience as a newsroom manager suggests many are so exhausted getting each day's edition out—without too many errors, libel, or dreaded OT pay—that there's no room for CAR."
- "Finally, CAR threatens some editors: It gives reporters more power over the agenda, and it forces editors to tell publishers that journalists DO need ongoing, formal training. That costs money."

Omaha World-Herald CAR specialist Carol Napolitano (personal communication, September 29, 1995) has some theories of her own about management attitudes toward CAR. She thinks there are at least four contributing explanations: "In my personal opinion, managers often are not supportive of CAR for one or more of these reasons:

- "They don't understand it, so they don't feel like they have control over the reporters who do use it, or they don't feel like they can fulfill a traditional supervisory role because they cannot advise the reporter."
- "They think it will cost too much money."
- "They think it will take too much time."
- "They have a fear or ignorance of computers and/or numbers."

She continued, "Support at my [former] newspaper has been spotty. It took almost two years to get the money and time to conduct training. After training, support seemed to dwindle again. We are expanding into new territory, creating more zoned editions and revamping our coverage philosophy, so right now it's pretty low on the list."

One of the journalists pointing to generational gaps in technical training is James Derk (personal communication, September 5, 1995), a computer columnist for Scripps Howard News Service and computer editor at the *Evansville Courier.* Offered Derk:

Newsroom managers = older men. This is a new science to them and they don't trust it initially. It means cash outlay with no guarantee of results. It means time spent online, spent reading Paradox manuals, time spent crunching numbers. What works is results. Do a project on your free time using a borrowed PC. Prove you're serious. Read some books. Collect reprints. Show them around. My news managers were not terribly excited until they sent three of us to Raleigh in 1993. I was city editor then, so I came back pumped, thanks to Frank Daniels III. I took a leave to set up CAR and never went back. Then we started a

BBS, then we became the town's dial-up Internet provider. So now we are making money with online and that gives CAR a boost.

Ray Robinson, a veteran reporter and projects editor for *The Press of Atlantic City* (personal communication, September 7, 1995) offers an additional perspective:

> I've never had a manager tell me that he or she doesn't support CAR. They all seem to want it. But some are afraid of the cost. And with so many tightwad publishers out there, that's a legitimate concern. Some are also afraid that CAR stories will turn into bottomless pits that suck up enormous amounts of staff time and never quite yield a story for the newspaper. And that has happened. It's also a legitimate concern. Management here has been very supportive in granting time and money to CAR. I've tried to respond by using the time and equipment not just to crank out huge, multi-part projects, but to help out wherever possible on daily stories and smaller projects. So far, it's worked.

> I also think managers are always worried that whoever is handling CAR in their newsroom is becoming more of a computer geek than a journalist. So when you're talking to them, it's important not to throw in too much techno-babble. Talk like a real person. Show them you're still a journalist.

4

Hardware Tools for Computer-Assisted Reporting

Ask anyone who works with computers and he or she will probably say that the computer's hardware matters. In the Windows 95 age of memory- and storage-hungry software, RAM and hard drive sizes matter. In the World Wide Web age of bulky graphic file downloads on the Internet, data transmission speeds matter. And in the "time is money" age, wasted effort due to lost information that was not backed up matters. It is also clear that each of these tools matter a lot to the success of any computer-assisted information endeavor.

Journalists seeking productive use of their computing tools for newsgathering must consider hardware specifications and capabilities somewhere in the process of getting started. A news researcher or a reporter trying to use the Internet at 9.6 Kbps to find information for a story will become very frustrated. A database editor trying to make sense out of a social services child abuse database for a local county will be annoyed with delays caused by a machine with slow processor speed, inadequate memory, or insufficient storage space to handle the database. It is one thing to want to do CAR; it is quite another to acquire and properly use the right hardware.

Of course, it is quite possible to use slow modems for most online work and slow processors, limited memory, or hard drive storage for data processing and analysis. However, these restrictions will also put a very low ceiling on the data, the software, and accompanying features that can be used. The bottom line is that hardware is one of the most important ingredients in the success formula for CAR. For newsroom managers and budget wizards, a successful CAR program will require a serious look at spending priorities because hardware and the training to use it cost precious budget dollars. For reporters, it means lobbying for the right CAR hardware as a priority. But hard decisions about priorities will have to be made at some point.

INFLUENCES OF THE COMPUTER INDUSTRY

The point was made in the opening chapter that CAR is heavily influenced by the computer industry. Technology companies located in places such as Redmond, Washington, along Route 128 in metropolitan Boston, and throughout the Silicon Valley of Northern California in large part determine the direction of computing in the nation and, of course, in newsrooms. The news business is no different from other industries heavily invested in computer technology. News organizations, like all other businesses, however, are at the mercy of the computer industry because news companies do not develop their own hardware and rarely develop substantial software used in CAR. The impact of this circumstance is significant.

What comes from Redmond, the home of Microsoft Corporation, each year, can be significant. The international stir caused by a software program called Windows 95 in fall 1995 was an example. But even the debut of a new edition of FoxPro or Access with new data massaging tools can send significant shock waves through newsrooms these days. The introduction of Windows 95 caused hundreds of meetings and discussions about use of this new operating system (OS) to replace DOS, Windows 3.x, Windows NT, OS/2, or any other product currently installed. If the decision was made to upgrade, then decisions related to upgrading hardware followed. It could be argued that some of the Fortune 500 corporations may have had significant influence on Microsoft's programmers as they developed Windows 95 and its various features from 1993 until its arrival. However, it is also safe to assume that most news companies, even the largest ones such as Gannett, Knight-Ridder, Scripps-Howard, Cox, the international wire services, the television network news divisions, and news magazines, were not significantly involved. Journalists, like many other professionals in other industries, work with what is developed for the corporate business world. There is little software and hardware in the PC market that is developed exclusively for the news business simply because of the high research and development costs involved, and few news companies see the investment worthwhile.

Some journalists recognize the influences of the computer industry on newsgathering, but most do not. Hardware firms such as Dell and Gateway 2000 build the computers on newsroom desktops and in briefcases. Software giants such as Microsoft, Computer Associates, Borland, Netscape, and IBM/Lotus provide the programs for writing, collecting data, and analyzing it. And online service vendors such as America Online, Nexis/Lexis, and DataTimes offer their products to the public at large, not necessarily to newsrooms. It is very difficult, if not impossible, to identify a computer-based product that was developed for news use that eventually wound up in use by the general corporate world or the public in general.

Journalists simply adapt these tools, to the best of their abilities, to their needs. In recent years, software companies have developed upgraded products that offer more and more customizability. This helps journalists with specific applications of these products in mind and provides a mechanism for individualizing these applications for particular newsroom uses such as ease in data entry or speed in data retrieval or report printing. Despite this, perception of the impact of the computer industry on CAR is mixed.

"Until recently, I would have answered that they were mildly influential. They are influential to the degree in which we reporters, as a group, pick a particular software package and use it. We reporters like to have our colleagues using the same software so that we can solve programming solutions when necessary," said Dan Browning (personal communication, October 16, 1995), CAR specialist for the *Saint Paul Pioneer Press*:

> Now, I'd say Microsoft, in particular, has come to dominate. At Knight-Ridder, we have signed some purchasing agreements that require that we use certain Microsoft products (Windows, Excel, FoxPro, or Access). That will limit experimentation by some newspapers, which will slow down the ability of reporters to find good alternative software. Knight-Ridder has done the same thing with hardware, incidentally. We must buy computers from certain manufacturers; we cannot buy cheap, off-the-shelf equipment. That limits the smaller papers because they cannot afford to get into CAR at the Hewlett Packard Pentium level. I suppose it does build in some chain-wide efficiencies, however.

These corporate-level influences are also felt in Seattle.

"The influence seems limited primarily to what products our newspaper buys," said Seattle *Post-Intelligencer* Systems Editor Paul McElroy (personal communication, October 13, 1995). "For example, our corporate spreadsheet is Lotus 1-2-3. After some internal debate, we made an exception and bought Excel for reporters because it effortlessly handles file transfers with Microsoft Access. We chose Access because many other newspapers use it and it seemed to be relatively easy to learn (more so than Paradox, anyway)."

Ray Robinson (personal communication, September 7, 1995) feels the influence is minimal:

> I don't think they play much of a role. The people doing CAR amount to a very small part of their market and I don't think they've taken much notice of it. When I talk to a hardware or software vendor and tell them I'm from a newspaper, they always assume that I work on the business side, doing market analysis, maintaining mailing lists, etc. When I tell them I work in news, they're surprised. They usually say they didn't think the news department would need PCs for anything but word processing and graphics. The one exception is mapping software vendors. They're very much aware of what newspaper reporters are doing with their products and seem interested in promoting it. I suspect that because their overall market is so much smaller than that of other vendors, they're more in touch with what people in highly specialized areas like CAR are doing.

This opinion is echoed by Knoxville's Jack Lail (personal communication, September 30, 1995):

> The influence of these companies is not any more than anywhere else. Newspapers have software guidelines just as other companies do, which means you might use Excel instead of Quattro Pro or FoxPro instead of Paradox. Actually, since newsrooms haven't been very good to buy CAR software, good shareware and freeware are popular. Programs that have been written by other CAR reporters are posted on IRE's CompuServe file library. askSam is a good example of how a small company has found a niche precisely because the big companies are that influential.

Derk, for the most part, sides with Robinson and Lail. "There isn't much influence on me, except for software I guess. I tend to follow the industry more closely because I also write the computer column for Scripps Howard. But CAR work doesn't rely on one brand or one type of system or software. Microsoft FoxPro works, but so does Paradox and dBase and SQL," Derk stated (personal communication, September 5, 1995).

THE DECLINE OF MAINFRAME COMPUTERS

For several decades, the only computers available for use in newsgathering were large systems known as mainframe computers. These are the highest level computing systems that can handle the most difficult and largest of processing tasks. Traditionally, mainframe systems were used by larger institutions such as corporations, educational institutions, government agencies, the military, and research centers. These high-end systems are designed for multiple users through time sharing. Mainframes are also most often associated with nine-track tapes, the storage tapes used for data generated and analyzed on mainframe system reel-to-reel magnetic tape drives.

For newspapers and other news media, mainframe systems were mainly used in the 1950s through the 1970s for purposes outside the newsroom. Companies large enough to have mainframe systems—such as the larger dailies, wire services, and networks—often used the mainframes for accounting, billing, customer record keeping, market research, and other business-side purposes. In the 1970s, some news companies began to use them for production-oriented activities such as typesetting in "cold-type" systems.

But these computers, as powerful and fast as they are, were rarely used for newsgathering. At some enlightened newspapers in the 1960s and 1970s, mainframes were used for some data creation and analysis, but mainly for projects such as political polls. A few database-oriented projects produced from government data copied onto nine-track tape, appeared during this era, but these were extremely rare.

Then desktop computing began to appear in the early 1980s. As these more affordable computers became more powerful, applications such as database and statistical programs that had been previously reserved for mainframes began to appear in PC versions. Gradually, into the 1990s, PCs, especially networked PCs, began to replace mainframes around the world. And slowly, use of computers in newsrooms increased because PCs were easier to use and affordable for all levels of newsgathering.

The result has been a decline in mainframe use around the world, especially in government data collection that previously depended on mainframes. At the same time, of course, there has even been a decline in the minimal use of mainframes by journalists for news stories. In the mid-1990s, only the largest of databases still require mainframes to be studied. The massive traffic ticket and driver record analysis of the *Houston Chronicle,* outlined in the preceding chapter, is an example of a project that still cannot be handled by desktop systems. But even projects of this type on mainframes are endangered. As hard drive capacities continue to grow past the 2 to 4 GB size available in 1995 and 1996, there will be even less demand for the power of mainframes.

"The decline of the mainframe and, less so, the minicomputer, has allowed CAR to prosper," stated Saint Paul's Browning (personal communication, October 16, 1995). "In the old days, only a few reporters could get access to the newspaper's mainframe. And only a few had the skills to do so. PCs have allowed CAR techniques to flourish by bringing the power into the newsroom."

At large newspapers such as *The Chronicle*, news magazines, the networks, and those other news media with national or large regional coverage areas, databases and analysis often involve massive projects of millions of records and hundreds of fields. *USA Today*, the *Wall Street Journal*, and *U.S. News & World Report*, for example, each need CAR stories with a national perspective and routinely use extraordinarily large databases. Locally focused CAR-based projects or stories often do not work for their audiences.

"[The decline of the mainframe] forces us to adopt a PC-based server to do big projects," noted Paul Overberg (personal communication, September 19, 1995), database editor for *USA Today* in Washington, DC, who works with projects involving very large federal databases. "It's a complicated tradeoff—it's easier than mainframes, but there are fewer experts to do the heavy lifting."

Another veteran editor with large database experience is Bill Casey, who supervises CAR projects for *The Washington Post*. "The decline in use of mainframes makes CAR easier," Casey (personal communication, September 22, 1995) believes:

> It hasn't got anything to do with analyzing data. When you are talking about replacing mainframes, the data contents of these systems are fundamentally the same. They may be more sophisticated today. But the movement away from mainframes is much slower and more painful than anybody would have imagined fifteen years ago. But it's happening. . . . The demise of the mainframe simply means that more data are available on diskette or downloadable or transferable without getting a tape. Getting a magnetic tape is a pain . . . it is a lot different from handling a couple of zip files on a diskette.

There is a decentralizing factor in the switch from mainframes to PCs for data management in government and other institutions. This should offer advantages for journalists seeking access to the information, Casey believes:

> I think, from a reporter's point of view, there is a human dimension to it, too. There are going to be more people who are in the business or operational side of organizations who are going to be dealing with data—that's happening already with all these machines spread out—it gives reporters more contacts. No longer do you have to find the exact technical person in the organization who is going to be nice to you. And there are a lot of them. Now you are going to have more opportunity, a bigger universe of people, who deal with the data and

can communicate with you about them. The conversion helps in that way, too.

This represents a movement from centralized data processing to distributed decision making. The centralized model has been a pretty good failure for thirty years. But there is no indication that the decentralized model is going to have any success because of the problems of change in organizations. It's more of a challenge because strict control of the data element definitions and files is loosening up as companies go to these different kinds of (storage) systems. That makes it a little more difficult, not hardware-wise, but software file formats. These are areas that could have some impact.

For most news organizations, the decline in mainframe use is not a major issue. "It affects us only in that government and private agencies that still use those methods to store data often cannot provide electronic information in practical formats," said Carol Napolitano, a CAR specialist at the *Omaha World-Herald.* "We must use print images or nine-track tapes or some other older medium, which can be time-consuming and costly to translate into today's computers and software."

Despite the decline of mainframes, there is still significant use of nine-track tapes. Often, state and federal government agencies still provide data on nine-track tapes when data are requested. This requires a news organization to have some means of transferring data from nine-track tape to another storage medium or to have a nine-track tape drive that can be connected to a desktop system. Heavy data analyzers in newsrooms are noticing some decline there also, though. "Fewer government agencies give you stuff on nine-track anymore. Yeah! And more people use desktops now, so when you ask, 'Can I get that on floppy?' they don't look at you as if you're from Mars now," explained James Derk (personal communication, September 5, 1995), computer editor for the *Evansville Courier.*

DESKTOP PERSONAL COMPUTERS AND CAR

The incredible growth of desktop personal computer systems since about 1980 is widely discussed and known (Garrison, 1995). In the past decade, there has also been a rapid growth in the use of portable PCs. In fact, most market studies show portables—with their increasing power and speed, taking a larger share of the total number of PCs sold each year in this decade. However, desktop PCs remain the foundation of CAR at almost all news organizations in 1996.

SWITCHING TO A NEWSROOM PC NETWORK

Many newspapers will be replacing aging dedicated word processing systems used for production in their newsrooms with networked personal computers in the near future. A number of newsrooms, such as the Waterbury *Republican-American,* Raleigh *News & Observer,* and San Jose *Mercury News,* have already made the transition. One newspaper planning the conversion in 1996 is *The Philadelphia Inquirer.* When the newsroom's new PC-based system is installed and running, it is likely to include the following hardware and software:

- Pentium-grade or better processor for each desktop station
- 32 MB of RAM per station
- Novell network
- Shared modems
- Access to the Internet through the newspaper's own node phillynews.com
- Windows 95 or a later version of the operating system
- Microsoft Office Professional for Windows 95 (Word, Excel, Powerpoint, Schedule+, and Access)
- Access to original and public databases
- Customized front-end software developed for easier database use by newsroom staff members

---

PCs operating under MS-DOS dominated the world's computer industry sales each year through 1995. Windows 95-based systems began to appear in 1995, however, beginning the end of MS-DOS. Yet despite that dominance, some journalists prefer other systems, such as Macintosh, for their newsroom work. Smaller news organizations, for instance, often have entire newsrooms based around networked Macintosh systems. At news organizations using MS-DOS-, Windows NT-, Windows 95-, or OS/2-based PCs, it is common in some graphics or advertising departments to find a room full of Macintosh systems. Some small publishing companies that produce newsletters and other forms of printed mass communication also prefer Macintosh systems.

Which PC systems are best for CAR? Which ones offer the most direct route to success with CAR? Although this might appear to be a difficult question to answer, the worldwide computer industry may have already answered it. Journalists, like others in the communication industry, use what is on the general computer market that is available to other businesses. Often, however, decisions about what to use are made at the corporate or chain level instead of in the newsroom or by journalists actually using the systems for particular tasks such as CAR online or with databases. If there is some freedom in choices to be made, there are numerous alternatives in each of the major categories of CAR tools.

In Table 4.1, data from the University of Miami national survey show the most commonly used processor for CAR stories or projects is a 80486-type processor that has been on the market since 1993. A total of 43% of all newspapers use "486s" for CAR in early 1995. This should change, of course, in 1996 and 1997 as 486s begin to disappear from retail outlets and more and more 80586-type processors are available at lower prices. In 1995, only a handful of newsrooms (3%) used the Pentium processor so far. A little more than 1 in 10 newspapers used Macintoshes for CAR (12%) and another 1 in 10 used older 80386 processors for CAR work.

Table 4.2 reveals changes in processors used in newsrooms for CAR in 1994–1995. As shown, there is some evidence of upgrading for CAR, moving toward higher end processors such as 80486s and 80586 Pentiums. Perhaps an important observation is that there continues to be a wide range of processors in use, with no apparent shifts in any particular direction between the 1994 and 1995 studies.

The differences in small and large newspapers are significant when the type of processor used is considered. Larger newspapers, for example, rarely use Macintoshes for CAR, but often use them for graphics and other purposes. Almost one quarter of smaller newspapers, however, use Macintosh computers for their CAR work. In fact, it is the second-largest category of processor for the smaller dailies and only by a small margin.

TABLE 4.1
Types of Processors Used, 1995

Type of PC Processor in Use	Large Dailies[a]		Small Dailies[b]		Totals	
80486-type	75	57.3%	24	24.2%	99	43.0%
Other	31	23.7	19	19.2	50	21.7
Macintosh	5	3.8	23	23.2	28	12.2
80386-type	11	8.4	12	12.1	23	10.0
None	1	0.8	13	13.1	14	6.1
Pentium	5	3.8	2	2.0	7	3.0
80286- or 8088-type	1	0.8	5	5.1	6	2.6
Don't know	2	1.5	0	0.0	2	0.9
Unix	0	0.0	1	1.0	1	0.4
Totals	131	57.0	99	43.0	230	100.0

Note. n = 287; missing observations = 57.
[a] Circulation over 52,800.　[b] Circulation under 52,800.

TABLE 4.2
Types of Processors Used, 1994-1995

Type of PC Processor in Use	1994		1995		Percentage Change
586 Pentium	2	1.0%	7	2.4%	+1.4%
486	64	30.8	99	34.5	+3.7
386	21	10.1	23	8.0	-2.1
286 or 8088	4	1.9	6	2.1	+0.2
Macintosh	18	8.7	28	9.8	+1.1
Other	31	14.9	50	17.4	+2.5
Missing/don't know/none	68	32.7	74	25.8	-6.9
Totals	208	100.0%	287	100.0%	

SUCCESSFUL HARDWARE CONFIGURATIONS

What hardware features make up an ideal CAR desktop system? Much depends on the purpose—whether the system is mainly used for online searching or for database analysis, or both, for example. Most experienced CAR supervisors have preferences for what desktop hardware they use, but there are certain must-have hardware tools for CAR. In 1996, these include:

- An 80586 or 80486 processor operating at 66 megahertz or faster.
- A processor box, such as a mini-tower style, with expansion capability.
- 16 MB minimum, but more random access memory (RAM) if possible.
- A 2 GB or larger hard drive, depending on sizes of databases to be used.
- A 6X speed or faster compact-disc drive (CD-ROM).
- A 14-inch or 17-inch color monitor.
- A 28.8 Kbps or faster fax/modem.
- A tape, high-capacity disk, or optical drive storage system.
- An uninterruptable power supply and surge protector.
- A black-and-white laser 8 page-per-minute printer.
- A nine-track tape drive.
- Options could include a flatbed scanner, a multimedia sound card, speakers, and PC Card slot.

USA *Today's* Overberg (personal communication, September 19, 1995) recommends upgrading to the best tools available for most CAR work. "A 486 or Pentium with 32 megabytes of RAM, a big SVGA screen, 6X CD and 1 to 2 GB of disk [is the ideal]," Overberg stated. "[You also need] a direct Internet hookup. The same can be had on the Mac side with a Power PC 608-based machine."

Seattle's McElroy offered his ideal system if there was no financial limit:

> If money is no object, I'd recommend a Pentium notebook PC with plenty of disk space (500 MB to 1 GB), 24 MB of RAM to handle large spreadsheets and databases, a modem and a cellular phone with the proper cabling to link with the modem. Plug the notebook into a docking station at the office so a regular keyboard and monitor can be used; unplug and take it on the road when necessary. That kind of setup could easily run $5,000 to $6,000; however, accessibility to the tools is once again a key to success.

> Consider this true story: A city official told a news conference that, in the interest of conserving money, he bought a desk for just $800. An alert reporter who saw the desk didn't think this was possible, so he used a spreadsheet program to call up the city budget during the news conference. He discovered that the $800 covered the desktop alone; the whole piece of furniture cost several thousand dollars. Armed with this information, he was able to ask the city official some rather pointed questions. The reporter [in this case] did not have a notebook PC, but he was able to walk across the hall to his bureau in City Hall and use his desktop PC to check the figures.

Similarly, Saint Paul's Browning (personal communication, October 16, 1995) feels a successful hardware configuration would include a very powerful base system with some database user-oriented peripherals. Browning recommends "a Pentium with 16 to 32 MB of RAM and two to three gigabytes of hard drive space, a 4X speed CD-ROM, an Iomega Zip drive, 1.44 MB 3.5-inch floppy drive, perhaps a Colorado tape backup, a 28.8-Kbps internal or external modem, a network card, and access to a nine-track tape drive."

NICAR training director and former database editor of *The Bergen Record* Neil Reisner also spends considerable time online, so his system reflects needs to work with databases and to work quickly on the Internet and commercial services. Reisner (personal communication, October 30, 1995), who is assistant system operator (sysop) for the Investigative-IRE section of the Journalism Forum on CompuServe, is a power user when defining his ideal system: "A Pentium 90, 16 MB of RAM, 1 GB hard drive or better, 17-inch monitor, 28.8-Kbps fax/modem or ISDN link, 4X speed CD-ROM (or even a small CD Jukebox) both floppy drives, some sort of serious backup—be it a Travan tape, a Bernouilli disk, or one of the newer ZIP drives—Windows 3.11, or Windows 95, or Windows NT."

OPERATING SYSTEMS USED FOR CAR

No matter what processor is in use, a computer's operating system, or OS, is the brains of any personal computer. Computer hardware cannot accomplish even the most basic task without an OS. An OS is software that performs a wide range of tasks that are necessary for a computer to work, but rarely interacts directly with the user. An OS is a collection of different computer programs that run whenever the computer is in use. Until a decade or so ago, most PC users used MS-DOS (Microsoft-Disk Operating System). Windows debuted as a graphical platform laid on top of MS-DOS. It was introduced in response to the Macintosh operating system that was more visually oriented. At about the same time Windows debuted, IBM introduced its own visually oriented OS, the latest known as OS/2, that was similar to the Macintosh system by combining the user interface with the OS.

Windows 1.0 and its later Versions 2.x and 3.x were operating platforms that were installed as a layer of software operating over DOS, not in substitution for it. But Windows, and to a lesser degree, OS/2, became popular with DOS users because of their graphical user interface that took advantage of an on-screen pointing device such as a mouse. For many office computer users not comfortable with command line operation of their PCs, Windows was a prayer answered by Microsoft. It has since dominated sales and OS/2 use has begun to fade. Windows' popularity grew with its presales installation in new computers that provided the product ready to run. In both the corporate and educational worlds, Windows had established itself by the beginning of the 1990s. It was only a matter of time before powerful and useful software originally written for DOS was rewritten with Windows conveniences and conventions. The same pattern will occur again at the end of this decade as new 32-bit software evolves for Windows 95, Windows 97, and beyond. The first wave was already occurring at the end of 1995 and in early 1996.

But there were performance problems with a DOS–Windows double layering on a PC. Windows was unstable. Error messages were common. Resource management was a nightmare for some users. There never seemed to be enough RAM. The Mac OS, IBM's new OS/2, and other systems did not require a second layer, were more stable, and had less overall trouble, many users of both systems believed.

Windows 95, originally to be named Version 4.0, combined with what would have been called MS-DOS 7.0. Microsoft promised that the Windows 2.0 and 3.x performance problems, such as high demands for memory, have been solved with more efficient use of memory. This seemed questionable only because of the rush to upgrade RAM and hard drive capacity for many existing PCs in 1995 and 1996. Thus, there was an enormous amount of anxiety connected to the new version of Windows. Should users upgrade to Windows 95 or its later editions? Should hardware be upgraded to take full advantage of the new product? Should other software also be upgraded? It is not too large an exaggeration to state that the big parts of the U.S. economy could be affected by this single product and the technology sector dominos that will be knocked down when it begins widespread use worldwide.

Windows 95 and Beyond

Computer users probably experienced the shift of an industry OS standard when Microsoft's Windows 95 debuted. The mass migration to the vastly changed new edition of Windows and its subsequent revisions is underway, although it may take a year or more. Since August 1995, computer users have been inundated with images of the now-familiar sky blue box, upgrade offers, and all the other associated marketing hype. Computer users take graphical user interface systems for granted, but Windows 95 was an important new operating tool for personal computers and their users. The effect, Microsoft said at the time of the system's debut, is a more productive computer for users. Windows 95 and its later editions have been marketed as more customizable for users and easier to configure when systems are upgraded or changed. It can be appealing to individuals needing connectivity also, through its networking and Internet capabilities.

The latest generation of Windows is a tool to enhance productivity with a PC, no matter what the task might be. Microsoft promoted the new operating system throughout 1995 and 1996 as more productive than other basic operating systems such as earlier Windows. It has the potential. Windows clearly increases performance speed and versatility. With its 32-bit processing, software will run faster. Products commonly used with CAR—Excel, Netscape, Approach, Access, FoxPro, and SPSS—each have 32-bit versions. Other products were on the way, debuting monthly in the first half of 1996. Microsoft officials have stated that the revised OS will make computers run 25% to 35% faster with the 32-bit processing. For number crunchers and data processors working on CAR projects, this means, simply, that more programs can run at the same time through what is the equivalent of a wider pipeline. This should lead to better quality multimedia such as sound and video from CDs.

Many journalists will wait and see with the Windows OS. Some have already jumped right in because they seek improved performance or have other motivations. Delaying the upgrade is not a bad idea, but there is no harm in moving up to Windows 95 for most users with most desktop and portable configurations. It is well documented in the computer industry literature from the spring and summer preceding the official release that Windows 95 will not support some software and some hardware. Perhaps much of that will be resolved for later editions of Windows.

What's different in this new operating system? Some of the most obvious changes from Windows 3.1 or Windows for Work Groups 3.11 are the appearance of the basic desktop itself and use of the pointing device. The Windows 95 desktop is not as cluttered with Windows or file groups as the 3.x systems. The key to the new software is a convenient "Start" button that resides in a toolbar at the bottom left of the user's screen. All clicking, by the way, is single click instead of double click. This is probably welcomed by individuals who always had trouble mastering that mouse skill.

The basic desktop has several new icons on it (see Fig. 4.1). Two of them are "My Computer" and the "Recycle Bin." "My Computer" leads to all the key elements of the computer such as the hard drive, CD-ROM drive, PC card or other removable drives, and the floppies. The "Recycle Bin" holds unwanted files until they are deleted. This is one of several new features that will remind Macintosh users of the numerous System 7.x-like features in Windows. The desktop is quite easily customized. Clicking on "Start" leads to one-click short-cuts to the programs and their groups and other key features of the operating system. The Start menu can also be customized in several ways, as can the shortcuts. For keyboard-oriented users or those with a wayward pointer, the Start menu can be fully operated by key combinations.

Perhaps the most interesting change in Windows for users who are heavy into file management is Windows Explorer. This replaces the familiar File Manager. Windows Explorer has some high potential when old habits can be broken. Explorer gives all sources of programs and data in one place. There are no multiple Windows nor is there as much clicking to do to move files around.

Another advantage of Windows Explorer is capacity for long file and folder names. Windows now uses them anywhere a longer name is needed. The old "eight-dot-three" filename format is gone, even though it can be still be used. File and folder names prepared under

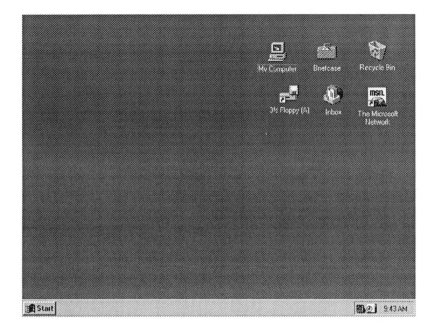

FIG. 4.1. Basic Windows 95 desktop configuration.

DOS 6.x or older versions are easily read. The longer file and folder names are another feature reminiscent of the Mac. For users who are hard-pressed to think of useful descriptive eight-character file names, this is a welcome improvement.

A third major desktop icon that will pop onto the desktop will be a one-click access to The Microsoft Network. MSN is a highly graphical, easy-to-use product that may soon rival CompuServe, America Online, Prodigy, and other commercial services for the general online consumer market. For serious online information gatherers such as news researchers and reporters, MSN is just another tool on the desktop so far. It was inexpensive at introduction and is still a relative bargain as commercial services go. MSN has a very slick look and a friendly user interface. The quality graphics and ease of use will make it appealing to many online customers. However, to take full advantage, users need fast modems, such as 9.6- or 14.4-Kbps, for starters. Like everything else that enhances performance by upgrading, a 28.8-Kbps or faster modem will give MSN a chance to do its best online service.

Windows has other strengths. Some quick and general observations:

- A document or file orientation in addition to the traditional program orientation.

- Working through the desktop to run programs and complete tasks is simple. Ease of use is increased.
- There are numerous system tools improvements, such as an improved control panel and a neat system properties option that quickly describes resources through a graphic that displays disk size and space availability. System properties also offer a device manager, hardware profiles, and instant performance status reports. Furthermore, tools include error checking, backup, and defragmentation status.
- An immediately observable change is improved printing speed. In Word, for example, the document begins printing instantly instead of waiting until the program has processed all pages. This is helpful for long documents.
- Much has been said about the instant hardware configuration potential of Windows, its "plug and play" capacity. The program is better able to diagnose existing hardware and software (e.g., drivers) during installation of Windows as well as able to add new hardware after Windows is in place.
- Windows seems to offer improved memory management. Crashes and those "general protection fault" error boxes that often popped up in Windows 3.x have disappeared.

No matter what aspects of Windows are most appealing or most troubling, the program takes some time to learn. It has numerous layers. Peel one back and another appears. The new look and significant changes in some of the basic concepts will require adjustment. For some people, the intuitive nature will make the conversion very easy. However, for others, there will be a steep learning curve. Practice makes perfect, as with any new software.

There are other downsides to upgrading to a newer Windows. First, it will require some users to upgrade hardware. Windows 95 will operate on 4 MB of RAM and 386 systems, but it is intolerably slow. For minimal performance, 8 MB of RAM is needed. Independent tests have shown that 16 to 24 MB is ideal and there is little gained in performance going beyond 24 MB except when using large graphics files. A larger hard drive may also be required because Windows 95 and the new 32-bit versions of existing software Windows 95 has spawned will be even larger than the 1994 and 1995 versions on the market. Multimedia demands, if any are needed for CAR work, will call for a larger hard drive also.

Second, Windows 95 may require CAR users to upgrade their software if they hope to make the most of the new OS and the advances of the 32-bit programs that were released in 1995 and 1996. Veteran PC users will remember the reluctance most people experienced when the original Windows debuted. Longtime command-line DOS users scoffed, saying it would never replace how they did their work. In 1996, those command-line users are truly hard to find. Like most adoption of new innovation, use of this program may take time to spread. It will become the standard for PCs. It already is the standard for new machines being purchased in late 1995 and beyond.

In short, Microsoft has created a new generation of operating systems. It is the computing present and future for most journalists using PCs. There may be some uneasiness at first, some of the familiar "if it ain't broke, don't fix it" thinking. It is obvious that experiences with this new system will vary considerably. Much will depend on the hardware that is brought into the mix. Even more will depend on the existing software to be used, not just software that will be acquired in the future. Ultimately, users will just have to put it on their own machines and try it.

Despite all of these new features and improvements, it remains unclear if Windows 95 and its later editions are the OS of the next decade. Some experts argue that Microsoft, the final determining force in the matter, may favor its high-powered Windows NT operating system when the base of computer hardware sold in the marketplace catches up with NT (Kalman, 1995). Because most PCs sold in 1996 were underequipped for Windows NT—it requires at least 16 MB of memory—Microsoft still marketed two main 32-bit OSs in 1996 and said in late 1995 that it would for the indefinite future. However, in the years ahead, it seems logical that only one of these will emerge for most PC users going into the next century and the third decade of desktop computing. Again, it is a wait-and-see situation.

Which Operating System Works for CAR?

For CAR and other newsroom applications, the most used operating system in 1995 was a combined DOS and Windows set-up. More than half of the newspapers responding to the 1995 CAR survey (52%) reported using DOS with Windows, as shown in Table 4.3. The combination referred to either Windows 3.x or Windows for Work Groups 3.11, or another version of Windows. Because the data in the 1995 survey were collected early in that year, prior to the debut of the vast Windows 95 beta program or the final release of the product, Windows 95 was not included in the 1995 study. However, it seems from group and individual discussions at the IRE–NICAR "CAR ROCK" conference in Cleveland in 1995 that many newspapers will be relatively slow to introduce the new version of Windows and any 32-bit versions of CAR-oriented software that gradually became available in late 1995 and early 1996.

TABLE 4.3
Operating Systems/Platforms, 1995

Primary CAR Operating System/ Platform in Use	Large Dailies[a]		Small Dailies[b]		Totals	
DOS/Windows	89	64.5%	32	33.7%	121	51.9%
Other	29	21.0	16	16.8	45	19.3
None	11	8.0	18	18.9	29	12.4
DOS only	5	3.6	11	11.6	16	6.9
Macintosh	0	0.0	13	13.7	13	5.6
Don't know	1	0.7	3	3.2	4	1.7
OS/2	2	1.4	1	1.1	3	1.3
Unix	1	0.7	1	1.1	2	0.9
Totals	138	59.2	95	40.8	233	100.0

Note. n = 287; missing observations = 54.
[a] Circulation over 52,800. [b] Circulation under 52,800.

Beyond DOS and Windows, there were a few other OSs in use, but none in any attention-grabbing proportions. About 7% of newspapers reported still using DOS only, interestingly, an artifact of slower and older hardware it appears. There were differences in small and large newspapers also, most likely due to the greater proportion of small newspapers using Macintosh systems in their newsrooms.

Table 4.4 shows the shifts in use of operating systems and platforms between 1994 and 1995. The change that is most noticeable is movement from DOS only to DOS with Windows. Use of DOS with Windows rose almost 21% in a single year, whereas DOS-only users dropped almost 9%. These numbers reflect the national shift in use of DOS-only software for data analysis to Windows-based programs that had been first introduced about 2 years earlier.

CAR AND COMPACT DISC DRIVES

One of the hardware peripherals that has rapidly grown in use is the compact disc drive (see Table 4.5). Beginning in 1995, most new desktop systems and a growing proportion of portables were sold with compact disc drives installed. This is due in part to the growing popularity of multimedia systems requiring CD-ROM, sound cards, and other devices added to the base processor and floppy drives. The most common type drive is the CD-ROM, which is a read-only storage drive. New information cannot be written to the drive and the existing files or data cannot be changed. These CDs have enormous storage capability, accepting as much as 540 to 680 MB of information, or about 74 minutes of audio playing time, and have become a major method for distributing games and software. More importantly for CAR, it is also a major means for distributing public databases such as those sold by the Bureau of the Census or the Federal Election Commission.

Another form of compact disc drive is known as a WORM (write-once, read many) drive. This type of drive is also called a CD-Recordable (CD-R) drive. These were in some use at news organizations needing to make permanent backups or to distribute data to newsroom staff members or to the public. WORM CD drives are highly valuable to newsrooms as data storage and long-term backup media. For newsroom archives that need to be duplicated and distributed in a limited manner or simply accessed easily on many newsroom PCs, these devices will become a necessity in newsrooms

TABLE 4.4
Operating Systems/Platforms, 1994-1995

Primary CAR Operating Sytem/ Platform in Use	1994		1995		Percentage Change
DOS/Windows	45	21.6%	121	42.2%	+20.6
Other	10	4.8	45	15.7	+ 9.9
DOS only	30	14.4	16	5.6	−8.8
Macintosh	8	3.8	13	4.5	+ 0.7
Don't know	0	0.0	4	1.4	+ 1.4
OS/2	5	2.4	3	1.0	−1.4
Unix	0	0.0	2	0.7	+ 0.7
None/Missing	110	52.9	83	28.9	−23.0
Totals	208	100.0%	287	100.0%	

TABLE 4.5
CD-ROM Drive Use in Newsrooms, 1995

CD-ROM Drives of Some Type in Use	Large Dailies[a]		Small Dailies[b]		Totals	
One in newsroom	52	37.7%	37	38.5%	89	38.0%
Two or more	67	48.6	11	11.5	78	33.3
None	17	12.3	45	46.9	62	26.5
Other	2	1.4	3	3.1	5	2.1
Totals	138	59.0	96	41.0	234	100.0

Note. n = 287; missing observations = 53.
[a]Circulation over 52,800.   [b]Circulation under 52,800.

in the near future as their prices have dropped considerably in 1995 and 1996 to much more affordable levels. CD-R cannot be used to make commercial CD-ROM molds, however, because that requires different compact disc recording technology (Gerber, 1995).

In 1995, CD-ROM drives were becoming more and more common in newsrooms. In the 1995 CAR survey, more than half of the newspapers reported using one or more CD-ROM drives. A total of 38% reported using one CD-ROM drive and another 33% reported using two or more CD-ROM drives, so more than 71% used a CD-ROM drive in some CAR capacity in their newsrooms. As with other hardware examined in the study in 1995, there are differences in large and small newspapers. Data in Table 4.5 show that large dailies typically have more than one CD-ROM drive, whereas smaller dailies are more likely to have only one drive and a much larger proportion had none.

Table 4.6 shows that in the 1994 data, 39% of the reporting newspapers used one or more CD-ROM drives. Of that, 36% reported using one CD-ROM reader and just 4% used more than one CD-ROM reader. This reflects a 23% growth in the number of newspapers with two or more CD-ROM drives and a 19% overall growth in the number of newsrooms with CD-ROMs in use for CAR overall.

OTHER IMPORTANT CAR HARDWARE

Hard drive capacities are growing. Modem speeds and capabilities to fax are increasing. More storage is required and different media for storage are being used. These are the trends in hardware. Some of the details are presented here.

Hard Drive Capacities

Hard drive manufacturers in 1995 and 1996 were making larger and faster drives and, at the same time, lowering prices on many of

TABLE 4.6
CD-ROM Drive Use in Newsrooms, 1994–1995

CD-ROM Drives of Some Type in Use	1994		1995		Percentage Change
One in newsroom	74	35.6%	89	31.0%	–4.6%
Two or more	8	3.8	78	27.2	+23.4
Other	0	0.0	5	1.7	+ 1.7
Missing/none	126	60.6	115	40.1	–20.5
Totals	208	100.0%	287	100.0%	

them. This meant that newsrooms using personal computers for CAR had greater capacity available to them, and they were taking advantage of the newer drives. The mean hard drive size is over a gigabyte (1,055 MB) in 1995. The sizes reported ranged from a very old 20 MB drive still in use to a 10 GB drive. The most frequent reported sizes in early 1995 were 1 GB (10%), 500 MB (5%), and 2 GB (4%). A year earlier, the mean hard drive size was considerably less at 853 MB for the newspapers reporting. The sizes ranged from a 20 MB drive in use to a 6.7 GB server in use for CAR.

Modem Speeds

There has been a shift in modems required by online users in newsrooms. The needs of World Wide Web, other Internet services, and commercial online service users have forced news organizations to upgrade modems in newsrooms. In late 1995 and early 1996, the standard was 28.8-Kbps and slower modems were rapidly being replaced as costs for 28.8- and 14.4-Kbps speeds dropped.

Table 4.7 shows the speeds of modems in use for CAR in 1995. The most popular modem speed in the 1995 data was 14.4-Kbps (49%) and 9.6-Kbps (22%), but 11% had 28.8-Kbps and about 2% used 57.6-Kbps connections. Perhaps differences in large and small newspapers' resources are evident in the speeds most often used when analyzed by circulation size. There are differences by size and, by reviewing proportions in Table 4.7, the proportions are one or more modem generations of faster speeds for larger dailies.

Data Storage Media

Much CAR that involves databases requires use of storage media beyond hard drives and floppy diskettes. These might be acceptable for some databases and some projects, but larger databases or limited capacities of hard drives require users to find alternatives for storage. Table 4.8 shows digital tape to be the most popular form of storage (31%), but it should be noted that an even larger percentage of all newspapers, 38%, do not use additional storage at all. Aside from placing the data at those organizations in jeopardy, there are probable resource pressures at those sites. Optical disks are also in use by about 9% of the responding newspapers and another 16% reported other forms of storage such as nine-track tape, Zip-type drives, Bernoulli-type drives, and various forms of CD-ROM drives. Again, there are noticeable differences in large and small newspapers and how each handles data storage problems. A much larger proportion of smaller newspapers has no additional storage media in use, although digital tape is the storage of choice when it is used. Regardless of what is in use, it seems clear that if

TABLE 4.7
Modem Speeds in Use in Newsrooms, 1995

Modem Kbps Speed in Use	Large Dailies[a]		Small Dailies[b]		Totals	
14.4	74	56.1%	26	35.1%	100	48.5%
9.6	26	19.7	19	25.7	45	21.8
2.4	12	9.1	16	21.6	28	13.6
28.8	18	13.6	4	5.4	22	10.7
1.2	0	0.0	6	8.1	6	2.9
57.6	2	1.5	2	2.7	4	1.9
0.3	0	0.0	1	1.4	1	0.5
Totals	132	64.1	74	35.9	206	100.0

Note. n = 287; missing observations = 81.
[a]Circulation over 52,800.   [b]Circulation under 52,800.

TABLE 4.8
Data Storage Media in Newsrooms, 1995

Type of Data Storage Media	Large Dailies[a]		Small Dailies[b]		Totals	
None	34	26.0%	51	55.4%	85	38.1%
Digital tape	55	42.0	15	16.3	70	31.4
Other	25	19.1	11	12.0	36	16.1
Optical disk	12	9.2	7	7.6	19	8.5
Don't know	5	3.8	8	8.7	13	5.8
Totals	131	58.7	92	41.3	223	100.0

Note. n = 287; missing observations = 64.
[a]Circulation over 52,800.   [b]Circulation under 52,800.

new storage technology develops, the database people in newsrooms check it out.

WHAT'S NEEDED NEXT? CAR SUPERVISORS' WISH LISTS

Journalists involved in CAR always seem to have hardware, software, and database wish lists. In 1995, what sort of hardware tools did they hope to acquire in the near future? Table 4.9 shows both hardware and software wish lists in the 1995 national survey,

TABLE 4.9
First Choice for Additional CAR Tools, 1995

First Choice for New CAR Tool	Frequency	Percentage	Adjusted Percentage
New personal computers	22	7.7%	12.8%
Upgrade existing PCs	17	5.9	9.9
MapInfo or Atlas GIS software	17	5.9	9.9
Internet access or improved access	15	5.2	8.7
CD-ROM drive reader	10	3.5	5.8
Any database package	8	2.8	4.7
New modem or upgrade	8	2.8	4.7
Nine-track tape drive	7	2.4	4.1
Network and server	7	2.4	4.1
FoxPro software, programming tools	6	2.1	3.5
CD-ROM writer/recordable	5	1.7	2.9
Visual Basic	5	1.7	2.9
Spreadsheet upgrade	5	1.7	2.9
Excel software, Excel training	4	1.4	2.3
Online service	4	1.4	2.3
Use resources better	4	1.4	2.3
More storage	4	1.4	2.3
Databases	3	1.0	1.7
New workstation	2	0.7	1.2
Paradox software, programming tools	2	0.7	1.2
Upgrade portable PCs	2	0.7	1.2
Training	2	0.7	1.2
Optical disk	2	0.7	1.2
Access and training	2	0.7	1.2
Statistics package	2	0.7	1.2
More RAM	1	0.3	0.6
Data visualization software	1	0.3	0.6
SPSS	1	0.3	0.6
Text manager	1	0.3	0.6
Presentation graphics	1	0.3	0.6
Full-time CAR position	1	0.3	0.6
Scanner, software	1	0.3	0.6
Missing	115	40.1	Missing
Totals	287	100.0	100.0

Note. n = 287; missing observations = 115.

revealing the most common preference was for new personal computers. It was often the complaint of editors, news researchers, CAR supervisors, and reporters that there were either not enough computers or none devoted to CAR work. In some cases, individuals wanted both new computers and upgraded existing systems.

Of the 172 newspapers reporting "wish lists" in 1995, new computers were at the top of the list for almost 13% of the newsrooms. Another 10% sought upgrades for existing desktop computers, pointing to a considerable hardware stress problem at almost one quarter of the newspapers. Third on the list, also about 10% of respondents, were two software products that permit users to merge databases with maps, commonly known as analytic mapping software. Internet access or improved Internet access (e.g., FTP or World Wide Web) was fourth on the wish list, at about 9% of the newspapers. Another hardware upgrade, adding a CD-ROM drive, was fifth on the list with about 6% of respondents seeking one or more drives. A very wide range of other hardware items follow on the list of "first choices" for new CAR tools.

These included such things as nine-track drives, local area networks for the CAR computers or the entire newsroom, additional RAM, optical disk drives, new workstations, and so forth. Software preferences included many that were database oriented such as relational database programs and programming tools for relational database programs, and statistical packages for more sophisticated analyses. Yet some news organizations revealed their "newbie" status by placing basics such as spreadsheets, online services, and databases on top of their wish lists.

5

Software Tools for Computer-Assisted Reporting

Syracuse Herald American/Herald-Journal reporters Erik Kriss and Jon Craig spent about 18 months studying how the New York state legislature spends taxpayer dollars. It was a story that needed to be done. Many New York journalists knew of the abuses, but no one had documented them in any systematic manner. The reporters, both veterans of politics and the state legislature reporting, knew something was amiss. Kriss, a veteran capital bureau and state government correspondent, and Craig, a government and politics reporter, decided a broad and deep investigation was necessary and, with the help of their newspaper's editors, they teamed to study thousands of documents and interview hundreds of sources for the project.

The result was an award-winning 11-part series that was published in 1994. Called "Secrets of the Chamber: How the New York State Legislature Spends Your Money," the project achieved what it sought: to make residents of New York more aware of how the legislature used tax dollars on itself. Kriss and Craig's stories were accompanied by editorial page editorials, editorial cartoons, photographs, informational graphics, a "whom to call" box, full-page "where the money goes" and legislative spending breakdowns and summaries.

Explained Kriss (1995):

> The New York state legislature has the biggest budget of any legislature in the nation, at $177 million, the biggest staff, the biggest of a lot of things. For years, it had been very difficult to get any kind of meaningful information about the legislature's budget out of the legislature or out of the state at all. So that's why we went ahead and decided to do this project. At the time we started into the project, we felt we had sufficient computer resources to be able to pull something like this off. Because of the magnitude of it, we knew we weren't going

to be able to do it just with old-fashioned shoe leather and traditional journalistic techniques.

Craig joined the project after it began because Kriss and his editor "were drowning in information" and Craig offered relief assistance to manage everything. "My role was to bring a fresh look and see what freedom of information requests weren't filled and see what gaps we had in our information," Craig (1995) explained.

Among the public information sources they used were:

- State accounting records of legislature transactions found both on computer and on paper.
- State comptroller building leases and lease summaries.
- Senate travel and expense vouchers.
- County clerk business partnership, corporation, deed, and other records in 20 counties across the state.
- More than 200 Department of State corporation filings.
- Payroll records for 4,600 legislative employees.
- Payroll histories over an 18-year period for more than 300 employees.
- Legislative commission meeting minutes.
- Legislative per diem and stipend summaries.
- Financial disclosure records of State Board of Elections.
- Legitech data.
- State Assembly legislative inventory.
- Legislature audits.
- Rules and laws about benefits, duties, and responsibilities of legislators.
- Department of Motor Vehicles automobile registrations and license records.
- State Department of Insurance documents.
- Legislature internal correspondence and memos.
- Out-of-state documents and reports.

Craig emphasized the value of planning for such a project. "Our project is only as good as the information we were given. I know that sounds incredibly simplistic, but New York's records are mainly paper reliant. . . . There were a number of things that were missing from our original databases. They had been too narrow." Craig explained that by combining paper records and the databases, a clearer and more complete picture of relationships began to emerge.

The newspaper's reporters and editors also created several original databases. These included databases of lawyers associated with legislators' law firms, names and affiliations of 56,000 people elected to political party committees around the state, losers of legislative races, and legislators' relatives.

"There was a total of about 175,000 cash transactions that we were able to make some sense out of with the computer and Paradox," Kriss explained. "That was step A. Step B was the juicy stuff. We wanted to use the computer to document and quantify what was basically unproved common knowledge about the legislative payroll—and that is that there is a whole lot of patronage, nepotism, and cronyism going on. We had heard of isolated examples, but we wanted to put the whole thing together and show just how pervasive that was in New York. We set up computer databases for each of these: patronage, nepotism, and cronyism."

The Syracuse project revealed that the state's lawmakers lived well. Benefits and perks were so common they were nearly uncountable. The stories were presented over a 2-week period to readers to permit time for them to digest the large amount of surprises and secrets. Among them included lavish spending on food and entertainment expenses, hundreds of political appointments on the legislature's payroll, relatives on the legislature's payroll, enormous pensions for members, higher than usual rents for office space, special tax breaks, postage paid for newsletters sent to registered voters only, broadcast studios for use by legislators, and expense-paid international trips.

"We didn't hang ourselves up on including every single detail of what we found in the computers," Craig stated. "The series, in the end, had a bigger impact because we kept our overall conclusions as simple as we could and we didn't get tripped up on specific facts. We also threw out things that we had not double or triple checked."

The reporters received considerable praise for their work in 1995. IRE presented them with the IRE Medal and the Society of Professional Journalists honored them with a Sigma Delta Chi Award.

TOOLS FOR THE NEW YORK LEGISLATURE PROJECT

Erik Kriss and Jon Craig used a number of computer tools for their study of the spending of the New York state legislature on itself. This is what they used:

- Epson Equity 386/20 with a 647 MB hard drive and 10 MB of RAM.
- Paradox relational database program to combine the state databases.
- Overland Data portable tape drive.
- Two nine-track tape databases from New York state government.

Kriss and Craig used highly sophisticated computer software tools for their successes as part of the "Secrets of the Chamber" project. Most helpful to Kriss and Craig was the ability to combine different databases to check for linkages in the major state databases they acquired and in their own original databases that were created. To accomplish this, journalists such as Kriss and Craig often use relational database management systems that have the capacity to review different data tables and match them with a common element such as a name or ID number.

In the case of the Syracuse project, reporters used database management software power to compare two nine-track tape 174,000-record databases from the state Comptroller's Office that contained records of cash transactions by the legislature over a 3-year period. The analysis was able to determine recipients of the legislature's spending on itself, when, and for what purpose. The software used also enabled the reporters to break down the spending into categories as was needed for specific analyses, such as spending by the Senate and by the Assembly. The two databases were obtained on eight different nine-track tapes from the state.

"Computers were an important part of this project, but certainly not the only part," Kriss emphasized. "There was still a lot of leafing through pages upon pages of payroll records, analyzing paper data, conducting lots of interviews, using sources to help us figure out where to go. . . . I don't know that anything we found was illegal. The legislature is very careful, both in making sure that everything it does is technically legal and making sure the law allows it to do the kind of things members want to do. . . . It was a little bit of a risky venture. We didn't know what kind of return we would get until we were done."

For several years, CAR has been dominated by a handful of buzzwords. Perhaps among the most used are *spreadsheets* and *relational databases.* Software is a critical element to successful CAR. Without the appropriate software tools for the task at hand, even the most powerful of computer tools are useless. This discussion investigates the most successful software tools used in CAR. What database programs are preferred by news organizations already involved in CAR? How are they used? What combinations of software work best?

TYPICAL SOFTWARE SET-UPS

The specifics of software configurations for CAR change each month as new products are placed on the market, tested, and adopted to newsroom news. But over the past several years, there has been an effective combination of software tools that have evolved in most newsrooms to form a "CAR software suite." These main categories of software in an ideal newsroom CAR suite include:

- Word processing program.
- Personal information manager and/or text database manager.
- Communications package and/or commercial online access proprietary software.
- Internet/World Wide Web browser/HTML editor.
- Spreadsheet program.
- Relational database management system.
- Statistical analysis package.
- Analytical mapping package.

There are numerous commercial enterprises selling products in each of these categories, with upgrades or completely new products introduced throughout each new calendar year. Many products in these categories are available in multiple platform versions, such as DOS/Windows, Windows 95, OS/2, Macintosh, and Unix. There are also inexpensive products available as well, often with fewer features, but they get much of the job done for much less money. Often these

---

SUCCESS WITH HANDLING DATA: AVOIDING TROUBLE

Inexperienced database handlers are perfect targets for data disaster. More experienced database users know there are certain basics steps to take when working with databases in electronic form:

- Back up databases and store backups in a separate location.
- Back up databases that are currently being used and analyzed on a basis that reflects use patterns (e.g., daily or more often).
- Decide whether data need to be password protected to assure integrity of the database.
- Designate one person at a time to work with (edit or update) a database.
- Use "read only" options with databases, if database access software offers this option, to avoid unwanted changes by users.
- Install a current antivirus software on the system to be used for analyzing the database and check on a scheduled basis for infections. Upgrade the antivirus software on a regular schedule.
- Develop a news department "security" policy for handling and storing key data. Make sure the policy is followed.

less expensive programs are parts of sets of several programs bundled together or programs available as shareware at little or no cost.

To help new users to get started with the products, including installation, software publishers offer technical telephone support. Many major software producers have help services online as well through such services as CompuServe, America Online, the World Wide Web, and bulletin board systems. Many telephone technical support services run for a period of time that begins on date of the first call. Typical support periods run 90 days or so. Support hotlines are often operated at no cost for the caller, other than the toll for long distance. Some companies charge for help at unusual times by requiring callers to use "900" numbers, credit cards, or other means. A list of the major CAR-related software publishers' technical support lines is contained in Appendix D.

The influence of the new Windows 95 operating systems and the 32-bit programming they permit is significant. The new product is already having a remarkable impact on software. In late 1995 and early 1996, there was a rush of new versions of existing mainstream programs to run under the new operating system.

So what do experienced directors of CAR prefer to use? Most, when asked, will identify a word processor, spreadsheet, relational database package, and perhaps one or two other specialized use personal favorites such as statistics or mapping programs (see Fig. 5.1). Three examples follow:

• Paul Overberg (personal communication, September 19, 1995), database editor for *USA Today:* "A good ASCII text editor like

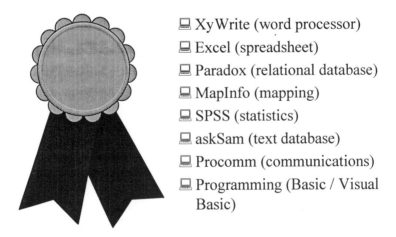

⊡ XyWrite (word processor)

⊡ Excel (spreadsheet)

⊡ Paradox (relational database)

⊡ MapInfo (mapping)

⊡ SPSS (statistics)

⊡ askSam (text database)

⊡ Procomm (communications)

⊡ Programming (Basic / Visual Basic)

FIG. 5.1. Most used CAR software.

XyWrite; SPSS, any decent spreadsheet, a database software that does query-by-example and has some programming power; data visualization software; accounts on all the online services; Netscape and an HTML editor."

• Dan Browning (personal communication, October 16, 1995), a CAR specialist for the *Saint Paul Pioneer Press:* "FoxPro, Access, Excel, askSam, Atlas GIS, Windows 3.11 or Windows 95, Lotus Word Pro or Microsoft Word, SPSS for Windows, and perhaps Lotus Notes; PKZip, Drag and View Gold, and Procomm Plus."

• Neil Reisner (personal communication, October 30, 1995), NICAR training director and former database editor for *The Bergen Record* in New Jersey: "Microsoft Office Professional for most purposes. A database even more robust than Access, preferably either FoxPro or Paradox for utility work. SPSS. Mapping software. Communications. PPP or better to the Internet. CompuServe for research. XyWrite/DOS (for ASCII data conversion). Various utilities, including back up software, anti-virus, conversion to and from Mac files—whatever you need to get stuff to your graphics department."

WORD PROCESSING TOOLS USED FOR CAR

Journalists unfamiliar with databases often think of them as large collections of numbers. This is only partially true, of course. Databases can often be a mixture of alphabetic and numeric information, or, going to the other extreme, can be only alphabetic, or simple text information organized in some logical manner. For this type of database, often special software is better used than the more quantitatively oriented programs for analysis of data. Advanced word processors offer database tools for searching, replacing, sorting or ordering, outlining, and other organizing among other things. There are also a handful of database programs that are best at manipulating large amounts of text. Consider the fact that a common CD-ROM disc can hold the equivalent of 330,000 8½-x-11-inch pages of text—55 feet high if stacked, or approximately 650 MB of information. Needless to say, if this is all text, such as reports and other documents from a criminal investigation, a powerful search and analysis engine is needed.

Rich Robertson (1995), a former *Arizona Republic* investigative reporter who became a reporter for KPHO-TV in Phoenix, offers an example:

> Text is also a database. We had a police sting operation in Arizona not too long ago that lasted a year and a half. There was 18,500 pages of

transcripts involved in that undercover operation. Several news organizations went down and got, through public records law, those 18,500 pages of paper. A big stack. They distributed them among a dozen reporters and had everybody trying to read all that stuff on deadline. Other enterprising reporters went down and said, "Wait a minute, these things obviously were done on a word processor. It's data, stored electronically. Give it to me on disk." It was six disks. Load it into your PC, run it through an indexing program and you can do searches. . . . I've kept those pages on my computer and frequently refer to it because there's a lot of prominent people in Arizona referred to in that string operation. It has become an archive source as well as a source for instant news.

There are a variety of word management tools, including word processors and text database managers. As shown in Table 5.1, XyWrite (27% in 1995 and 20% in 1994) remains the most used word processor and text editor in newsrooms for purposes related to CAR, but Microsoft Word (20%) and Corel's WordPerfect (14%) are becoming more common as newsrooms move to PC-based systems and adopt the leading office "suites" produced by Microsoft and Corel. Diversity in word processing seems to be the growing trend, however. There are a number of other products used in newsrooms for CAR as well. There are word processor usage differences that occur when looking at preferences broken down by newspaper size. XyWrite, Word, and WordPerfect are the top three, in that order, for both sizes of newspapers, but smaller newspapers tend to use other word processors such as those used exclusively on Macintosh systems.

Table 5.2 shows changes in word processor use from 1994 to 1995. Perhaps the most significant changes were brought about by

TABLE 5.1
Word Processors in Newsroom Use, 1995

Word Processor	Large Dailies[a]		Small Dailies[b]		Totals	
Other	29	21.2%	42	38.5%	71	28.9%
XyWrite	41	29.9	26	23.9	67	27.2
Microsoft Word	32	23.4	17	15.6	49	19.9
Corel WordPerfect	24	17.5	11	10.1	35	14.2
None	7	5.1	12	11.0	19	7.7
Lotus Word Pro	4	2.9	1	0.9	5	2.0
Totals	137	55.7	109	44.3	246	100.0

Note. n = 287; missing observations = 41.
[a]Circulation over 52,800.   [b]Circulation under 52,800.

TABLE 5.2
Word Processors in Newsroom Use, 1994-1995

Word Processor	1994		1995		Percentage Change
Other	36	17.3%	71	24.7%	+7.4%
XyWrite	48	23.1	67	23.3	+0.2
Microsoft Word	12	5.8	49	17.1	+11.3
Corel WordPerfect	15	7.2	35	12.2	+5.0
Lotus Word Pro	5	2.4	5	1.7	−0.7
Missing/none	92	44.2	60	20.9	−23.3
Totals	208	100.0%	287	100,0%	

shifts from "missing" to a particular word processor. This could have been caused by respondents who did not know the type of proprietary software in use in the newsroom. More respondents knew what was in use in 1995 and reported it. Clearly, there is a shift toward PC-based software such as Microsoft Word, but almost all individual categories increased slightly.

SPREADSHEET TOOLS USED FOR CAR

Many journalists venturing into the more quantitative and database sides of CAR for the first time do so with a spreadsheet program. Spreadsheets have considerable database building and computational power and they provide a solid base for fast learning. Because users can learn the basics of database construction and data processing with a spreadsheet and because they also offer a variety of database manipulation features such as formulas, sorting, advanced bivariate and multivariate statistics, they are ideal for most beginners. Regardless of whether the users only use the spreadsheet for simple roster databases or if they advance to importing an agency's database into a spreadsheet for analysis, the tool is one that should not be missing from a newsroom's CAR arsenal.

Which spreadsheet programs are best for CAR? There are numerous products on the market and opinions vary according to the more advanced features each offers. Success with a spreadsheet and the right choice for the spreadsheet depend on the purposes of the program. What will it be used for? If there are a wide range of anticipated purposes, then a full-service package such as Microsoft Excel (example screens shown in Fig. 5.2), Lotus 1-2-3, or Corel's Quattro Pro should be chosen. For less sophisticated applications

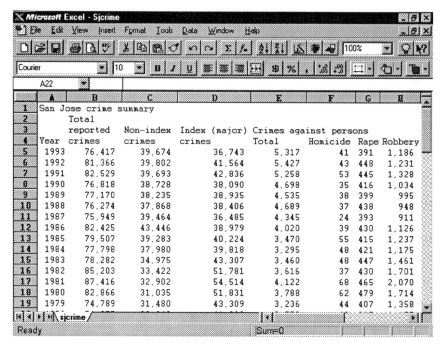

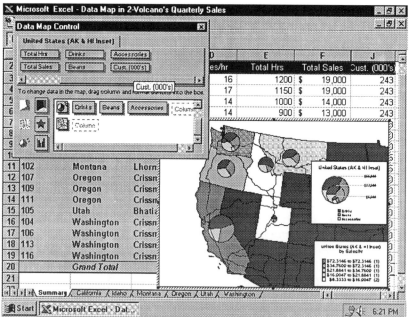

**FIG. 5.2.   Example screens from Microsoft Excel,
the most popular CAR spreadsheet.**

of spreadsheets, less expensive and more basic spreadsheet programs such as those available as shareware might work well.

Table 5.3 reveals that Microsoft's Excel has become the dominant spreadsheet (31% of those reported using spreadsheets) in 1995, but many journalists use 1-2-3 (20%) and Quattro Pro (17%). However, even larger proportions than these did not use spreadsheets or did not respond to the question. In 1994, Excel did not have as large a preference lead. The single greatest difference in large and small daily newspaper use of spreadsheets is not so much the products selected as the use of spreadsheets at all. A total of 33% of smaller dailies did not use spreadsheets, whereas only 8% of larger dailies did not use them.

Table 5.4 displays the growth of Excel as the favorite spreadsheet in newsrooms for CAR. Excel's use grew 9% in a single year, whereas Corel's Quattro Pro and Lotus 1-2-3 grew about 1% each. The fact that there was a 16% drop in "missing/none" responses in the single year indicates more awareness of products in use as well as more use of spreadsheets that began in the past year. The growth of none

TABLE 5.3
Spreadsheets in Newsroom Use, 1995

Spreadsheet	Large Dailies[a]		Small Dailies[b]		Totals	
Microsoft Excel	45	33.3%	29	27.1%	74	30.6%
Lotus 1-2-3	28	20.7	21	19.6	49	20.2
None	11	8.1	35	32.7	46	19.0
Corel Quattro Pro	32	23.7	9	8.4	41	16.9
Other	19	14.1	13	12.1	32	13.2
Totals	135	55.8	107	44.2	242	100.0

Note. n = 287; missing observations = 45.
[a]Circulation over 52,800.   [b]Circulation under 52,800.

TABLE 5.4
Spreadsheets in Newsroom Use, 1994-1995

Spreadsheet	1994		1995		Percentage Change
Microsoft Excel	35	16.8%	74	25.8%	+ 9.0%
Lotus 1-2-3	34	16.3	49	17.1	+ 0.8
Corel Quattro Pro	27	13.0	41	14.3	+ 1.3
Other	12	5.8	32	11.1	+ 5.3
Missing/none	100	48.1	91	31.7	−16.4
Totals	208	100.0%	287	100.0%	

in use is a reflection of more specific answers provided. It is assumed that many of the respondents that would have reported none in 1994 simply did not answer the question at all.

RELATIONAL DATABASE TOOLS USED FOR CAR

For news organizations already using spreadsheets and those need-ing to go beyond analysis of data in single tables, more advanced tools exist. These are relational database management systems, or relational database software. There are quite popular for what is commonly called "database journalism."

Table 5.5 reveals that in 1995, Novell's Paradox was the preferred (24%) software, but Microsoft's FoxPro (21%) was also widely used (see Fig. 5.3). Another Microsoft relational database program, Ac-cess (see Fig. 5.4), is growing in popularity as part of the Microsoft Office suite "Professional" edition, and was used by 5% of newspa-pers in 1995.

Table 5.6 shows a similar pattern in shifts to that observed with spreadsheets in Table 5.4. More specific answers, even those report-ing none, occurred in 1995. Respondents were not as likely to skip questions in the software section of the questionnaire as they were a year earlier, perhaps reflecting more knowledge of tools in use or that tools were being used for some database functions at all. Most product categories increased slightly, but FoxPro experienced the most growth, almost 6%, in the year.

TABLE 5.5
Database Management Systems in Newsroom Use, 1995

Database Manage-ment System	Large Dailies[a]		Small Dailies[b]		Totals	
None	15	10.9%	48	47.1%	63	26.4%
Borland Paradox	41	29.9	16	15.7	57	23.8
Microsoft FoxPro	37	27.0	14	13.7	51	21.3
Other	30	21.9	12	11.8	42	17.6
Microsoft Access	9	6.6	4	3.9	13	5.4
Borland dBase	4	2.9	4	3.9	8	3.3
Lotus Approach	1	0.7	4	3.9	5	2.1
Totals	137	57.3	102	42.7	239	100.0

Note. n = 287; missing observations = 48.
[a]Circulation over 52,800. [b]Circulation under 52,800.

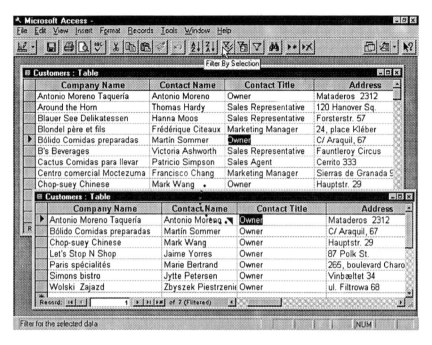

FIG. 5.3.   Example screen from Microsoft Access, a relational database program.

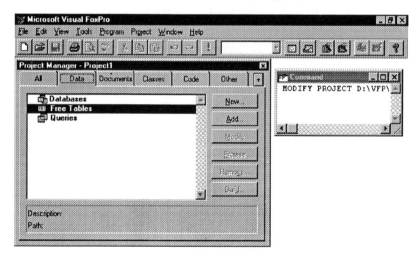

FIG. 5.4.   Example screen from Microsoft Visual FoxPro relational database program.

TABLE 5.6
Database Management Systems in Newsroom Use,
1994-1995

Database Management System	1994		1995		Percentage Change
Borland Paradox	41	19.7%	57	19.9%	+0.2%
Microsoft FoxPro	25	12.0	51	17.8	+5.8
Other	22	10.6	42	14.6	+4.0
Microsoft Access	2	1.0	13	4.5	+3.5
Borland dBase	10	4.8	8	2.8	−2.0
Lotus Approach	—	—	5	1.7	—
Missing/none	108	52.0	111	38.7	−13.3
Totals	208	100.0%	287	100.0%	

The dominance by Paradox and FoxPro in newsrooms dates from the early 1990s when they were two of the leading DOS-based relational database products. dBase, the original database program created in the early 1980s for DOS desktop systems, lost most of its users when it was slow to develop a Windows version of the product early in the 1990s. There were differences in database software use by size of newspaper, but as was the case with spreadsheets, the most glaring difference was in use. Almost half of the smaller dailies, 47%, did not use the tool. Only 11% of the larger dailies in 1995 did not use a relational database program in their CAR.

ANALYTICAL MAPPING TOOLS USED FOR CAR

Analytical mapping tools, as discussed in chapter 4, are high on the wish lists of many CAR supervisors. Many newspapers so far in the mid-1990s have added many CAR software tools to their list of resources, but mapping programs have not yet gained widespread use. One of the major reasons, until recently, has been the high cost of the software. Originally priced at over $1,000 per package, some producers have lowered their prices. This should increase use in the next several years if no other factors change because the demand seems to be there, according to the 1995 survey.

Most newspapers (71%) were not yet using computer mapping products, as demonstrated in Table 5.7. But the decrease in this figure shows signs of some growth in use. Of those newsrooms using geographic information systems (GIS) software, MapInfo (15%) and Atlas GIS (9%) are the most widely used. There were also differences in use by size. Larger newspapers (43%) use the product far more than smaller ones (10%).

Table 5.8 shows changes in mapping software use between 1994 and 1995. As shown in Tables 5.4 and 5.6, shifts in response patterns account for much of the change in this software category between 1994 and 1995. More specific responses explain the major shifts, but there are other noted shifts. MapInfo gained in use, about 7%, whereas Atlas GIS did not change in proportion of use over the year.

STATISTICAL PACKAGES USED FOR CAR

Another growth area in CAR software is use of packages designed for statistical analysis. As demands for CAR projects grow, so do the analytical power needs. Several years ago, a spreadsheet's statistical power may have been enough for most projects done in newsrooms that required data analysis. This limited analysis to frequency counts and descriptive statistics generally of a univariate nature. In recent years, with simpler projects completed, more and more complex ideas and projects have been undertaken. Statistical pack-

TABLE 5.7
Analytical Mapping in Newsroom Use, 1995

Mapping Programs	Large Dailies[a]		Small Dailies[b]		Totals	
None	76	56.7%	95	89.6%	171	71.3%
MapInfo	31	23.1	4	3.8	35	14.6
Atlas GIS	20	14.9	2	1.9	22	9.2
Other	7	5.2	5	4.7	12	5.0
Totals	134	55.8	106	44.2	240	100.0

Note. n = 287; missing observations = 47.
[a]Circulation over 52,800. [b]Circulation under 52,800.

TABLE 5.8
Analytical Mapping in Newsroom Use, 1994–1995

Mapping Programs	1994		1995		Percentage Change
MapInfo	10	4.8	35	12.2	+7.4%
Atlas GIS	16	7.7	22	7.7	0.0
Other	9	4.3	12	4.2	–0.1
Missing/none	173	83.2	218	76.0	–7.2
Totals	208	100.0%	287	100.0%	

ages, which have existed since the 1950s on mainframe systems, have become more useful for CAR projects in more contemporary Windows or OS/2 desktop form. Two of the oldest and most widely used mainframe statistical packages, the Statistical Package for the Social Sciences (SPSS; see Fig. 5.5) and the Statistical Analysis System (SAS), have grown in popularity in their PC versions in the past decade.

However, as was found with analytical mapping software, not many newspapers (just 16%) used statistical software in 1995, as shown in Table 5.9. Among CAR editors and reporters using statistical packages, SPSS is the most popular at 9% use. SAS, 3%, and other programs, 4%, are used by very few daily newspapers for CAR. The differences in large and small newspapers are again characterized by the nature of CAR projects and the need for the most powerful analytical tools. Smaller newspapers (3%) do not use statistical packages often. By comparison, 27% of larger newspapers use them.

Table 5.10 shows virtually no change in use of statistical software during 1994–1995. There is no noticeable increase in use in that period of time. Because there were so few newspapers using statistical packages in 1994 and 1995, it is worthwhile to note that the total number using statistical software increased from 30 to 39 newspapers in the 1-year period.

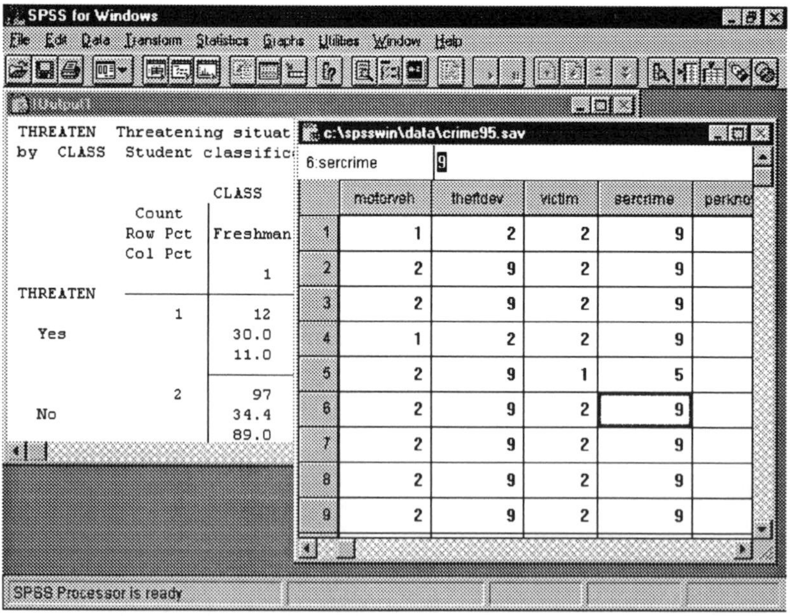

FIG. 5.5. Example screen from SPSS, the leading statistical software for CAR.

TABLE 5.9
Statistical Packages in Newsroom Use, 1995

Statistical Package	Large Dailies[a]		Small Dailies[b]		Totals	
None	97	72.9%	104	97.2%	201	83.8%
SPSS	20	15.0	1	0.9	21	8.8
Other	8	6.0	2	1.9	10	4.2
SAS	8	6.0	0	0.0	8	3.3
Totals	133	55.4	107	44.6	240	100.0

Note. n = 287; missing observations = 47.
[a]Circulation over 52,800. [b]Circulation under 52,800.

TABLE 5.10
Statistical Packages in Newsroom Use, 1994–1995

Statistical Package	1994		1995		Percentage Change
SPSS	15	7.2%	21	7.3%	+0.1%
Other	10	4.8	10	3.5	−1.3
SAS	5	2.4	8	2.8	+0.4
Missing/none	178	85.6	248	86.4	+0.8
Totals	208	100.0	287	100.0	

DATABASE MANAGERS, PIMs USED FOR CAR

Stephen C. Miller, a reporter for *The New York Times*, is like many reporters. He has an information management problem. But he is unlike many reporters in at least one way. He has solved it or, at least, he is on his way to solving it. Miller (1995) has discovered tools he can use on his computer that help him get control of the information he receives each day:

> On my beat, for example, I get about two dozen phone calls a day and 20 or 30 pieces of mail and two or three unsolicited faxes. I have five electronic mail accounts and average about 50 pieces of E-mail a day. In addition, I'm on a dozen or so electronic mailing lists and I routinely monitor about 20 or 30 forums, Usenet newsgroups, and bulletin board systems. My World Wide Web bookmarks are up to nearly a hundred. In addition, I have 1,200 individuals, nearly 600 companies, and about a dozen projects to keep track of at all times. The list keeps growing. The info-floodgates have opened and if you haven't piled up your digital sandbags yet, be prepared to evacuate. While specialized database programs, called personal information managers (PIMs), are

best for handling your personal data needs, you probably have programs that can be used to mimic many of the most powerful PIMs. It takes some manual intervention, discipline, and creativity, but it can be done with good effort. (p. 1)

Television reporter Mike Wendland, a member of the investigative team at WDIV-TV in Detroit, uses a bound planner book in combination with a computer-based PIM to organize his sources and other information needed on a daily basis. "I use a Franklin Planner (Monarch size) to keep track of stories, take notes, schedule appointments, write down futures. I found their Ascend program, which allows you to keep detailed phone numbers and set up extensive note files in their 'Red Tabs' [to be helpful]," Wendland (1995a) explained. "Every month or so, I print out the phone file and carry it in the planner. It's a system that works better than anything else I've messed with in 25 years. If you try Franklin planner, I strongly suggest you get their audio tapes on how to set up and use it. It's quite a system."

In addition to PIMs, Miller, Wendland, and others who use information management software also use word processors, spreadsheets, and text database managers for these tasks. But, so far, Miller and his colleagues constitute only small proportion of all journalists using CAR. Only 21% have discovered use of full-text database managers or personal information managers—the software day planners that organize appointments, addresses, and other information.

Although these information management tools (see Figs. 5.6 and 5.7) make sense for reporters and editors to use, they have not found their way into newsrooms in 1995 in any substantial levels, Table 5.11 indicates. But there is some growth, as Table 5.12 shows. In

TABLE 5.11
Text Editors/Personal Information Managers in Newsrooms, 1995

Text Editor, PIM	Large Dailies[a]		Small Dailies[b]		Totals	
None	88	67.2%	88	83.8%	176	74.6%
askSam	21	16.0	4	3.8	25	10.6
Other	16	12.2	8	7.6	24	10.2
Lotus Organizer	4	3.1	5	4.8	9	3.8
Lotus Smartext	2	1.5	0	0.0	2	0.8
Totals	131	55.5	105	44.5	236	100.0

Note. n = 287; missing observations = 51.
[a]Circulation over 52,800.   [b]Circulation under 52,800.

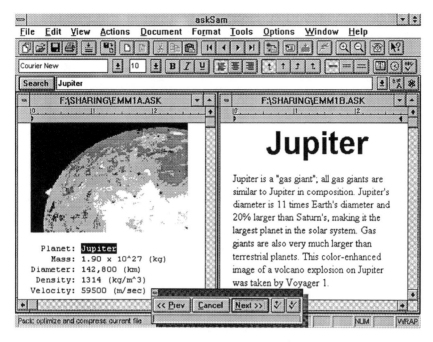

FIG. 5.6. Example screen from askSam, a database manager software package.

FIG. 5.7. Example screen from Microsoft Schedule+, a PIM software program.

TABLE 5.12
Text Editors/PIMs Used in Newsrooms, 1994-1995

Text Editor, PIM	1994		1995		Percentage Change
askSam	4	1.9%	25	8.7%	+6.8%
Other	10	4.8	24	8.4	+3.6
Lotus Organizer	1	0.5	9	3.1	+2.6
Lotus Smartext	—	—	2	0.1	—
Missing/none	193	92.8	228	79.1	−13.7
Totals	208	100.0	287	100.0	

1994, 93% did not use PIMs or text managers, compared to 79% a year later. askSam was used by 2% of respondents in that year. Use of askSam grew about 7%, but use of other products was minimal.

SOFTWARE DEVELOPMENT, PROGRAMMING TOOLS USED FOR CAR

Perhaps the highest level of computer literacy in a newsroom is to become a competent programmer. There are numerous software development and programming tools on the market and they vary in complexity and computing power. Regardless, most journalists involved in CAR do not program. Some of the most sophisticated users do some original programming, but these are a very small group in newspaper newsrooms across the United States.

As shown in Table 5.13, very few newsrooms (20%) in 1995 used any form of original programming software. Among those in use, Microsoft Basic (5%) and Microsoft's newer Visual Basic (4%), for use with Windows, are gaining some use. As with most of the other software products discussed in this chapter, there were major differences in use according to the size of the newspaper. Programming tools, the limited use of them noted already, are almost exclusively the province of larger newspapers. Whereas 28% of larger newspapers used some form of programming software, only 10% of smaller dailies used them.

Table 5.14 shows minimal growth in use of development and programming tools from 1994 to 1995. There is a small amount of growth in using Basic and Visual Basic, the data show. But many CAR journalists who do programming typically use the macros of their spreadsheet or database programs and these uses are not measured.

COMMUNICATIONS SOFTWARE USED FOR CAR

For CAR that involves online research, e-mail, or other tools available on a remote computer or computer system, a communications package is essential. Many commercial online services and most World Wide Web access providers on the Internet have proprietary software or Web browsers required for communications to connect, but some sort of software is necessary. Users of America Online, CompuServe, and Nexis/Lexis, for example, are well familiar with their own software that permits use of the services. Similarly, Web

TABLE 5.13
Development Tools Used in Newsrooms, 1995

Development Tools	Large Dailies[a]		Small Dailies[b]		Totals	
None	90	72.0%	92	90.2%	182	80.2%
Other	14	11.2	5	4.9	19	8.4
Microsoft Basic	9	7.2	3	2.9	12	5.3
Microsoft Visual Basic	8	6.4	1	1.0	9	4.0
Borland C++	3	2.4	1	1.0	4	1.8
Borland Turbo Pascal	1	0.8	0	0.0	1	0.4
Totals	125	55.1	102	44.9	227	100.0

Note. n = 287; missing observations = 60.
[a]Circulation over 52,800. [b]Circulation under 52,800.

TABLE 5.14
Development Tools Used in Newsrooms, 1994–1995

Development Tools	1994		1995		Percentage Change
Other	13	6.3%	19	6.6%	+0.3%
Microsoft Basic	2	1.0	12	4.2	+3.0
Microsoft Visual Basic	4	1.9	9	3.1	+1.2
Borland C++	—	—	4	1.4	—
Borland Turbo Pascal	—	—	1	0.0	—
Missing/none	189	90.9	242	84.3	–6.6
Totals	208	100.0%	287	100.0%	

users are well familiar with the different forms of Mosaic and products such as Netscape. But what about access to other services, bulletin board systems, and simply connecting to the home system back at the newsroom? These computing tasks require a more generic communications package. There are many on the market, but most newsrooms that are successfully linking to the outside world with computers use only one program, Procomm Plus (see Fig. 5.8).

As shown in Table 5.15, Procomm Plus clearly dominates newsroom preferences. In 1995, about 45% of newsrooms using communications software reported using Procomm Plus. All other programs—such as Crosstalk, Windows Terminal, Smartcom, and others—reported constitute only about 39% of the respondent newspapers. However, one in six newspapers, 16%, do not use any communications software. In 1994, Procomm Plus also was the software package of choice (30%). Crosstalk, Smartcom, or other communications software accounted about 34%, but 36% did not use any software to go online.

As with other software, usage of communications packages is a function of size of the newsroom. The primary difference, again, is not as much in the product used as it is whether the category of product is used at all. Whereas only 6% of larger dailies did not use a communications package, 30% of the smaller dailies did not use

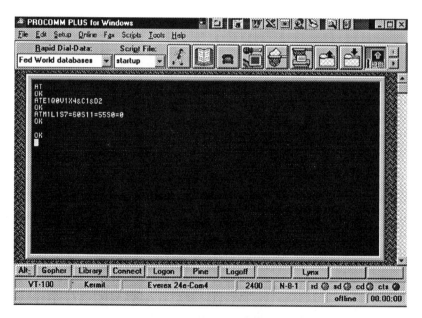

FIG. 5.8. Example screen from ProComm Plus, the leading communications software for CAR.

TABLE 5.15
Communications Packages in Newsroom Use, 1995

Communications Package	Large Dailies[a]		Small Dailies[b]		Totals	
Procomm Plus	75	58.1%	26	27.4%	101	45.1%
Other	20	15.5	29	30.5	49	21.9
None	8	6.2	28	29.5	36	16.1
Crosstalk	12	9.3	2	2.1	14	6.3
Windows Terminal	7	5.4	7	7.4	14	6.3
SmartCom	7	5.4	3	3.2	10	4.5
Totals	129	57.6	95	42.4	224	100.0

Note. n = 287; missing observations = 63.
[a]Circulation over 52,800. [b]Circulation under 52,800.

TABLE 5.16
Communications Packages in Newsroom Use,
1994-1995

Communications Package	1994		1995		Percentage Change
Procomm Plus	64	30.8%	101	35.2%	+4.4%
Other	25	12.0	49	17.1	+5.1
Crosstalk	11	5.3	14	4.9	−0.4
Windows Terminal	3	1.4	14	4.9	+3.5
SmartCom	11	5.3	10	3.5	−1.8
Missing/none	90	43.3	99	34.5	−8.8
Totals	208	100.0	287	100.0	

communication software. Whereas Procomm is the favorite product of larger dailies, other products, such as those designed for Macintosh systems, are more often favored by smaller dailies. Datastorm Technologies, the Missouri-based maker of Procomm, did not sell a Macintosh edition of its product on the market at the time of the 1995 survey.

Table 5.16 shows there was not much change between 1994 and 1995 in terms of communications software in use. With no breakthrough products introduced, there were some minor shifts. Procomm Plus gained about 4% in use to increase its domination in newsrooms. The number of newspapers not reporting or not using a communications program dropped about 9%, however.

WHAT NEXT? CAR SUPERVISORS' SOFTWARE WISH LISTS

In Table 4.9, a summary of new computing tools newspaper respondents hoped to add in the coming year for CAR was offered. The discussion in that chapter referred primarily to hardware improvements. When asked what software was high on a CAR supervisor's "wish list" in early 1995, the responses were clear: high-end analytical software.

The second overall choice was analytical mapping software such as MapInfo or Atlas GIS, noted as a first preference by 10% of the news organizations responding. Improved access to the Internet, which includes updating World Wide Web browsers, was fourth at slightly lower than 9%. Database packages constituted a variety of preferences also, including such things as "any database package" (5%), or specific relational database programs such as FoxPro (4%), Access (1%), or Paradox (1%). A sophisticated programming tool by Microsoft, Visual Basic, which permits programming for Windows and can be linked to databases for data entry or retrieval as well as other purposes, also rated high. Some news organizations sought spreadsheet software upgrades, acquisition of statistical packages such as SPSS, text database managers, scanner software to accompany scanners—presumably for data entry—and data visualization software.

3-D COMPUTING: AN APPLICATION FOR NEWSGATHERING?

A developing software category that may have CAR applications is three-dimensional computer software. As newer, higher performance computers debut each fall, there are also new ways to use them. Among the growing uses are three-dimensional products for a variety of applications. Although it has not yet found its way into many newsrooms, 3-D is widely used in other fields for research and data analysis. Fields such as medicine and other physical sciences, advertising animation, engineering, video game entertainment, and the military use three-dimensional software.

But for journalism? For database analysis?

Three-dimensional software is a new class of data analysis applications that has begun to appear in some specialized forms. These products are often used in scientific environments, but are also finding their way into business uses. Because many advanced CAR projects use tools originally designed for the academic world as well as the business world, it makes sense to look at 3-D for possibilities in newsrooms. Some software companies are developing 3-D applications for Internet browsers, also.

One category of 3-D software is data visualization technology. This software enables users to visualize database queries in graphical format. Some experts feel data visualization software is the next generation of decision-making software for many industries (DeJesus, 1995; Ricciuti, 1995; Schroeder, 1995).

Software such as Themescape, published by Pacific Northwest Laboratories, based in Richland, Washington, displays data linkages in documents as hills and valleys of a landscape. Themescape accomplishes this form of displaying the links in a three-dimensional format by graphing overlap in keywords in the documents or other characteristics of the data.

AVS Express, a product of Advanced Visual Systems in Waltham, Massachusetts, presents data as 3-D images instead of two-dimensional columns and rows. For instance, a national crime database by region might be displayed in 3-D map form with crime statistics superimposed on each state (Ricciuti, 1995).

"Today's 3-D is a new variation on a familiar theme: ever more powerful and cheaper computers. The fanfold paper printouts of yesteryear gave way to screens with monochrome text, followed by windowing software and simple graphics. Now, the windows are being thrown open," noted *Business Week* writers Peter Coy and Robert D. Hof (1995, pp. 71–72).

The prospects for use of such software in newsgathering may prove to be the next frontier in data analysis. Most 3-D software users feel the visualization makes understanding easier. Humans live in a 3-D world. The two-dimensional format of most database software limits comprehension and understanding, some experts feel. For most users, including scientists, the 3-D experience stimulates thinking (Coy & Hof, 1995).

Data visualization software, because it is new, is very expensive and requires high-performance systems. It is likely, of course, that time will make this tool more accessible for news organizations. Prices will eventually drop, if other high-end software pricing histories, such as analytical mapping, are any indication. And, of course, PCs increase in performance with each generation developed. Another disadvantage of 3-D software is the sluggish performance of some computers that run it. The software can produce animation that needs power, storage, speed, and memory. As this new tool begins to find its way to other types of data beyond text, it is likely to become more usable by social scientists and journalists. One example is 3-D data mapping. The potential for these graphics is enormous, it seems.

3-D applications are also expensive in that the software remains pricey and the hardware required to run it is high-end and expensive, usually top-of-the line workstations. However, experts expect prices to drop in the next several years, opening it further to some newsrooms for possible use. Like other computing products that debuted, prices should go down and the capabilities of the products should rapidly increase.

6

Online Services and the Internet

Today's newsroom research centers feature gleaming PCs, rich-colored large-screen monitors, lightning quick modems, speedy CD-ROM readers, fast laser printers, and skilled, online-savvy researchers. This model has replaced the old morgue, which is passing rapidly from newsrooms around the world. These newsroom facilities are experiencing a transitional period, yet it may be hard to find a glue pot, clipping or photo files, or very many books in a truly modern news organization's research and reference center these days. Everything is going digital (Paul, 1993; Semonche, 1993). In fact, there is even debate on what to name these areas that are so important to journalism. More and more, reporters are becoming researcherlike in their work. Conversely, more and more researchers are becoming more reporterlike (Garrison, 1995; Leslie, 1994).

"Electronic sources have essentially bought newsrooms the luxury of time," observed Barbara Hijek (personal communication, November 9, 1995), deputy library director for the Tampa bureau of the *St. Petersburg Times:*

> How many times have reporters rushed to crime scenes of tragic accidents or double-murders? How many times have reporters become frustrated when authorities refuse to "confirm or deny" the identity of a victim until relatives or significant others are contacted? How many times have reporters become frustrated when the next-of-kin is notified only thirty minutes before deadline? Two major breakthroughs have occurred that have helped us diminish this level of frustration. The first is the cellular phone; the second is twenty-four hour access to government information.

Perhaps the single most important reason for this information gathering evolution in newsrooms is the changing desktop computer. Online searching and the power and reach of computing have rewritten the rules of this important game. Instead of using books or clip files, electronic libraries have information available in accessible online databases, CD-ROM, or other digital storage media. Originally the transition focused on text materials, but in recent years interest has focused on digital graphic imaging—storage of photos and graphics in digital form as well.

There are two major subdivisions of online computer resources that journalists use in their information gathering. The first is the commercial online service. These include the basic consumer-oriented services such as CompuServe, America Online, and Prodigy. But it also includes more specialized services such as Nexis/Lexis, Information America, Dialog, and DataTimes. The number of these highly specialized online information services seems to be growing on a weekly basis. Some longtime users of these tools have labeled the commercial networks that have recently linked to the Internet as the "outernet" to indicate their relation to the international network of computer systems. The second major subdivision, of course, is the Internet. The Internet includes a wide range of linked computer systems originally anchored in the defense industry, government, and the academic world. This system has grown remarkably in the past several years to include seemingly countless commercial links as well. The Internet has a wide range of access forms and tools to use the resources on this vast network, including the World Wide Web, Gopher, newsgroups, and much more.

News organizations are using both of these types of online services to enhance their reporting reach. For example, *The Arizona Republic* is one of dozens of large metropolitan dailies that regularly use online services in day-do-day reporting. News researchers conduct dozens of online inquiries daily. In 1995, the newsroom budget was increased by almost 10% to accommodate growing online use, from $80,000 in 1994 to almost $88,000. The Phoenix-based newspaper, with circulation at 400,000 daily, coordinates its online research through the newspaper's newsroom library. Among the services used by researchers are America Online, Dialog/Knowledge Index, Lexis/Nexis, PACER, Burrelle's Broadcast Database, DataTimes, CDB Infotek, DataQuik, Dow Jones News/Retrieval, FedWorld, NewsNet, various government BBSs, and other online resources such as those offered by the Federal Election Commission.

POPULAR ONLINE NEWSGATHERING TOOLS

Perhaps the most used online commercial newsgathering services are Nexis, DataTimes, and Dialog, says *Arizona Republic* Library

Manager Paula Stevens (personal communication, January 27, 1995). Most often, it is staff members of her department who do the searches for reporters and editors. Like most larger newspapers with high-volume online searching, especially involving expensive services, professional news researchers are more cost effective and most searches are produced by news librarians.

"While no one doubts the importance of online searching/research for major and long-term investigative projects, it should also be remembered how online searching is much more frequently used for the quick background check, company data, biographical material, and so forth," Stevens emphasized.

Typical of this sort of online research success at *The Arizona Republic* are searches conducted by librarians for factual information for stories. A recent story by reporter Eric Miller discussed the prospects of Phoenix acquiring a Major League Baseball franchise. Librarians assisted by checking facts and background information for Miller. Librarians often also do "more esoteric research" from time to time, Stevens noted. She pointed, as an example, to a recent article by *Republic* columnist Steve Wilson that discussed ethics in the United States and required librarians to find the exact words of a comment reported about William J. Bennett in a *New York Times* article.

The *Richmond Times-Dispatch*, about half the size of *The Arizona Republic* with daily circulation of 210,000, also uses online research on a regular basis. The newspaper spends considerably less—about $30,000 in 1995—according to Associate City Editor Joseph Gatins (personal communication, February 2, 1995). The newspaper's librarians coordinate online services and their use, but Gatins says reporters and editors also do searches with online tools "depending on the story."

The newspaper most often uses online services to connect with Weatherdata, but also uses Dialog frequently to access the newspaper's own electronic library. Knight-Ridder-Tribune Graphics is also a major online provider for the newspaper. But its online success has been based on diversity. The newspaper regularly uses AP Graphics Net, Lexis/Nexis, Prodigy, Presslink, professional and college sports statistics services, local government online services, and government, commercial, and private bulletin board systems as well. Online searches are often done with Crosstalk or proprietary software with a 14.4-Kbps modem, Gatins reported. However, he also said the newsroom needs more personal computers and more training to increase access and skills for newsroom staff members. "Generally, our newspaper's biggest successes have been securing—and manipulating—data not handily retrievable any other way," Gatins explained.

CELLULAR PHONES AND ONLINE NEWS RESEARCH

Barbara Hijek, deputy library director for the Tampa bureau of the *St. Petersburg Times,* says her job as an online news researcher has changed remarkably in recent years. One reason is the cellular telephone. What is happening at her newspaper on a regular basis for breaking stories is a sign of how two high-tech tools can be "married" for high-tech reporting.

"These days a reporter is sent to the scene equipped with a cellular phone. Cellular phones are considerably more private that the old hand held radios. Less risk of competitors able to overhear conversation or pick up radio waves. The reporter now can phone a news librarian/researcher when he arrives at the scene. Known facts are conveyed to the researcher: location, tag numbers of automobiles, and so forth," Hijek (personal communication, November 5, 1995) stated. Hijek continued:

Recently a fairly prominent doctor was found brutally murdered at his apartment complex. The neighbors were insisting that the victim was a doctor. The police were tight-lipped. The reporter phoned Kitty Bennett, news researcher of the *Times.* Kitty was able to verify the victim's name via a tag search. But she discovered that the tag info was wrong. Kitty then phoned the reporter back and told him "something is wrong—the tag doesn't check out with make of car." Police began shooing media away—but our reporter was able to hurry and take a second look at the vehicle. This time he read the correct tag info to Kitty over the phone. If he had waited to come back to the newsroom to give the info to the library staff it would have been over.

(continued on next page)

Some of the *Times-Dispatch* staff writers and editors use their own America Online, CompuServe, Delphi, and Internet access accounts, also, on their home systems, he noted. "Not enough of our staffers are comfortable with the medium, however, largely for lack of hardware."

A typical use of online services came during the 1995 earthquake near Kobe, Japan. *Times-Dispatch* staff writer Andrew Petkofsky used online tools to search contacts and resources on the Internet for information about the devastation of the earthquake. Not only did Petkofsky report about the earthquake in his story, he relayed Internet addresses for readers to use on their own to find additional information.

Just as the newsroom researcher, news research itself, and the news library/research center are experiencing benchmark changes annually in this decade, so are the tools being used—those examples

(continued from previous page)

But on-the-scene-teaming scored a victory. Indeed the victim was a doctor. We then ran the victim's name through our twenty-four hour county government access database. What emerged was a paper trail of civil litigation between the doctor and his ex-wife that included allegations of domestic violence, separations, and divorce. We found a lawyer's name that was handling the divorce. Kitty was then able to run the address through AutoTrack to determine if other autos were registered at this address. Bingo. Another name emerged.

Still the police refused to confirm or deny. Later that evening the reporter confirmed the identity through a hospital spokesperson. Still the police refused to confirm or deny or release details. We had confirmation of the victim's identity. It was a "higher" profile murder—certainly not a local celebrity, but someone known in the medical community. We felt certain that by the time the morning paper hit the driveway his next-of-kin would have been notified. Ethically, we look at these sorts of situations case-by-case.

The next morning we ran a fairly in-depth account of the murder. We were able to contact the lawyer who confirmed the divorce was hostile. If this murder had occurred only a few years prior, we would have had to wait to go to the courthouse the next day for a typical records search. Our initial story would have lacked all the rich detail we were able to provide. The doctor's wife was convicted months later.

in Phoenix and Richmond illustrate the point. Online research is an extraordinarily valuable part of CAR and has become integrated into the daily routines of many newsrooms in North America. Its rapid acceptance has, in part, been due to the improvements in interface for users, the power of search engines used to manipulate the databases, greater ease in downloading information or in printing reports, and steep declines in pricing for some services. Online services are becoming more popular and less expensive, recent studies show (Eng, 1995). One estimate by Dataquest Corporation stated that there would be 25 million subscribers spending $3.2 billion by 1997, up from 15 million users and $2.5 billion in 1995. However, the per-member spending is forecast to drop from $172 a year in 1995 to $132 in 1997. The growth is due mainly to the surge in popularity of the Internet (Eng, 1995).

Journalists are responding to these changes with exponential growth in use of commercial services, bulletin board systems, the World Wide Web, the Internet, and other online tools. Although journalists are part of a growing group of information professionals who know how to find and use online information, it seems that the rest of the computer world is recognizing this at the same time. The growth rate in membership in services such as America Online and CompuServe, often used by journalists to locate and distribute information, has been rapid in the past several years—well into the millions of members. Where there once used to be significant variations in the content of the leading products, there is not as much in 1996. America Online (AOL), for example, debuted as a home and recreational computer user system aimed at the family market. CompuServe (CIS) was originally created to serve business customers with business-oriented news and information. This, in part, may explain CIS's continuing appeal in many newsrooms, but AOL has rapidly grown in popularity among news organizations in the middle of this decade. In the past 2 years, as the competition has heated up in the general online services industry, the leaders have become more and more alike. Much newer, relatively untested, services such as Microsoft Network are also trying to satisfy information access needs in 1996. Adoption of these computerized information sources is growing at a rapid rate in newsrooms around the nation, research shows (Davenport, Fico, & Weinstock, 1995; Garrison, 1995).

"If you haven't really used the Internet before or done much reporting in cyberspace, I think the commercial online services are an excellent way to start," stated Bill Loving (1995), CAR editor for the *Minneapolis Star Tribune*. "The Internet has been described as an unruly jungle, very confusing, hard to get around. It doesn't have to be that way, but for a lot of people, in their first experience, it is overwhelming . . . an unregulated free for all. But that is where most of the 'meat' is in cyberspace."

Loving feels the advantage for beginning with a commercial service is its organization of resources. Because of this, for journalists just learning online newsgathering, commercial services are very helpful and less intimidating. He also feels the proprietary software used by such services as CompuServe or America Online makes it even easier to click and go to a feature of the service.

Selecting the right product for a newsroom may not be an easy decision, especially if budgeting requires that only one can be used. There may be corporate factors, such as a chain or group involvement with one company or another. Access to specific information may be a major factor as well. Some of the services continue to offer exclusive "gateway" access to other computer systems containing certain databases that appeal to some reporters, news researchers, and their editors.

For many news organizations just beginning to work with CAR resources such as online tools, two of the biggest factors will be

World Wide Web and Internet access and e-mail. For any news organization today without an e-mail address of some kind, the basic monthly access price of a service such as AOL or CIS is worth the expense. It is, these days, a CAR tool no news organization should be without. All major services offer these within certain known limitations that vary from service to service. However, even the limitations are slowly dropping from the fine print with each new edition of the service's proprietary interface software.

The mass market commercial services are becoming easier to use with their own proprietary software and this can be reassuring to beginners in newsrooms who may be a little fearful of their computers. Most services are visually oriented and offer Windows-type point-and-click manipulation.

Another attractive change for smaller news organizations on limited budgets is more bang for the buck. Cost-conscious newsrooms can gain World Wide Web access, other Internet tools, and the usual package of information services through the commercial online services. Many services have flat-rate pricing for most content and, for the premium databases, per-use fees. Because these online providers offer general interest content, but often helpful specific content as well, some reporters and editors find them helpful. They make a superior starting point for a newsroom with limited resources but the urge to begin online CAR. At the very least, they provide inexpensive access to the Internet and e-mail communication.

"The on-line world is growing fast and changing fast—and it's changing dramatically," observed *PC Magazine* Editor Rick Ayer and Executive Editor Robin Raskin (1995, p. 108). "The commercial services . . . have gotten bigger, both in the number of users they claim and in the amount of content they offer."

Carol Napolitano (personal communication, September 29, 1995), a veteran Internet user and CAR specialist at the *Omaha World-Herald*, is sold on the way online tools speed and enhance her reporting: "Information can be instantaneously obtained and updated. The Net has the potential for virtually limitless depth and is in a standard format that allows easy searching. It lifts the spirits of reporters to use it, because it is fun. It makes them want to learn more. Some of our most entrenched reporters who wanted nothing to do with CAR changed their minds after learning to surf the Internet."

For one Minnesota news research expert, going online means breadth and depth of information gathering. "The major benefit [of online reporting] is the exponential increase in the numbers, variety, and quality of information sources (both people and documents) that inform news reports. Having access to online sources of infor-

THE MOST COMMON START-UP SERVICES

There are dozens of companies offering Internet access and dozens of other online services that offer connection to the online world. The following list is for news organizations interested in getting off to a successful start with a basic online service. Pricing information, always subject to change, should be obtained from the vendors. New users are also cautioned to check minimal hardware and software requirements for each service because they will vary. There are minimum modem speeds for many services, minimal processor speeds, and several services require Windows or another GUI to operate their proprietary access software.

- America Online—8619 Westwood Center Dr., Vienna, VA 22182-2285; 800-827-6364 or 703-448-8700.
- CompuServe—5000 Arlington Centre Blvd., Columbus, OH 43220; 800-848-8199 or 614-457-8600.
- Delphi Internet—620 Avenue of the Americas, New York, NY 10011; 508-323-1000.
- Dow Jones News/Retrieval—P.O. Box 300, Princeton, NJ 08543-0300; 609-452-1511.
- GEnie—401 N. Washington St., Rockville, MD 20850, 800-638-9636, 301-251-6475.
- Microsoft Network—One Microsoft Way, Redmond, WA 98052; 206-882-8080.
- Lexis/Nexis—9443 Springboro Pike, Dayton, OH 45401; 800-543-6862.
- Prodigy—445 Hamilton Ave., White Plains, NY 10601, 800-776-3449.
- The WELL (Whole Earth 'Lectronic Link)—Suite A200, 1750 Bridgeway, Sausalito, CA 94965, 415-332-4335.

mation allows librarians and reporters to put what seem like isolated events into context, to see patterns and connections, to understand that what is happening may not be unique to that community or that person or that institution," stated Kathleen Hansen (personal communication, September 19, 1995), a national authority on online research who teaches at the University of Minnesota. "Also, it allows reporters to get beyond the 'golden Rolodex' of usual suspects and tired old sources for interviews, expertise, analysis, and commentary on the day's events. And it gives the newsroom access to primary documents, original reports, the actual language of a specific bill or declaration or treaty, rather than relying on some source's interpretation and spin."

There is no doubt that online searching is faster and more thorough than the old-fashioned methods of an earlier era. However, there is some research evidence that using online services may take more time than using a printed index, especially for inexperienced searchers (Neuzil, 1994). This is one reason some news organizations do not permit reporters or editors to search costly services without training.

"If you don't have a large, well-staffed news library in your organization and would like to do a lot of your own media clip searches and research, these online services can be a very powerful tool," said Minneapolis' Loving (1995). "You can do it yourself and not necessarily wait for a librarian."

GROWTH AND USE OF ONLINE RESOURCES

Computer industry experts readily acknowledge it. Online services and resources are one of the most dynamic portions of the industry in the middle of the decade, halfway into the second decade of the personal computing revolution. Combine this with the increasing use of online tools to distribute news and information and there is no doubt of the importance of networked computers and users in the future for the news industry.

"*Information everywhere* is the catchphrase of the computer age, and on-line services and the Internet continue to be the most exciting parts of the computer world. Just look at how much interest there now is in using the Internet and setting up Internet pages and sites," stated *PC Magazine* Editor-in-Chief Michael Miller (1995, p. 4).

Many online experts may note that 1995 was the year of the World Wide Web. It may be that 1996 will be remembered as the year of the *online publication*. There is significant growth in electronic newspapers, magazines, and newsletters. Many news organizations, even broadcasters, are exploring the prospects of electronic products in a serious manner. The Newspaper Association of America (NAA, 1995) said that in 1995 it found 60 newspapers already offering full online newspaper operations to the public. NAA forecast an additional 30 newspapers would add online products by the end of 1995. NAA, the nation's leading organization of newspaper publishers, also stated that there were about 30 newspapers with home pages on the Internet's World Wide Web. Another 25 newspapers, NAA said, sold their electronic archives to the public in CD-ROM format. Many more were expected to offer the product by the end of 1995.

These early products are probably the tip of an iceberg. This new wave of electronic products that will likely incorporate heavy doses of CAR into their newsgathering effort, has just begun in 1995 and 1996.

On the information-gathering side of going online, newspapers often move to online services as a first step into CAR. This requires minimal tools and some level of budget for online expenses. Environmental reporter Whit Andrews is an experienced online user. He needed some fast statistical information for a story he was preparing about water safety at a national recreational area on Lake Michigan. Andrews, a veteran freelance reporter who formerly covered the environment for *The Times* in Munster, Indiana, turned to the Internet for the answers. He explained how he did it:

> I used the Internet to obtain daily rainfall totals for a watershed in Northwest Indiana. I then compared those totals to E. Coli tests at the Indiana Dunes National Lakeshore—obtained in spreadsheet format—to show that high test results were nearly always coincident with major rainfalls. This proved a familiar truism, that the tests rose when the rains fell. It also allowed us to demonstrate that the Lakeshore's testing program often failed to protect swimmers from dirty water. (personal communication, October 6, 1995)

In 1994, reporters, news researchers, and editors at about 57% of daily newspapers in the United States used some form of online services to solve informational problems just as Andrews did in Indiana, but that level of use was in the process of changing. A year later, 1995 data show a 7% growth to 64% of daily newspapers using some type of online services in the newsroom—ranging from government bulletin board systems to commercial services to the Internet. Data reported in Table 6.1 provide details of this growth.

The differences in size in ability to use CAR are evident in the use of online services. Differences in large and small newspaper use of online services are quite evident when basic use is analyzed by size in Table 6.2. Larger dailies, which are far more resource rich, have almost completely moved into online tools for reporting. More than 90% of the newspapers reported using online tools in 1995, overshadowing the 40% use level of smaller dailies.

TABLE 6.1
Use of Online Services in Reporting, 1994–1995

Uses Online Tools in Reporting	*1994*		*1995*		*Percentage Change*
Yes	119	57.2%	183	63.8%	+6.6%
No	83	39.9	96	33.4	–6.5
Missing	6	2.9	8	2.8	–0.1
Totals	208	100.0%	287	100.0%	

TABLE 6.2
Use of Online Services in Reporting, 1995

Uses Online Tools in Reporting	Large Dailies[a]		Small Dailies[b]		Totals	
Yes	128	90.1%	55	40.1%	183	65.6%
No	14	9.9	82	59.9	96	34.4
Totals	142	50.9	137	49.1	279	100.0

Note. n = 287; missing observations = 8.
[a]Circulation over 52,800. [b]Circulation under 52,800.

TABLE 6.3
Reasons for Not Using Online Services, 1995

Reason Offered	Large Dailies[a]		Small Dailies[b]		Totals	
Just starting	5	41.7%	10	20.0%	15	24.2%
No hardware/soft-ware	2	16.7	12	24.0	14	22.6
Not yet online	2	16.7	12	24.0	14	22.6
Money or budget	1	8.3	7	14.0	8	12.9
Not a high priority	2	16.7	3	6.0	5	8.1
No expertise	0	0.0	4	8.0	4	6.5
Dragging our feet	0	0.0	1	2.0	1	1.6
No interest	0	0.0	1	2.0	1	1.6
Totals	12	19.4	50	80.6	62	100.0

Note. n = 287; missing observations = 225.
[a]Circulation over 52,800. [b]Circulation under 52,800.

Among the small number of newspapers still not using online services in 1995 (n = 62) that offered explanations for their status, some reported they were "just starting" (24%), as shown in Table 6.3. Others noted the rather hollow explanation that they were "not yet online" (23%). Another group had no equipment, such as a computer with a modem, or the right software (23%) to go online. Another 13% said it was a financial issue. Surprisingly, 8% stated that online reporting tools were not a high priority and 6% stated that their newsroom lacked someone with the expertise to use online resources.

If a news organization has an online service, it is used. Table 6.4 shows 33% of daily newspapers searched one or more times daily in 1995. A total of 25% of dailies searched once a week or more often, but not daily. Another 11% searched once a month or more often,

TABLE 6.4
Frequency of Use of Online Services in Newsrooms,
1995

Frequency	Large Dailies[a]		Small Dailies[b]		Totals	
Daily or more often	74	54.0%	9	8.0%	83	33.2%
Weekly or more often	35	25.5	28	24.8	63	25.2
Never used	10	7.3	50	44.2	60	24.0
Monthly or more often	15	10.9	13	11.5	28	11.2
Less than monthly	3	2.2	13	11.5	16	6.4
Totals	137	54.8	113	45.2	250	100.0

Note. n = 287; missing observations = 37.
[a]Circulation over 52,800. [b]Circulation under 52,800.

TABLE 6.5
Frequency of Use of Online Services in Newsrooms,
1994–1995

Frequency	1994		1995		Percentage Change
Daily or more often	57	27.4%	83	28.9%	+1.5%
Weekly or more often	23	12.1	63	22.0	+9.9
Monthly or more often	8	3.6	28	9.8	+6.3
Less than monthly	3	1.4	16	5.8	+4.4
Other	36	17.3	—	—	—
Missing/never used	81	38.9	97	33.8	–5.1
Totals	208	100.0%	287	100.0%	

but not weekly. A total of 6% searched less than monthly and 24% said they had never used online services.

Table 6.5 indicates several developments. First, fewer newspapers are not using online services at all or are at least reporting the fact. Most importantly, those newspapers that used online services infrequently in 1994 have increased their use in 1995. Each of the use categories has increased from 2% to 10%, with use on a weekly or more frequent basis increasing the most, just under 10%.

There are, again, substantial differences in search frequency based on newspaper size. Larger dailies, logically, with more resources, search more often. Whereas 54% of larger newspapers searched online daily, only 8% of smaller dailies have similar research habits. Only 7% of larger newspapers had not used online tools, whereas 44% of smaller ones had never used online tools.

TYPICAL ONLINE SET-UPS IN NEWSROOMS

There probably was no "typical" online set up at daily newspapers in the United States in 1995; but it is helpful to look at how five daily newspapers of varying sizes have established their online services for use in the newsroom:

Detroit Free Press

- *Daily circulation*—535,000.
- *Most frequently used services (top three)*—Lexis/Nexis, Information America, the Internet.
- *Other major online services used*—CompuServe, Dialog/Knowledge Index, PACER, commercial and government bulletin board systems, and local government online services.
- *Who does searches?*—News researchers and reporters working on the assignment.
- *Annual online budget*—Not disclosed.
- *Sample stories helped with online research*—ProfNet helped identify sources for story on marriage and the movies, researchers downloaded Consumer Product Safety Commission recall notice for dangerous baby cribs for a story.
- *Online success*—Broadening the newsroom's source base.
- *Online failure*—Reluctance on the part of staff members to use online research.
- *Source*—Ron Dzwonkowski, projects editor and CAR supervisor (personal communication, January 31, 1995).

Indianapolis Star

- *Daily circulation*—230,000.
- *Most frequently used services (top three)*—Lexis/Nexis, DataTimes, Internet.
- *Other major online services used*—America Online, local government online services.

- *Who does searches?*—Librarian or news researcher.
- *Annual 1995 online budget*—$21,000.
- *Sample stories helped with online research*—Indiana airline accident, proposed Congressional Internet limitations.
- *Online success*—Finding sources, such as pilots and aviation experts, for an airline accident in northwest Indiana.
- *Online failure*—Locating sources and sending inquiries over the Internet, but not getting responses until several day˜ after the story is published.
- *Source*—Mark Nichols, assistant city editor and computer projects supervisor (personal communication, January 31, 1995).

Citizen Times, Asheville, North Carolina

- *Daily circulation*—70,000.
- *Most frequently used services (top three)*—Internet, CompuServe, and Prodigy.
- *Other major online services used*—None.
- *Who does searches?*—Anyone in newsroom who knows how to search.
- *Annual 1995 online budget*—Not disclosed.
- *Sample stories helped with online research*—Child support enforcement series backgrounding, local antidissection activist profile research, methods of teaching reading research.
- *Online success*—Access to Library of Congress data on federal legislation to cover local congressman, information for profiles we did not get from sources or subjects of the stories by looking at their hometown newspapers online.
- *Online failure*—Reporters have been slow to learn how to use online tools with their already-heavy workloads.
- *Source*—Mark Barrett, staff writer and investigative reporter (personal communication, January 2, 1995).

Herald & Review, Decatur, Illinois

- *Daily circulation*—45,000.
- *Most frequently used services (top three)*—Business Database Plus (CompuServe), Magazine Database (CompuServe), Disclosure.
- *Other major online services used*—CompuServe, FedWorld, government bulletin board systems.
- *Who does searches?*—Assistant city editor.
- *Annual 1995 online budget*—Not disclosed.

- *Sample stories helped with online research*—Backgrounding on a casino company proposing a riverboat casino, research on derivatives and municipal finances.
- *Online success*—None reported.
- *Online failure*—Not making wider use of online resources, not doing enough research for stories.
- *Source*—Bill Ruminski, assistant city editor and online researcher (personal communication, January 4, 1995).

The Chronicle-Telegram, Elyria, Ohio

- *Daily circulation*—35,000.
- *Most frequently used services (top three)*—Federal election commission online, local Freenet.
- *Other major online services used*—None.
- *Who does searches?*—Reporters working on assignments.
- *Annual 1995 online budget*—$50.
- *Sample stories helped with online research*—Campaign finance stories.
- *Online success*—Campaign finance stories.
- *Online failure*—Too much online material to be used, too little money for it.
- *Source*—John Kohlstrand, staff writer and CAR project reporter (personal communication, January 5, 1995).

NEWSROOM USES AND BENEFITS OF ONLINE TOOLS

The Oregonian, the major daily newspaper in Oregon with a circulation of 360,000 from Portland, has experienced its most effective use of CAR in online tools. Dee Lane, a family and children team staff reporter (personal communication, February 27, 1995), uses CAR in her own stories and she works with other reporters on CAR matters. She described how it has impacted her newsroom: "The biggest CAR growth here has been in use of online resources, including the Internet. The techniques are easier for most reporters (who generally are computer illiterate) and the payoff is faster. In the long run, only a handful of reporters will learn to use relational databases, spreadsheets, and GIS programs, but everyone will use the Internet."

James Derk, computer editor at the *Evansville Courier* (personal communication, September 5, 1995) believes online tools such as the Internet and the World Wide Web have changed reporting forever.

"It's a whole new world. Not only do we make money from sign-ups, making the bosses happy, the reach of information is incredible. Look at the Web pages I wrote for our newsroom http://www.evansville.net/courier/scoop. Every time a reporter sits down at a newsroom PC and clicks on INTERNET, this is what comes up. Can you imagine this kind of information available even a year ago? Me neither."

Small dailies can benefit from online links as well. *The Battle Creek Enquirer,* a 28,000-circulation daily in Michigan, is one example. Newsroom staffers are developing a direct online link to local government databases to enhance access to records and data at the city and county levels. The result, of course, is data that wind up in news and feature stories.

"The biggest promise [of CAR] is a link by modem between our newspaper's AS-400 mini-mainframe and the AS-400 used by the city and county," observed Bill Miller (personal communication, March 5, 1995), the *Enquirer's* computer projects coordinator:

> All important data available to us just by asking. So far, we used it to get two years' worth of police incident reports. We've used it twice more in the past six months [in 1995]:
>
> (1) To download city parking-fines data. That produced a two-day report showing the worst offenders were a handful of employees at a downtown insurance company office. The "parking ticket queen" was a woman with more than $700 in unpaid tickets. When I called to ask her about the tickets, she went ballistic, threatened to sue, etcetera. Turned out she had kept it a secret from her husband for years and was scared to death he'd find out.
>
> (2) To download city bicycle-registration data. The numbers helped a story showing that bike thefts have been rising the past couple of years, in part because there are more high-priced machines around.
>
> The truth is, it takes a tremendous amount of my time (and others who help) to get this stuff over to our PC and into useable form. For a small-city newsroom, such projects are often a luxury when most of our time goes into daily reporting. I haven't given up on it, though, and hope that systems will gradually become more compatible as time goes on. (personal communication, November 2, 1995)

MOST USEFUL ONLINE SERVICES IN NEWS RESEARCH

The Internet, especially the World Wide Web, is growing and quickly became the preferred online tool for newsrooms in 1995. In 1994,

TABLE 6.6
Use of Online Services in Newsrooms, 1994–1995

	1995		1994		
	Frequency	Percentage	Frequency	Percentage	Percentage Change
America Online	109	38.0%	36	17.3%	20.7%
Internet	128	44.6	52	25.0	19.6
DataTimes	77	26.8	31	14.9	11.9
Prodigy	46	16.0	25	12.0	4.0
Westlaw	5	1.7	0	0.0	1.7
CompuServe	113	39.4	79	38.0	1.4
Commercial BBSs	46	16.0	31	14.9	1.1
Newsnet	14	4.9	8	3.8	1.1
Datalink	3	1.0	2	1.0	0.0
Delphi	30	10.5	23	11.1	–0.6
Lexis/Nexis	81	28.2	60	28.8	–0.6
Burrelle's Broadcast	9	3.1	8	3.8	–0.7
Credit services	16	5.6	13	6.3	–0.7
GEnie	2	0.7	4	1.9	–1.2
Private BBSs	52	18.1	43	20.7	–2.6
Dialog/Knowledge Index	64	22.3	55	26.4	–4.1
Dow Jones News	35	12.2	34	16.3	–4.1
Government BBSs	90	31.4	81	38.9	–7.5
Local government online	78	27.2	—	—	—
FedWorld	57	19.9	—	—	—
PACER	56	19.5	—	—	—
Information America	11	3.8	—	—	—
Interchange	3	1.0	—	—	—

Note. n = 287 in 1995; n = 208 in 1994.

the Internet was rarely cited as a newsgathering tool, but in the 1995 survey, it was used by 45% of the responding newspapers, Table 6.6 indicates. This was the highest proportion of any online newsgathering tool. A year before, 25% reported using the Internet in newsgathering functions. CompuServe (see Fig. 6.1), widely recognized for its useful information content, is the second-leading service, used by about 39% of newspapers reporting in 1995. It had been the top choice in 1994.

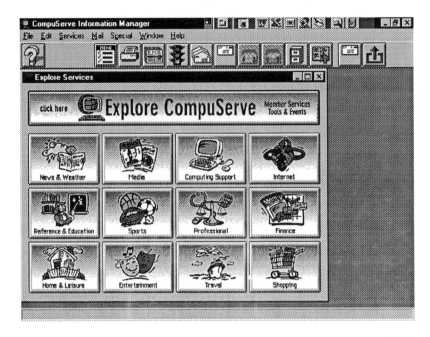

FIG. 6.1. Main menu screen from CompuServe Win-CIM Ver. 2.0.1.

FIG. 6.2. Main menu screen from America Online Ver. 2.5.

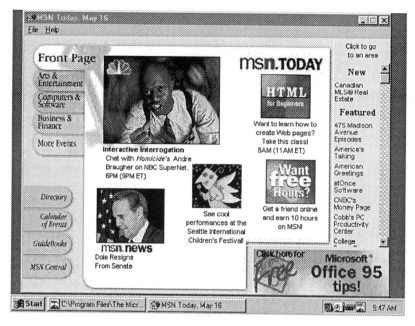

**FIG. 6.3.   Front Page screen from the
Microsoft Network.**

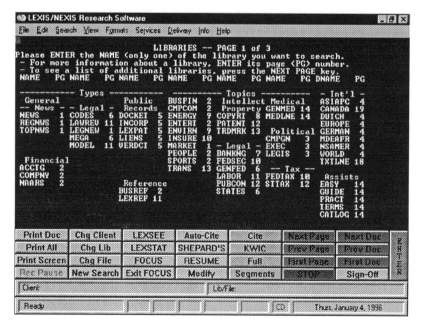

**FIG. 6.4.   Sample libraries menu screen from
Lexis/Nexis.**

However, the fastest growing online tool in newsrooms has been America Online (Fig. 6.2). This service was used by 17% in 1994, but more than doubled in proportion of use to 38% in 1995, a gain of 21%. Another fast-growing service was DataTimes, which gained 12% from 15% of newsrooms in 1994 to 27% in 1995. Other services gained less than 5% or lost proportion of usage.

Other widely used services in 1995 (see Figs. 6.3 and 6.4) included various government BBSs (31%), Lexis/Nexis (28%), local government services online (27%), Dialog/Knowledge Index (22%), Fed World (20%), and PACER (20%). The services that lost usage the most in newsrooms between 1995 and 1994 were government BBSs, Dow Jones, and Dialog. One likely reason for drop in use of BBSs, of course, is the conversion of many BBSs to World Wide Web or Gopher access through the Internet.

SUCCESS WITH THE INTERNET IN THE NEWSROOM

The Internet is a reporting resource with yet-unrealized potential. Most newsroom users are only beginning to recognize its capabilities. With or without the World Wide Web, the Internet is an amazing reporting resource. Ask any news librarian or database editor. Ask any editor or reporter who has used it for finding sources, locating background information on a relatively obscure subject, or getting current data from an institution or government agency. But this is the way most journalists think of the Internet as a newsroom tool. A growing use of the Internet for database editors, for example, has been file transfer protocol (FTP). Some editors use FTP to access government computer systems and to locate and download text and database files.

Even the more conventional commercial services have realized the need for full Internet access and have been moving toward that goal since 1995. Use of the World Wide Web, newsgroups, FTP, Telnet, and other areas of the Internet are their goals. "Without a direct gateway into the Internet, the proprietary services are totally dead," believes Bill Casey (personal communication, September 22, 1995), CAR supervisor at *The Washington Post.* "Without it, you cannot get at any of the links and nobody wants to be on a separate system any more. . . . It's definitely changing. I am not an online person, but I am more than willing to recognize people do spend tremendous amounts of time on them."

The Internet, no matter how it is accessed, actually has two primary benefits to journalists that can move them toward success in CAR:

- First, the Internet permits journalists to gather information through its many information retrieval tools.
- Second, the Internet also will allow journalists and their news organizations to go one step further—to be information distributors through the same computer network used to gather information.

Chris Callahan (1995), assistant dean for the College of Journalism at the University of Maryland, believes the wide range of resources on the Internet make it a necessary resource for journalists: "It is by far and away, the single richest resource in the world. It has more information than any library, more information than any commercial service. It has an enormous diversity of information available. Because it is growing so much, the Internet itself is becoming a news story . . . it has become so much of a part of society we need to be covering it."

Whit Andrews (personal communication, October 6, 1995), a free-lance writer in Nebraska and a former Internet trainer for Northwest Indiana's *Times,* said his former newspaper uses the Internet extensively:

We have relatively little online use that is not Internet-related. I will note that online business databases have been *very* valuable in last-minute backgrounding of major—and not so major—corporations. Internet research has added a valuable dimension to our research capabilities. The Internet has three major features that make it attractive for journalism research: (a) information may be kept

---

NATIONAL INTERNET SERVICE PROVIDERS

There are numerous access providers for journalists who want to use the Internet in their newsgathering. Fees and minimum hardware and software requirements will vary and should be checked with the individual vendors. A few of the leading national access providers are:

- *Global Enterprise Services*—3 Independence Way, Princeton, NJ 08540; 609-897-7300.
- *IBM Internet Connection*—3405 Dr. Martin Luther King Jr. Blvd., Tampa, FL 33630; 800-455-5056.
- *InternetMCI*—3 Ravina Dr., Atlanta, GA 30346; 800-353-3545.
- *PSI Net*—510 Huntmar Park Dr., Herndon, VA 22070; 800-774-0852.
- *NetCom Internet*—3031 Tisch Way, San Jose, CA 95128; 800-353-6600.
- *SpryNet*—Internet Division, 316 Occidental Ave., Suite 200, Seattle, WA; 800-777-9368.

up-to-date to the minute (although that is not always the case); (b) there is capacity for nearly endless information depth; and (c) that information may be searched rapidly using keywords and even full-text searches. When the information is obtained via the Internet, it is already digitized. That means that it can be imported fairly easily into applications as simple as raw-text word processors and as complex as spreadsheets and database managers, or even image manipulators such as Photoshop.

In the past year or two, more and more news organizations have been testing and trying the potential of this worldwide computer network for providing information to audiences. It makes sense, especially for print-oriented news organizations with space limitations, to make some of their information that is not published in an edition of the newspaper, magazine, or newsletter available online. This might include such detailed information as story source lists, databases for individual checking, and archives. Some news companies are already doing this for their readers and audiences. And, of course, the Internet provides another channel for readers and viewers to communicate with editors, producers, and other news staff members.

How do some journalists get the most out of the vast resources of their Internet access? Many journalists are using the Internet for these purposes:

- Personal and group communication through e-mail.
- Instantaneous communication through Internet Relay Chat and similar services.
- Professional communication and education through specialized distribution lists such as topic-oriented list serves.
- Specialization and beat subject monitoring through distribution lists.
- Research for stories through various search resources in Gopher and the World Wide Web.
- Identification of potential sources for stories through e-mail, distribution lists such as list serves, Usenet newsgroups, and expert source-oriented services on the Internet such as ProfNet.
- Locating and downloading resources such as files and programs through FTP or other similar services.
- Using resources of remote computer systems through Telnet or other similar services.
- Access to government and other public institutional resources.

A directory of Internet distribution lists, or list serves, that offer content focusing on one or more aspects of CAR, is given in Appendix

E. There are a number of these Internet mailing lists that offer advice about CAR issues, methods, problem solving, and software advice for subscribers. A list of CAR methods and tools-oriented sites on the World Wide Web is contained in Appendix F. These sites can be reached with any Web browser.

"The major advantage of the Internet is getting a reporter up to speed in a hurry on a subject he or she knows little about," said *USA Today* database editor Paul Overberg (personal communication, October 19, 1995). "It opens story research beyond Big Print—major newspapers and magazines. It allows finding people knowledgeable on a very specific subject in a hurry."

For some journalists, certain features of the Internet serve as a window on the rest of the world, permitting access to places hard to see or places half a world away. Through Usenet newsgroups, distribution lists, and e-mail, for example, journalists can get the pulse of the global community, their city or region, their neighborhoods, of other journalists, and even their own newsrooms.

Stated Minnesota's Kathleen Hansen (personal communication, September 19, 1995):

> Right now, and for the foreseeable future, I see the main advantage of the Internet as a method for informally monitoring the world, the latest information on the topic of a particular beat, a specific community, or whatever. I do have a real problem with the total lack of quality control on the Internet (my librarian roots are showing). But as a means for reporters, editors, news librarians, and everyone else to keep up with an interest area, there is nothing like the Internet. I believe every reporter on a specific beat should be subscribing to at least a few of the most relevant listservs, newsgroups and discussion areas in her/his topic. And they should know how to use the Internet to find primary documents in that subject area. And they should know how to communicate with sources and audience members via Internet resources. In other words, it is a "what's happening?" tool rather than a formal method of information-gathering, in my opinion.

Maryland's Callahan (1995) also notes there are problems with the Internet, mainly its disorganization level when compared to the well-planned commercial services:

> Because of the way the Internet has grown, it is very difficult to find information quickly. The Internet . . . is simply this hodgepodge of computers that have grown over time without anybody, any Internet company, trying to figure out what it should look like. The result, quite frankly, is a mess. From a journalistic perspective, it is much more difficult to navigate than commercial services. There's no single

SUCCESSFUL SEARCHING ON THE WORLD WIDE WEB

Finding useful information on the World Wide Web on deadline is one of the biggest challenges to journalists on the Internet. Unless users know a particular location, fast information retrieval is often difficult. However, a number of search and/or indexing tools have recently evolved on the World Wide Web that list resources by topic or search through registered Web sites with key words, or do both. The search tools often search the address, the name of the site, and a short annotation about it for key words related to the subject. Here are some of the best search site uniform resource locators (URLs):

- *All-in-One Internet Search*—
  <http://www.albany.net/~wcross/all1srch.html>
- AltaVista—<http://www.altavista.digital.com>
- Excite—<http://www.msn.com/access/excite/html>
- *Lycos Search Engine*—<http://lycos.cs.cmu.edu/>
- *Netscape Internet Search Page*—
  <http://home.netscape.com/home/internet-search.html>
- *WebCrawler Searching*—<http://webcrawler.com>
- *WWWWorm*—
  <http://www.cs.colorado.edu/home/mcbryan/WWWW.html>
- *Yahoo*—<http://www.yahoo.com>

or comprehensive way to search the Net, so you never actually know if what you are looking for is out there.

Callahan believes introduction of the World Wide Web several years ago has made use of the Internet feasible for most daily journalism-oriented reporters and editors. It offers easier, visually oriented use of resources on the Internet. He said this may be the best way for beginners to learn to use the resources of the Internet and to turn it into a useful newsroom resource.

BULLETIN BOARD SYSTEMS AS NEWS RESOURCES

Bulletin board systems (BBSs) are one of the oldest ways computer users link to other computers to use online resources in gathering information. In the early 1980s, BBSs were commonly used to share information such as posted messages in public areas and private messages, and to provide a common site for other electronic information such as files or programs. There are two main types of BBSs. There are thousands of local BBSs that serve special topical interests and/or specific organizations in a community or region and there are national BBSs—such as the Well—that have broader content, wider interests represented, and more members.

Access to bulletin board systems is rapidly changing. Originally designed for direct connection with a dedicated telephone number, numerous public and private BBSs are becoming available through Internet access. Most commonly, government and some commercial BBSs are now part of the Internet as World Wide Web resources or as Gopher sources.

"It's obvious that the 80,000 computer bulletin boards around the country and the World-Wide Web will someday merge to form a sort of mega-network offering an on-line smorgasbord. You'll be able to access the Web via your local BBS and access the BBS via the Internet," predicted *PC Magazine* columnist John C. Dvorak (1995, p. 91). "Eventually it will be hard to tell the difference. The BBS community will help bring paid services to the Web, which collectively has been giving information away. If people were paying for Web access, *we'd see better sites*. As it now exists, most Web sites are nothing more than advertisements for T-shirts, coffee, and magazine subscriptions."

In 1996, some news organizations still found BBSs to be the answer to the high cost of online CAR. However, in Sandpoint, Idaho, where the tiny *Daily Bee* is published, BBSs are not an answer because editors feel their content is just not useful to the reporters and editors. "We are mostly concerned with local news," said Managing Editor Bill Buley (personal communication, February 25, 1995). "There are a few local BBSs in the area, but they don't usually have any newsworthy material on them; mostly nonsense."

The *Minneapolis Star Tribune's* Bill Loving (1995) feels BBSs can be very useful to journalists, especially those on an online budget:

> Every community has dozens, if not hundreds, of local bulletin boards. It is an often-overlooked resource in cyberspace. It takes a little work to negotiate your way around in them. They're not mass media consumer services like the online services, they're designed for small and local interest groups. But it is an entire world that's hidden from most main stream media organizations and it's a good thing to look into. Dial up some local bulletin boards. Find ones that have interesting subject areas and you might stumble across some interesting people or story ideas in your own community.

WHO IS INVOLVED IN ONLINE REPORTING?

The online world is still the newsroom researcher's domain, but at some daily newspapers, searching is done by anyone who knows

TABLE 6.7
Individuals Conducting Online Searches in Newsrooms,
1995

Position/Title of Person	Large Dailies[a]		Small Dailies[b]		Totals	
Librarian/ researcher	51	38.1%	5	5.7%	56	25.3%
Reporter	33	24.6	19	21.8	52	23.5
Anyone in the newsroom	24	17.9	26	29.9	50	22.6
None	5	3.7	27	31.0	32	14.5
Other	15	11.2	8	9.2	23	10.4
Editor	6	4.5	2	2.3	8	3.6
Totals	134	60.6	87	39.4	221	100.0

Note. n = 287; missing observations = 66.
[a]Circulation over 52,800. [b]Circulation under 52,800.

how. This is especially true at smaller news organizations, such as local television stations with smaller staffs. Often even major market television stations in 1995 were still without a full-time news researcher position.

Table 6.7 shows the responsibilities for conducting online searches in newsrooms. Of those that conduct searches, one quarter (25%) of newspapers reported that librarians did the online research. Others conducting searches included reporters themselves (24%), editors (4%), and anyone in the newsroom (23%).

NEWSROOM SPENDING FOR ONLINE SERVICES

Data collected about online spending by newspapers in 1995 offer some interesting numbers. The data from 1995 show contrast to 1994. The 1995 respondents reported 1994 spending at $24,384 and 1995 spending at $21,915. Of those newspapers that are online in the newsroom, an average of $16,534 was spent in 1993. In 1994, 67% did not use or plan to use online resources. But of those using them, spending increased to $17,210. One explanation for the drop from 1994 to 1995 in the latest data is the increased number of responding newspapers that reported lower levels of spending in

1995 that did not report spending or did not spend any budgeted funds in 1994. The differences in 1994 figures over the 2 years could, perhaps, be caused by a larger proportion of larger newspapers reporting spending compared to the previous year.

In either year, this amounts to monthly spending of about $1,400 a month. Some large newspapers, in fact, reported spending more than $50,000 annually on online services in the 1994 data and as much as $250,000 in the 1995 data. Newspapers are, however, reluctant to reply to questions such as this. About two thirds of the newspapers responding did not report their spending habits.

USING ELECTRONIC MAIL IN NEWSGATHERING

Reporters and editors have discovered electronic mail (e-mail). With a growing number of newsroom PC networks and individual PCs linked to the Internet, use of e-mail is expanding in a variety of different ways. Some journalists use e-mail to correspond with their editors or other staff reporters over in-house local networks. Some, however, find e-mail makes communicating with reporters at other news organizations easier: no phone tag, for example.

A fast-growing group of journalists are also using e-mail to locate and communicate with news sources. Some journalists find sources by using e-mail to receive information from distribution lists, or list serves, on their coverage specializations (e.g., medicine or the environment), on the subject of journalism itself, or their specialization within journalism (e.g., copy editing, photography, investigative reporting, etc.). This makes keeping up with issues and locating sources easier, especially for sources and subjects not concentrated in a single geographic area. Furthermore, an increasing number of public relations organizations have discovered e-mail to be a faster means of distributing information such as press releases to reporters whose addresses are kept in distribution lists.

The nature of e-mail is changing as well. The content of e-mail, for veteran users, has always been strictly unenhanced text. This works for pure messaging functions, but it limits the potential and power of electronic messages. E-mail systems are now capable of transferring files attached to e-mail messages and of using enhanced text with fonts, sizing, formatting, color, and graphics.

E-mail also means even more, and this has important implications for reporting in print and broadcast newsrooms. The most sophisticated systems include video and audio as well. The possibilities for use of the newest forms of e-mail in newsgathering as well as the absolute delivery of news seem vast.

Neil Reisner, NICAR training director and former database editor at *The Bergen Record* in New Jersey and an avid online user, finds e-mail to be extraordinarily valuable to his newsgathering on a daily basis. Reisner (personal communication, October 30, 1995) says he uses e-mail

> anyway I can. I use it to find sources, to do research, to network with colleagues, to interview known sources, and reach out to new sources. Sometimes even to interview unknown sources.

> For example, I interviewed a Japanese CompuServe sysop right after the Kobe earthquake when it became clear from traffic on the CIS Japan Forum that this person was doing a lot to help folks in the U.S.

MAKING E-MAIL WORK IN THE NEWSROOM

Some basic elements of e-mail that assure better and more effective communication:

- *Happy returns.* Always include a complete return name and address. Some e-mail management software will permit automatic headers and footers for correspondence.
- *Capital idea.* Do not type messages in all caps. Internet mail etiquette suggests this is interpreted as screaming.
- *Hot news.* Keep flaming (inflammatory messages) at a minimum. Send e-mail content that would be acceptable in face-to-face conversation.
- *Invaded privacy.* Remember there is no complete privacy with e-mail on the Internet and on newsroom networks. Many systems make automatic backups of all messages even if the sender and receiver have deleted the message.
- *Efficiency expert.* Develop use of e-mail software tools to facilitate message sending and receiving and, simply, to save time. Many programs have shortcuts that save time and effort.
- *It's a habit.* Manage e-mail efficiently. Check mail regularly and delete unwanted messages on a regular basis and store those to be saved in a separate directory or queue.
- *Spread out.* Use distribution lists. These tools permit mass transmission of mail to groups of individual receivers.
- *Networking.* Learn how to use local newsroom network links to the outside world.
- *Take out the trash.* Know the storage capacity of the electronic "mailbox" used. Some have definite capacities that limit the amount of mail that can be received, opened, or unopened at a given time and limit the amount of messages that can be stored over long periods of time. For some systems, when a mailbox fills, the system cannot be used until it is emptied and this may require a visit with a systems operator.
- *Insecurity.* If security is needed to avoid electronic eavesdroppers, use encryption software.

get information to or about friends in Kobe. I didn't know who he was, but could see what he was doing. Took advantage of the time difference to shoot him some questions and got answers in time to meet deadline. Paired with a phone interview with a local who had posted a message seeking info on a friend in Kobe. Made for a nice "here's how folks are using cyberspace" piece that was very timely.

Omaha journalist Carol Napolitano (personal communication, September 29, 1995) also depends heavily on e-mail. "We use e-mail to find sources through services like ProfNet and find interesting new sites on the Internet through e-mail services like I-Watch. We use it to communicate with sources, often as a follow-up to phone or in-person interviews or conversations. We use it to communicate with fellow journalists for advice, feedback, and so forth, on professional lists like CARR-L, IRE-L, NICAR-L and SPJ-L."

"With the advent of the Internet, what you are dealing with is a major communication tool that can put you in touch with sources that you may have had to spend weeks and months locating otherwise. Everything from ProfNet . . . to real specific areas of interest. You have, let's say, a hang-gliding accident in your community. Get on America Online and you will find people who are safety experts in hang gliding around the country in a matter of an hour," offered Jonathan Krim (1995), assistant managing editor for the *San Jose Mercury News.*

"I belong to discussion forums that are conducted via Internet e-mail, first of all. This helps me stay current on Internet developments, among other things. I have joined, generally, Internet discussion groups that include subjects of my articles in their missions," stated Nebraska free-lance environmental writer Whit Andrews (personal communication, October 6, 1995):

Examples include MOSQUITO-L, which I listened in on while working on a story about the potential invasion of Tiger mosquitos into our region, and NABOKV-L, where I unsuccessfully sought information about where Vladimir Nabokov's lepidoptery papers reside. I have used ProfNet, the expert location service run out of "vyne.com". That's become more prosaic than it was a year ago, and one can use a telephone number instead.

But sometimes I have successfully used E-mail to communicate with sources obtained using ProfNet, and in some cases I have re-contacted them after a story has run. For example, I wrote a story last spring about the collapse of yellow perch population in Lake Michigan. I obtained the names of several perch experts, including field scientists, via ProfNet. I corresponded with several via E-mail at the time. To follow the story up after the summer's tests were to have been completed, I tried to get in touch with one of the scientists via telephone, but she was often out. Finally, I posed her a list of three questions via her email. Two weeks later, she answered, in detail, and I had a story. I did reach her by telephone again—but she had no time to talk. I used the E-mail interview and talked to one of her assistants for data. Scientists in particular are often more comfortable communicating via the written word.

There are risks using e-mail for information gathering. Rose Ciotta, veteran CAR editor for *The Buffalo News* and a former Knight Fellow at Stanford University, explained her concerns:

I actually do interviews on E-mail, but only with people I know and then only to start the conversation. It's useful to get someone to write down their thoughts. You probably get higher quality information than when you just ask them to start talking to you. I reserve the right, of course, to call them and get them to elaborate on what they said—especially if they dropped a juicy thought and didn't pursue it. Of course, the drawback in doing an E-mail interview is you don't have the opportunity to spontaneously get them to react to your question. But, it does save time especially when you need to survey several people.

I would caution against using E-mail interviews with people you don't know. It's too dangerous, especially considering how easy it is for people to mask their identity on-line. I would use E-mail to find people in newsgroups or on-line forums or ProfNet or any other on-line source, but I ask for a telephone number so I can listen to the voice. That's important for accuracy's sake.

Some news organizations also use e-mail to keep in touch with readers. This is popular with television stations, especially as a promotional tool, and for newspapers' and magazines' editorial or opinion pages to receive letters to the editor and contributed articles. Most reporters and editors appreciate it when readers or viewers communicate with them by telephone, but e-mail gives readers still another level of equally immediate feedback to the reporting process, especially after the initial stories are published.

Whatever the use of e-mail might be in newsrooms, it has a down side. Privacy may be one of the major concerns. With e-mail, no message is assured to be private unless it is encrypted. Users concerned about message content privacy should investigate encryption programs such as PGP (Pretty Good Privacy) because few e-mail programs for online services or the Internet offer encryption utilities. In competitive situations, privacy may be a problem, although no known episodes of raided e-mail by competing news organizations have been widely publicized.

Even when a privately sent e-mail message is deleted, it is not always destroyed. Most computer systems have backups, putting most messages into archival storage if left in the system after 24 hours or so. Some corporations regularly monitor e-mail content, but this practice has not been widely reported in any newsroom electronic mail systems. And, in a few cases, e-mail messages stored in company archives have been subpoenaed for use in litigation. Early court cases opposing such management practices have been won by the employer (Peyser & Rhodes, 1995; see also Angell & Heslop, 1994).

Another problem is the form of the message transferred. It is often difficult to transfer some types of documents, such as those embedded with formatting codes or objects such as graphics or other images, depending on the capacity of the e-mail software or the mail system used. The quality of the document is often lost if sent only as text. And, finally, not everyone checks his or her e-mail as regularly as conventional mail is checked. This often defeats the speed advantage.

A FEW SUCCESSFUL USES OF ONLINE REPORTING TOOLS

One of the much-heralded newspapers that has embraced computing is the Raleigh *News & Observer* in North Carolina (Garrison, 1995). The newspaper is often used as a model for the newsroom of the next decade that merges computer-literate journalists with the act of newsgathering in a growing region anchored by the state's capital and government agencies. What is happening in Raleigh that works so well? How are computers, online services, and databases serving journalists there? What is the formula for success?

Former *Baltimore Sun* business editor Philip Moeller (1995) offers one possible explanation:

> It sounds so simple. Begin with a typical metropolitan newspaper newsroom—perhaps the staff is a little younger than at peer papers, but not noticeably different in most respects. Now, give serious thought to the computer and communication equipment that promises to revolutionize the news, information and entertainment industries. What if staffers could master these machines, making their use routine inside the newsroom rather than merely a topic they write about? Welcome to the Raleigh *News & Observer.* (p. 42)

The newspaper, Moeller argues, offers "a comprehensive look at how digitized information and new approaches to reporting and writing stories could reshape the nation's newsrooms."

What makes news organizations, such as the *News & Observer,* successful in using online research in the newsroom? There seem to be at least six components for its success:

- Teamwork on all stories involving reporters, editors, and news researchers.
- General encouragement from management, positive management attitudes toward computing and online research.
- Training and high computer literacy levels among all newsroom staff members beyond the news research center.
- Success in identifying and hiring qualified researchers and staffers.
- Adequate computing and online resources including services and budget.
- Rewards for successful use of the tools in stories.

Sometimes even the obvious approaches to using online tools are overlooked, but it is often these obvious uses that serve online services users best. For example, it seems logical to regularly and systematically check certain online services for local references for story ideas and to make certain stories by other news organizations are noticed by editors and reporters. Barbara Hijek, deputy news library director for the Tampa bureau of the *St. Petersburg Times*, offers a tip for using a full-text online database service:

A utility of databases is their ability to sift through information that may escape an editor's eye. Every day I sign onto Nexis and perform a "filter search." For example, I enter the word "Tampa" and look for references from other publications to our locality. It is a rich source of business information. I find information about company re-locations that editors do recognize. Editors look at slugs on the wires for recognizable local companies. They could not possibly read every story completely on the financial wires. Many times they will skip a story because the company is based in New York. However, the bottom of the story mentions the fact that the company has narrowed it relocation sites to Tampa and Dallas. We've been able to scoop local competitors using this technique. For example in June of 1994, I found a news wire on Nexis that said Citicorp was relocating 100 jobs to Tampa. (Hijek, personal communication, November 15, 1995)

AND A FEW FAILURES USING ONLINE SERVICES

In most endeavors, losses come alongside the victories and failures come alongside the successes. The same principle applies with the online tools journalists use in their daily newsgathering. One common mistake made by beginning online users is the belief that, if information is contained in a computer database or other form available by a telephone connection, information is perfect. Not so, any experienced user will say. Read on.

Online Database Problems

One expert has labeled it the "misinformation explosion." Christopher Feola (1994), news systems editor at the Waterbury, Connecticut, *Republican-American*, has concluded that online database misuse has reached such extremes that it is a serious journalistic problem. Some journalists, he says, "can become addicted" to online services (p. 42). "Fueled by the growing popularity of both commercial and in-house computerized news databases, journalists have found that it is much easier to repeat errors or rely on the same tried anecdotes and experts," Feola (p. 39) explained. These two biggest problems related to use of online services in news reporting, repeating errors and repeating use of the same experts, may have grown in weight because of computing speed and database comprehensiveness, Feola suggested.

Mary Kate Leming (personal communication, September 15, 1996), assistant managing editor and a veteran news librarian at the *Palm Beach Post*, feels accuracy is a concern with online CAR:

> Accuracy is always an issue. There the only real key is understanding the source. If you understand the source of where your data is coming from, you have a feel for it. There shouldn't be a question in people's minds about where a service gets its information. Reporters know whether sources are valid or not. Sometimes news researchers will tell them whether we feel an electronic source is more or less valid than another source.

A News Researcher's Views of Online Flaws

Sperry Krueger (personal communication, July 29, 1995), a news researcher at the Raleigh *News & Observer*, offered some examples of her recent online experiences that caused problems in the information gathering process:

> I think the quality of online databases is pretty good in general. There are problems on all levels though. The first thing I thought of is how things that are problems aren't fixed as soon as I think they should be. For example, we often have to search the *Greensboro News & Record* on Nexis and every single story I've gotten from them has the last letter of the reporter's name missing. So, if I'm looking for a story by Kelly *Thompson*, it's in their database as Kelly *Thompso*. I've never reported this to anyone because I assume that Greensboro knows about the problem and is trying to fix it with Lexis/Nexis.

Another thing that I've noticed recently [is that] *The New York Times* has more corrections than any other paper I search. It's amazing. It almost looks like *The New York Times* has more problems, but I'll guess that it's just that they do a better job of getting corrections in to Nexis. I don't trust most coding that newspapers do. I think that this is a pretty big issue for most newspaper libraries . . . it would be nice if subject or keyword lists worked, but I don't think they do.

As for other types of online databases, I've seen a variety of problems. The FAA's [Federal Aviation Administration] database caused problems when there was a plane crash in Charlotte last July because the tail number was assigned to more than one plane. I wasn't really involved in the details on this, but my understanding is that it was an FAA problem rather than a problem for the company who provides the database online.

On a public record database, I was trying to get someone's driver's record. My request in the online database came back negative—no record for that driver. When I called the North Carolina DMV [Department of Motor Vehicles] to get the record, they faxed it to me. The online database company gave me credit for that search, but I never got an answer about why there was no record for the subject.

A List of Online Trouble Spots

Veteran *Miami Herald* News Research Editor Elisabeth Donovan says there are numerous problems with online services, but often reporters and editors do not realize the dangers:

We see them so frequently that we and most reporters are pretty able to deal with the errors and attribute most of them to clerical input or false information given to police, etcetera. I can't remember a time when errors have really made it into print, or caused serious problems with stories. We do find that we need to advise younger or new reporters on the hazards of relying on online data: particularly when a reporter excitedly announces that he's found two people using the same Social Security number! Or a company or lawyer that has dozens or hundreds of corporations! In those cases, we patiently explain, the error is probably (a) a person who doesn't always quite remember his SSN and puts it down on applications with digits reversed or such; or (b) a company or lawyer who files incorporation papers for others (explaining that a registered agent is different from an officer).

Each database has its particular margin of error and we also must explain that, for example, real estate records on DBT [Database Technologies] Autotrack may not be as current as on ISC [International Systems Corporation] or the county database. Or that a recent real estate sales figure may be based on document stamps and might not quite reflect the exact sale price.

We are lucky in that most of our reporters know to question a record (ask a researcher) before they take it at face value. It helps that most reporters have had experience looking at county records at the courthouse and recognize limitations. I worry, though, about the inexperienced that demand their own access to these databases but might not have the savvy to question a record they pull late at night or on the weekend when there's no one to ask. I try to include any anomalies I've found in my monthly information newsletter and in my database research manual, but worry that everyone doesn't read those. (personal communication, August 1, 1995)

Donovan offers a helpful list of what she called the most "egregious problems" with online services that she has found:

1. *County criminal records:* "We find often that an arrestee has given his DOB [date of birth] differently each time he's been arrested, so we find multiple DOBs next to the same name with variations of a year or month from the actual."

2. *Real estate records:* "Official county records are not updated quickly enough, and the commercial service we use [ISC] is very up to date but has addresses missing. Records on DBT, although statewide, can be a year out of date. Other providers of statewide or out-of-state records (Lexis, TRW, Information America) are updated much less frequently. Sales history never goes back through all owners of property."

3. *County court records:* "Are purged two years after last action on case. So I worry that reporters think they're getting full record when they're not. This includes divorce records."

4. *Driver license records:* "Are updated differently in each database. DBT may be six weeks out of date, others may be even more. CompuServe is the most current but reporters don't use it much since you can't search easily on it. Same for motor vehicle registrations."

5. *Federal court records (PACER):* "Only go back about three years and reporters not always aware of that."

6. *Court decisions on Lexis:* "All cases are not included. There are some that aren't published and we've never really understood the distinction. (This is one of those cases when I wish I had more training in legal research). On occasion we can't find a case a reporter has requested and can't give a good reason why."

7. *Credit header checks:* "Lots of errors here. A record pulled for Dexter Lehtinen when he was interim U.S. Attorney said his current employment was student at Stanford, previously Florida legislator.

Sometimes two or three names come up on a SSN search. Employment data is unidentifiable as far as when that employment occurred. I try to warn each reporter when I do these searches."

8. *Sales figures and other corporate data on Dun & Bradstreet or other corporate information databases (S&P, Moody's):* "It's not always accurate and if you try to use these databases, for example, to get largest employers in Dade ranked by employee, sometimes the list doesn't match what we know to be true; figures may reflect total employees of a company worldwide instead of in the local headquarters."

The Internet's Fallibility

Because of all the national and international media attention it has received in recent years, the Internet has grown both in general consumer use and in newsrooms. Most of the time, the industry literature's attention touts all the advantages of the network, but seldom discusses its shortcomings.

What are they? The Internet does offer much to reporters in locating information, but it can cause reporters problems in the area of verifying information found in the many thousands of Internet sites worldwide. "For journalists, one of the Net's worst failings is its lack of verifiability," stated NICAR staff member Gwen Carleton (1994a, p. 5). "Much of the 'official' information flowing through the Internet must be double-checked. . . . The federal government takes no responsibility for mistakes that are transmitted through Fed-World, for example."

Carleton also notes that the Internet's fluid nature can be troublesome for journalists. "Internet vagaries, from disappearing databases to access overloads, are all part of the experience," she observed (p. 5).

Finding information is still another problem. Despite Gopher search engines—such as Veronica—and several powerful tools on the World Wide Web—such as Yahoo—finding the information that is out there may be the single biggest frustration among journalists using the Internet.

Dan Browning (personal communication, October 16, 1995), CAR specialist for the *Saint Paul Pioneer Press*, feels the Internet and its research-oriented users are just taking their first steps. "Research on the Internet is in a fledgling stage. The data are there, but finding it can be time consuming. Sometimes, old fashioned source work will produce better results quicker. The Internet can't be beaten for accessing various special interest groups, however. It's quite useful to read the newsgroups. And E-mail remains as one of the great communications mediums ever invented. It allows access to individuals who might never return phone calls."

Carleton agrees. Internet success for journalists is all in the searching. "[K]nowing how to find what you need, and how to get it, consistently—that's the sticking point," Carleton (1994b, p. 2) stated. "For journalists with little patience and even less time, the result can be frustration."

7

Portable Computer-Assisted Reporting

Elizabeth A. Marchak is one of thousands of journalists who go on the road to cover news. Her work as a reporter for the Washington, DC, bureau of *The Plain Dealer* requires her to travel frequently to cover major stories of regional and national interest. Marchak, who has specialized in the aviation industry and campaign finances in recent years, frequently moves around the country in addition to her regular commutes between Washington and Cleveland, where the newspaper is based. As a bureau reporter with a heavy travel schedule, she frequently depends on a portable computer to keep in touch with e-mail, to write stories, to file stories with her editors in Cleveland, and to check the home newsroom computer system for in-house messages, for background information, for stories by other reporters, and to check her own stories after they have been edited before they are published.

Marchak, who joined *The Plain Dealer* in 1993 after 10 years as an editor with the *Washington Times*, specializes in computer-based projects. One of several *Plain Dealer* reporters with database and online skills, Marchak often uses her portable PC to take her CAR work on the road. When she joined the newspaper, she bought the first portable she could find and quickly outgrew it. She finally upgraded after 2 years of struggling with inadequate hardware and software.

In that short period of time, Marchak developed a nationally recognized specialization in aviation safety reporting through her analysis of Federal Aviation Administration (FAA) data. Her FAA database work focuses on accidents and other incidents related to aircraft safety. She has also worked extensively with national and regional campaign finances through her analysis of Federal Election Commission databases in recent years. Throughout 1995, for instance, she wrote stories about the FAA's inability to control use of junk aircraft parts, aircraft parts scams that even affected President Clinton's Air Force One, use of unapproved parts by the aircraft industry, lack of FAA policing bad parts, counterfeit parts, and even the very poor quality of the FAA's own databases that keep records of these parts, aircraft repairs, and other critical aviation industry information. One of her recent stories from the year-long series, cowritten with *Plain Dealer* Washington reporter Keith C. Epstein, focusing on the poor quality of the FAA's database is reprinted in Appendix G.

Her aviation database projects require large storage and her IBM PS Note laptop was too small for much of it, so she has to combine her laptop work with her desktop system at *The Plain Dealer's* Washington bureau office and her desktop PC at home. Both of those systems permit her to download data from government nine-track tapes for storage on hard drives and analysis with a database management system such as Microsoft FoxPro, her favorite database program for her work.

"When I go on the road, I take only what I need," Marchak (personal communication, November 1, 1995) explained. "I work with the data in the office and I know what I need. I cull it down and work that way."

Marchak uses Microsoft Excel as her spreadsheet software and Microsoft FoxPro for her database analysis software. She uses Microsoft Word to write. She accesses online services with Procomm Plus. She upgraded her portable computer at the beginning of 1996, but before that she was forced to be highly imaginative to get her work done with the smaller, less powerful IBM system with which she started. That computer had less than 100 MB of space on the hard drive, forcing her to work with an additional external hard drive. Her new system has adequate space for many of her database projects, she says. Marchak carries her portable PC in a computer "backpack," a special case that she says is better than the conventional portable computer travel case because it has more space for her peripherals, a camera, and whatever documents she needs.

However, even the largest database projects can be advanced toward completion with her portable systems—either her older one or her new one—because of her overall approach to portable computing. Marchak's experiences taught her a valuable lesson of database-oriented computing: Adjust and make things work no matter what hardware and software you have available. Database analysis can get done with even limited tools.

With the smaller system she used for 2 years, she was forced to reduce data by converting it to tables small enough that she could store them on floppy disks or on the external hard drive when she traveled. Working with these subsets of the larger database, it was not unusual for her to travel with a half dozen or more diskettes containing data, she explained. Furthermore, she frequently ran DOS versions of her programs, even though the portable had Windows, to save space because the DOS versions were much smaller than their Windows counterparts in terms of hard drive space requirements. She even worked with an older version of FoxPro, she said, to save space.

"I've learned to triage my time and efforts. I have learned to work with what I have. You make due. In many ways, it was a jerry-rigged system," she explained. "At work and at home, I would do what I could not do with the portable. But if I got in a real jam and needed to travel with a more powerful laptop, I'd borrow one of the others in our bureau."

Marchak will take her data tables on the road for several reasons. She can continue to work with her data while traveling, of course, but she has found an additional advantage of portable CAR. Much of the time, she says, her sources do not know the database nor what is in it. More than once, she says, she has shown data from a query or an individual case to a source for comment by opening up her laptop and running the data on screen or by showing a source a printed copy of the data:

> A computer and data are a great way to get your foot in the door. I take the data with me and show it to sources when I am doing interviews. I did that once on a ride-around with some cops in looking at homicides and they were stunned with what I had found. The computer and data get them to talk about it. Most people have not seen the data I work with. It is an amazing way to get people to talk when they see the data. It has helped me many times in dealing with aviation industry sources.

The moments of discovery and discussion about her data that she shares with her expert sources are still other aspects of her computer-based reporting that excite her, Marchak said. She also uses her portable to build databases from original keypunch entry from time to time, but mostly uses databases loaded from tapes. In a difficult situation with no electronic data available, she is ready to use the portable to enter data. Marchak is a self-taught computer journalist. In many ways, her success has been the result of her willingness to spend time learning how to use the computer to help her with stories:

> I got into it heavily after the IRE New York meeting [in 1993]. I began to teach myself. I also groveled at the feet of a lot of good people through IRE. I volunteered to get involved and made presentations

about my work at professional meetings. That forced me to learn more in an intense manner. I had to find out what's new, what's out there that is fresh. It was a lot of work and a lot of long weekends in front of the computer. I also found some databases that no one has looked at in a comprehensive fashion. People look at FAA data by checking a tail number or something similar. I'm taking a more complete look. In the past year, I've even trained people in government about their own data.

Marchak feels her portable computer has broadened the scope of her work with databases and helped her stories in several ways. "I'm having fun doing this. And the paper's very supportive," she said.

TAKING COMPUTERS TO THE STORY

The Waterbury *Republican-American* in Connecticut has turned its entire newsroom into a CAR facility. In fact, it may be the first newspaper to become a fully portable CAR newsroom. The newspaper equipped all full-time reporters/writers with laptops during 1995 and the newspaper was in the process of converting desktop PCs to portables at the beginning of 1996. "It is our publisher's view that laptops empower reporters, which makes for a better paper," explained Chris Feola (personal communication, November 14, 1995), CAR editor for the *Republican-American.*

The newspaper's philosophy is to incorporate CAR into daily reporting at all levels by all reporters in all departments. "All of the computer-assisted reporting coming out of the *Waterbury Republican-American* is done on laptops; all of our regular CAR-ites already have laptops. This week's installment: A sports reporter's analysis of college coach salaries, comparing men's coaches to women's coaches to other state employees. In recent weeks: Election coverage, including tax and spending analysis."

At the end of 1995, the *Republican-American* had the following systems:

- Nine AST 386SX laptops.
- Three AST 486 laptops.
- One Toshiba 386SX laptop.
- Five Toshiba 486 laptops.
- Seven IBM 486 Think Pads.

"We have Texas Instruments Extensa 486s on order. We're hoping to have laptops for all our reporters by the end of the year [1995]. One Toshiba has an active matrix color screen; two ASTs have dual scan color. All the 486s have 8 MB of RAM or better, and 200+ MB hard drives. The 386s—which are obviously older—have 4 MB of RAM and smaller hard drives. Those are falling back to lighter use; the 486s are our primary machines," Feola explained.

Feola, who also oversees computers in the newsroom, has equipped the portable systems with Windows 95 and Microsoft Works 95, a package of office-oriented programs that includes word processing, spreadsheets, and database tools for most reporters. "Those who do heavy duty CAR work get Microsoft Office. We don't allow variations or user installed software," Feola stated.

Reporters and writers can file their stories or transfer data using a modem. "We have a comm server that automatically routes stories dumped by modem or floppy," Feola said. "We have PC-CARD bus 10-Base-T connectors for the 486s, which we'll hook up as soon as the permanent wiring reaches them."

Although the Waterbury newspaper's extensive use of portable computers throughout its newsroom is still an exception, portables are catching on as CAR tools for many individuals. *Asbury Park Press* reporter Rick Linsk, for example, uses his portable computer for a variety of newsgathering and story-filing purposes for his New Jersey newspaper. One of them is CAR. His newspaper is not using portable computers for CAR in any widespread manner yet, he says, but there are a growing number of situations where portables typically used for writing and filing stories are being used for more than just those basics:

> We haven't really integrated portables into CAR. Portables are, as is true elsewhere, tapped for traveling or late-night assignments, such as when the Pope came to the New Jersey/New York area. But they are scarce, often end up getting adopted for indefinite periods by certain departments, and we don't even have one specifically assigned to the CAR program. Having said that, we have had a few special occasions where reporters on CAR stories went out of their way to acquire a newsroom portable and use it to key in records. In 1993, Ames Alexander and Mark Lagerkvist used, I think, a Tandy 100 to key in records showing how much New Jersey charitable organizations spent on fundraising versus actual programs. A few months ago, I used a Toshiba—our Statehouse bureau chief's, lent to me as a favor—to key in state records detailing amusement ride injuries in New Jersey. This was an interesting case because we obtained their database of accidents, but the database (according to the state at least) didn't contain important information like an explanation of how the accident occurred and of the rider's injury. And for one year's accidents, the database lacked names. I used Excel on the laptop to key in the missing data for 218 of the 784 accidents that occurred over a three-year period. I would have done them all, but the state

balked at the time spent chaperoning me through the file cabinets, and I had enough to prove my point anyway. It enabled me, among other things, to show that the state had incorrectly coded dozens of serious injuries, including concussions, as "non serious." (personal communication, November 2, 1995)

What Is PCAR?

The relatively small collection of journalists involved in portable computing, such as the work Linsk described, is gradually getting larger. Each year, more journalists travel with portable computers and an increasing number leave the office on local assignments with portable computers, or carry them home to continue to report or write. Industry-wide, more and more portable computers are being sold and the proportion of all computers sold is growing as well. One reason, of course, is the growing capability of portable computing hardware. Another reason is the increasing affordability compared to a few years ago.

It makes sense to some, at least, that portable computing would have a ready-made application in CAR. In this manner, journalists can take their computing power to the data, if necessary, instead of the more conventional opposite situation. Imagine reporters key-punching budget information, voting records, or health care statistics into their laptops and notebooks at the offices where these records are kept, perhaps only in paper form. Portable computers, linked with wireless networks, may be the next generation of computing for newsrooms, but they had not quite become the newsroom norm and they were not yet a major resource for CAR in 1996.

A clear avenue of expansion and growth in CAR is *portable computer-assisted reporting* (PCAR). Many news organizations are only beginning to explore the possibilities of computers in their daily reporting and some of those newsrooms are beginning to use portables for online and database-oriented newsgathering.

Use of Portable Computers Is Growing

A recent study of personal computer sales estimated that by the beginning of the next decade, portable computing will account for more than one third of all sales of PCs. BIS Strategic Decisions projects sales growth to jump from about 25% in 1996 to over 35% in 2000. In terms of the primary PC used by portable users, the numbers are even more dramatic. In 1996, only 33% of all portable PC users used the portable as their primary system, but by 2000 the figure is expected to change to 80% because of major use shifts expected by then (Ablondi, 1995b; Anonymous, 1995a). By 2000, of the almost 22 million portable PCs in use, more than 17 million of them will be primary systems and not backup systems to desktops. A major computing work style change among computer users in the United States in general is on its way, it seems, and it will only be a matter of time before it comes to newsrooms, but it seems likely to occur within the next 10 years, if not sooner.

Computer Industry Focuses on Portables

There are hot spots in the computer industry. One of them is the Internet. Another is wireless communication. Still another is portable computing. A remarkable sign of the increased legitimacy of portable computing is the fact that the first PC operating system has been developed with an awareness of the needs and uses of portable computers such as notebooks and laptops. Windows 95 and its subsequent editions offer a set-up option screen that included a "portable" configuration alongside the "typical," "compact," and "custom" configuration options. What this means to the next generation of Windows users is a set of tools that makes the basic set-up of a portable system better suited for the uses of that PC. For many journalists, though, it means much greater convenience in connecting to newsrooms from remote locations. The Windows 95 system includes tools for communication with networks and other systems with a few clicks of a pointing device. For journalists on the road and those involved in CAR at a remote location, this will make connectivity a breeze compared to earlier configurations that made setting up a portable more difficult. Windows 95 provides the needed software for network connections or for simple hook-ups with the newsroom system using Hyper Terminal, the OS's own communications program (for a complete technical discussion of the Windows 95's remote access tools, see Rigney, 1995). With the new Windows lead, it seems other operating systems may soon also recognize the need to serve portable users more readily. The move toward portable computing and portable PCAR is slowly beginning.

BUT . . . PORTABLE
COMPUTER-ASSISTED REPORTING?

To some, using a portable computer for CAR may seem like a silly idea. To those individuals, portable computers are inadequate substitutes for desktop systems. They simply no longer fit that description. Portable computers are every bit as fast, powerful, and capable as most desktops. Portable computer engineering and technology made a wide range of leaps forward in the mid-1990s to catch up. As a result, a shift may occur in the years ahead in CAR. For some more routine CAR applications, at least, laptop and notebook computers will take on a new role with their increased capacity and lower prices. As existing portables are replaced and new ones are added to newsroom resources, it seems natural that these systems will begin to be used for daily and small-project CAR. And with wireless links to use server resources, there will be no limits to what PCAR can do. The convenience of movement of the system to the data, instead of moving the data to a newsroom desktop CAR system, among other benefits, makes the step an easy one to take.

"Your next big number-crunching computer may not be so big. In fact, you may be able to carry it with you to your local government agency," observed Associated Press CAR consultant and former NICAR staff member Drew Sullivan (1995, p. 6). "Notebook computers are steadily gaining in speed, capability and adaptability. It might be time to take another look. . . . [A] new group of notebooks is hitting the market that meet the reporter's need for large RAM and storage memory, as well as the flexibility to attach peripherals such as tape drives and take advantage of upgrades in bus speeds."

Empowerment: CAR Anywhere, Anytime

A number of journalists feel portable PCs should be in the hands of journalists in newsrooms to enable CAR tools to be used on daily stories anywhere at any time. Neil Reisner (personal communication, October 30,1995), NICAR training director, is one of them:

> To every reporter, a portable! Portables could be the workhorses of journalism and are getting inexpensive enough to be so. Imagine a newsroom in which every reporter is issued a portable, a desk with a voice line and a data line, and a docking station that includes a full-sized monitor and keyboard. That reporter would be prepared to work in the office and work in the field. He could, say, load it with a database of the voting records of local legislators and look information up on deadline for a story. He could type in last year's municipal budget and the right formulas and produce a quick-and-dirty analysis of the new budget the instant it's released by a town council. And file it on deadline.
>
> It'd be kind of sadistic to force reporters to work exclusively on portable screens and keyboards, not to mention that it would likely result in causes of action for various ergonomic ailments. But the kind of docking station arrangement described above could result in a situation where reporters have maximum flexibility to do their jobs.

Editors, however, should likely continue to use full desktops for ergonomic reasons.

Rose Ciotta, CAR editor for *The Buffalo News*, thinks CAR would be enhanced with portables—if journalists had them to use:

> Arm every reporter with a laptop loaded with software and the data they need for their beat. We're a long way from doing that if everyone is going to wait for someone in a central position to do it. This is a question of spending money on hardware, software, data development. What's the payoff? Better, quicker stories. It's an ideal scenario, I think, but I don't know that anyone can justify the expense across the board right now. You certainly have this happening in pockets in the newsroom. Sports reporters and political reporters—i.e., those on the road a lot—have learned to make use of their laptops as a source of data as well as a writing tool. The ideal, I think, is to equally arm the suburban reporter and the city hall reporter.

> I doubt they will replace desktop PCs completely, but I do see a day when we become more of a roomless newsroom than we are. The technology certainly exists to send every reporter "into the field" armed with the tools to gather information, write, and send copy to the paper. Why do most newspaper reporters report to a central office or bureau everyday and use desktop PCs? The answer is probably habit, tradition, the need to actually see people show up for work. We're moving in the portable direction for reporters, but I don't see that happening in the editing arena unless the nature of what we do drastically changes. (personal communication, November 22, 1995)

Cost Will Be the Major Barrier

Jack Lail (personal communication, September 30, 1995), assistant managing editor/technology, for the *Knoxville News-Sentinel*, thinks portable computing has much potential for use for CAR. "Pentium laptops are here so we definitely have the power for advanced computing, but more importantly I think laptops ought to allow reporters to have more organized information. (But) they just aren't as handy to use. The keyboards are often cramped, the screens more difficult to read."

However, Lail feels that there are economic issues that prevent PCAR from wider use in newsrooms today. "It is the cost/benefit problem. Managers feel they are getting enough value from cheaper methods to stay competitive. Whether true or not, that's what they believe. Photographers may get a digital camera, but our reporters don't have cell phones."

Reisner agrees with Lail's economic concerns. "Although, as costs decline, many journalists are using portables more. Beepers and cellular phones are no-brainers because they're easy to use and their benefits are easily seen. Laptops, though, are still primarily used as fancy word processors. Until journalists understand that they can be used for much more (as can desktops, for that matter), we'll not be using the technology we have to its fullest capacity."

Seattle Post-Intelligencer Systems Editor Paul McElroy (personal communication, October 13, 1995), believes that there are barriers to widespread use of PCAR, but he feels it could catch on in newsrooms. "Perhaps, but only if companies are willing to invest in docking stations, regular keyboards, and monitors. Using a notebook PC keyboard and built-in monitor is fine on an airplane or for a city council meeting, but I sure wouldn't want to be stuck with it all the time.

McElroy feels PCAR has not caught on because of its innovative nature and its cost. "My guess is that the technology is still relatively new, expensive, and occasionally unreliable. It's also a function of return on investment. Most newspaper publishers are reluctant to spend money unless they see a real pay back. The intangible promise of better news stories is a hard sell at budget time."

In Saint Paul, *Pioneer Press* CAR specialist Dan Browning (personal communication, October 16, 1995) sees cost problems as the continuing barrier to the advantages of portable computing by journalists in all contexts:

> Expense is the major barrier. Loss and theft have also been a problem. Some portables can be used to replace some PCs in newsrooms. But the screens are too small and they're too expensive in comparison with PCs. We'll still need to buy those expensive video terminals to plug into the laptops when we're back at work. And we'll still need PCs with mega hard drives. Portables can be used to gather data at the site when government refuses to provide it on a portable medium. It can also be used as a way to infect the newsroom with the skill, as it gets around the problem of limited hardware at the various work stations.

Although some capable high-performance portables were selling for under $2,000 in mid-1996, there were many on the market, those with top-of-the-line configurations and maximum capacities, selling for $5,000 and more. However, older 486 portables were selling for as little as $700 in late 1995. There is no doubt that most news organizations will not invest in many portables at those high-end prices.

Breaking Some Very Old Habits

Even the newsrooms with the most portable resources will not leave the desktop base yet. Bill Casey is director of CAR at *The Washington Post*, which had about 300 newsroom portables in use in late 1995. He is not so sure that portables, such as laptops and notebooks, will become the dominant PC in newsrooms for several reasons.

"First of all, a lot of people do write at their desks. And they don't want to write on a portable screen. People want a larger screen, even a seventeen-inch. There is the issue of monitors. And they are more expensive. Anyone who is running an SII system needs a special card for an IBM machine, also," Casey (personal communication, September 22, 1995) stated.

NEWSROOM USE OF PORTABLE COMPUTERS

Portable computing—laptops, notebooks, and handheld palmtops—has given journalists the ability to take CAR with them on the road for a major event or down the street to city hall. Some

---

DEFINING PCAR HARDWARE TERMS

- *Laptop*—An older portable system weighing approximately 10 to 15 pounds. The term is sometimes used to refer to any portable computer.
- *Notebook*—This is the weight class for the vast majority of portable computers on the market today. Notebooks weigh between 5 and 10 pounds and are approximately the size of a wirebound paper notebook, though thicker. They come with hard drives, QWERTY keyboards, and LCD screens.
- *Palmtop*—Computers small enough to hold in one hand and operate with the other, usually weighing less than 2 pounds. Palmtops run on off-the-shelf batteries and often feature a PC Card slot for expansion.
- *Personal digital assistant*—A handheld computer that serves as an organizer, electronic book, or note taker and includes features such as pen-based entry and wireless transmission to cellular or desktop systems.
- *Subnotebook*—A full-function notebook computer that weighs less than 5 pounds. Because of the unflattering associations with the prefix *sub*, manufacturers often use the term *ultralight* to describe their subnotebook computers.
- *Transportable*—The granddaddy of portable computers. Weighing between 15 and 35 pounds, transportable computers are barely portable, but usually pack plenty of power and expansion possibilities.

Source: Costa (1995b), p. 84.

of the first journalists to use portable computers were sports reporters at games and political reporters on the campaign trail, both often writing and reporting on tight deadline turnarounds. With the continuing demand for fieldwork, it made sense to equip them with portables to make story filing more efficient. Thus, more than a decade ago, first-generation portables were making their way into newsroom for the sole purpose of permitting reporters to file stories in electronic form from a remote site. It was more efficient than dictating to a clerk, another reporter, or a copy editor. The original motivation was to preserve keystrokes. As portable computing simultaneously became more powerful and more inexpensive during the first half of the 1990s, it became feasible for journalists to do much more with portable computing than just file stories.

Paralleling development of portable computer engineering came improvements in communications hardware and software that made remote communications easier and faster. More modem power for less money sounded a loud call to many portable users to increase their use of portable PCs for more than just writing and filing stories. These changes encouraged increased remote use of commercial online services and the Internet. At the very least, it means new ways, such as e-mail, for reporters and editors on the road to keep in touch with the newsroom and with sources.

During the late 1980s and early 1990s, paralleling the rapid development of portable computing was an extraordinary growth in other forms of portable communication. As these devices became more readily available, more portable, and less expensive, they became more attractive to editors and reporters for routine use instead of special events use that may have previously dictated their use, if at all.

Table 7.1 reveals that 83% of all newspapers responding in the 1995 CAR survey used portable computers in some way. Larger daily newspapers, with the additional resources that come with size, used portable PCs much more than do smaller daily newspapers in 1995.

TABLE 7.1
Field Use of Portable Personal Computers, 1995

Field Use	Large Dailies[a]		Small Dailies[b]		Totals	
Yes	124	90.5%	98	75.4%	222	83.1%
No	13	9.5	32	24.6	45	16.9
Totals	137	51.3	130	48.7	267	100.0

Note. $n = 287$; missing observations = 20.
[a]Circulation over 52,800. [b]Circulation under 52,800.

CHOOSING A PORTABLE COMPUTER

Finding the right portable computer is not easy, especially for individuals not too interested in the details of computer hardware. And, because there are certain requirements for portables for use in CAR, there are a few things to consider:

- "Test drive" as many portables as possible before buying. Go to stores and do not depend solely on catalogs or magazine advertisements. Most stores have hands-on displays to try a system. Review the screen display, the mouse type and design, and the keyboard, especially, to determine if each fits personal needs.
- Decide on the best processor and system speed for the job. If the uses are mainly for online research, this is not as important as, say, modem speed and the ease of telephone line connection. But if the portable will be used for database work, faster is better for processors. Check Pentiums, for instance. The cost may be worth it.
- Look for RAM capacity. Start with an absolute minimum of 8 MB, but 16 MB to 20 MB is preferred for use with Windows 95 and for the long-range life of the system, especially if database software such as Access will be run under Windows 95. The expandability of RAM will determine, in part, how long the system will remain useful to you.
- Buy a color screen system, but decide whether you need the best color (active matrix) or if you can settle for something less expensive (dual scan). Monochrome screens were very hard to find in 1996, but will be much less expensive.

(continued on next page)

While 91% of larger newspapers reported using them, only 75% of smaller dailies used them.

Table 7.2 shows a considerable shift from limited use of portable computers in newsrooms for newsgathering and writing from 1994 to 1995. About 64% used portables in 1994, but the figure jumped to 77% in 1995. There was also an increase in the number of newspapers not using portables, from about 9% to 16%, but there was considerable reduction in the number of newspapers not reporting in the 1-year period.

Using portable computing is a necessity for any sort of journalistic success in the mid-1990s, for certain, but there are only minimal configurations that seem to represent consensus about how to use portables in the field. News organizations most often use their portables for preparing stories and for transmitting them back to the newsroom's production system for editing and typesetting. In order to use a PC for this purpose alone requires a minimal

(continued from previous page)

• Determine how long the system will run on its batteries, but be aware of estimates from manufacturers. These are always too high. Talk to someone who has a similar system, if possible, and get their experience. Lithium-ion batteries are longer charge life batteries than the more common nickel-cadmium.

• Be sure the system has an internal 3.5-inch floppy drive.

• Be sure the system has at least one, but preferably two, PC Card (PCMCIA) slots for modems, fax cards, flash memory, and other purposes. These can also be used to add external CD-ROM drives or other peripherals for access to data stored in other formats. Usually portable systems come with one Type II and one Type III slot or two Type II slots. One of each will provide greater flexibility.

• Determine use patterns before deciding on hard drive size. For portables used mostly online, there is no real need for an larger-than-normal (500 MB) hard drive. For serious database work, do not get a drive with less than 1 GB, but consider investing in the largest available for that particular model (usually 1 to 2 GB). Removable hard drives can also be more easily upgraded when the time comes to do so.

• Check into whether the system has removable components such as hard drives or floppy drives that can be used for other purposes (e.g., additional batteries or CD-ROM drives).

• Decide if an internal CD-ROM is needed with the portable system. It will add more to the cost, but will add multimedia and data versatility for that price. At the same time, consider whether a sound card and speakers are needed.

configuration of some sort of operating system such as DOS or DOS with Windows, a word processor, an internal or external modem, and communications software.

Some news organizations are beginning to use their PCs for other purposes also, but these organizations are not nearly in agreement

TABLE 7.2
Field Use of Portable Personal Computers, 1994–1995

Field Use	1994		1995		Percentage Change
Yes	134	64.4%	222	77.4%	+13.0%
No	18	8.7	45	15.7	+8.0
Missing	56	26.9	20	7.0	−19.9
Totals	208	100.0	287	100.0	

about how or what should be done in 1995. These differences are discussed in the following section.

EQUIPPING PORTABLE COMPUTERS FOR CAR

Data in the following tables display in somewhat dramatic form the considerable variation in hardware and software configurations of portable PCs used in daily newspaper newsrooms. In Table 7.3, it is clear than online services are not yet in widespread use on newsroom portables. Most portable computers with hardware equipped for transmitting stories to the newsroom can also be used to go online from the field. Online services have a number of potential purposes for journalists in the field—such as e-mail, database access for research, background from current news on wire services, travel, and weather information—but they are not being used. In 1995, only 16% of newspapers used any type of online services or Internet access from remote locations with portable PCs. Among the newspapers that do use remote online access, it seems to be the exclusive province of larger dailies. More than one quarter of larger dailies (28%) provide such access to their traveling journalists, but only 4% of smaller dailies offer it as part of the portable computing package for the road.

When asked how their portable computers were configured, it became clear that word processing and transmission of stories are the primary purposes of portable PCs used on news assignments. More than 9 in 10 large newspapers used word processing, with the remaining few newspapers either not reporting accurately or using basic text managers for writing stories, Table 7.4 reveals. Smaller dailies used word processors 7 in 10 times.

Communications software was used by 65% of news organizations overall, but by a considerably greater proportion of large dailies (79%) than smaller ones (50%). But after word processing and

TABLE 7.3
Online Services Use with Portable Computers, 1995

Use	Large Dailies[a]		Small Dailies[b]		Totals	
Yes	38	27.5%	6	4.5%	44	16.2%
No	96	69.6	125	93.3	221	81.3
Don't know	4	2.9	3	2.2	7	2.6
Totals	138	50.7	134	49.3	272	100.0

Note. n = 287; missing observations = 15.
[a]Circulation over 52,800. [b]Circulation under 52,800.

TABLE 7.4
Software Use with Portable Personal Computers, 1995

Software Category	Large Dailies[a]		Small Dailies[b]		Totals	
Word processors	124	91.9%	91	70.0%	215	81.1%
n = 287;						
missing observations = 22						
Communications	106	78.5	65	50.4	171	64.8
packages						
n = 287;						
missing observations = 23						
Spreadsheets	16	11.9	10	7.8	26	9.8
n = 287;						
missing observations = 23						
Database managers	13	9.6	4	3.1	17	6.4
n = 287;						
missing observations = 23						

[a]Circulation over 52,800. [b]Circulation under 52,800.

communications software, there was little other use of portable PCs in 1995. Table 7.4 also shows that spreadsheets (10% of all newspapers) and relational database or other database managers (6% of all newspapers) are not yet popular for journalists on the road. Whereas there were significant differences by size in database manager use, the use differences by size for spreadsheets were not significant. It is apparent from these data that database tools are the new frontier of portable CAR. Although journalists have been comfortable using portable computers with online tools for some time, they have yet to adapt to the new power of portables for such things as database creation, editing, and analysis in remote locations. Portable PCs may not yet be powerful enough to handle the largest of data processing jobs that run into gigabytes in size, but portables can clearly handle any database management jobs for routine databases.

OTHER PORTABLE NEWS REPORTING TOOLS USED

Journalists at larger newspapers are beginning to discover how to successfully use communication tools with their portable computers while on assignment out of the office and while on the road. One major change is a gradual switch from two-way radios to cellular telephones. On-air time is lower priced in many metropolitan areas because of competition and growth of the cellular system than when the systems were first marketed, but the cost of telephones is also much less inexpensive and, in some cases, telephones are given away and are not even a factor in deciding to use the service. With the lower prices for pagers and beepers and pager and beeper services, even newspapers with stretched and restricted newsroom operating budgets can afford to use them in limited ways—such as keeping in touch with editors, key beat reporters, or photographers.

The growth of portable communications tools is, perhaps, even more impressive than the growth of portable computing discussed earlier. Several areas of growth include two-way portable communication through cellular telephones and two-way pagers and beepers. In a recent national study of professionals, portable computer users were likely to also be portable communicators. About half of those using portable PCs used cellular telephones and approximately another 30% used pagers or beepers (Anonymous, 1995b).

Individuals with portable computers often use them to go online. A 1995 national study of portable computer users determined that the majority of them use them to access computers elsewhere, such as mainframes, but almost as many users link up to check e-mail or to connect with a network server at a remote location. The study also determined that 74% of users had modems in their portables and 71% used the modems to connect to their offices (Ablondi, 1995a).

One-way paging has been used extensively in newsrooms for more than a decade, especially with reporters and photographers in the field, but there will be growth in the next decade in the next level of paging, two-way mobile data services. One estimate placed growth in this new communication tool from about 1.4 million subscribers in 1996 to 5.2 million in 2000 (Anonymous, 1995e).

Table 7.5 shows that slightly more than half of the newspapers (54%) using portable PCs use them with modems. A greater proportion of large dailies (66%) use them than smaller dailies (34%),

TABLE 7.5
Field Use of Modems with Portable PCs, 1995

Field Use	Large Dailies[a]		Small Dailies[b]		Totals	
Yes	90	66.2%	53	41.1%	143	54.0%
No	46	33.8	76	58.9	122	46.0
Totals	136	51.3	129	48.7	265	100.0

Note. n = 287; missing observations = 22.
[a]Circulation over 52,800. [b]Circulation under 52,800.

TABLE 7.6
Field Use of Fax Cards with Portable PCs, 1995

Field Use	Large Dailies[a]		Small Dailies[b]		Totals	
Yes	5	3.7%	0	0.0%	5	1.9%
No	131	96.3	129	100.0	260	98.1
Totals	136	51.3	129	48.7	265	100.0

Note. n = 287; missing observations = 22.
[a]Circulation over 52,800. [b]Circulation under 52,800.

TABLE 7.7
Field Use of Cellular Telephones, 1995

Field Use	Large Dailies[a]		Small Dailies[b]		Totals	
Yes	78	57.4%	39	30.2%	117	44.2%
No	58	42.6	90	69.8	148	55.8
Totals	136	51.3	129	48.7	265	100.0

Note. n = 287; missing observations = 22.
[a]Circulation over 52,800. [b]Circulation under 52,800.

however. It is interesting to note, however, that newspapers have been slow so far to upgrade modems to fax capability. This may be because of cost or it could be because of a perceived lack of need with e-mail and other communication services available, but Table 7.6 shows virtually no use of fax capabilities of portable computing by news organizations in 1995. Only 2% of all newspapers answering the question use fax modems, but the figure could be even smaller if missing data are included and no response is interpreted as not using the device. No smaller dailies reported using fax capabilities in the 1995 national survey.

Cellular telephones are much more commonly used than fax modems at U.S. daily newspapers in 1995, as shown in Table 7.7. Overall, 44% reported using them for one or more purposes related to newsgathering. However, cellular telephones are still a tool of the wealthier news organizations, generally, if size is an indicator. Almost twice as many large dailies (57%) reported using cellular telephones than did smaller dailies (30%).

One-way pagers and beepers, more affordable means of portable communication than cellular telephones, are, interestingly not as widespread. Although two-way pagers and beepers are available, these are not in noticeable use by news organizations for newsgathering. This might suggest that news organizations that had spent money on beepers now spend it on cellular telephones, instead, rather than using both devices. Overall, as shown in Table 7.8, 29% of news organizations responding to the survey used pagers and beepers. There are size differences in beeper use as well. Almost twice as many large newspapers (36%) use pagers and beepers than do smaller newspapers (21%).

Use of two-way radios is another communication tool that has helped reporters and photographers in the field for a much longer period than cellular telephones or pagers and beepers. Table 7.9 shows that use of two-way radios remains important to one in five daily newspapers for remote, and presumably, local reporting. Overall, 20% of newspapers use two-way radios and there is no difference in use levels determined by newspaper size.

Taking available technology to the next level would be the natural combination of available portable communication and computing technology. Practically speaking, this would simply involve linking laptop and notebook computers with cellular telephones. The available technology does not require digital cellular telephone service, nor does it require a cellular modem, although these more advanced devices make communication more reliable. Table 7.10 reveals that only 5% of newspapers were using this potential in 1995 and there is no difference in the use of this technological advance by newspaper size.

TABLE 7.8
Field Use of Pagers and Beepers, 1995

Field Use	Large Dailies[a]		Small Dailies[b]		Totals	
Yes	49	36.0%	27	20.9%	76	28.7%
No	87	64.0	102	79.1	189	71.3
Totals	136	51.3	129	48.7	265	100.0

Note. n = 287; missing observations = 22.
[a]Circulation over 52,800. [b]Circulation under 52,800.

TABLE 7.9
Field Use of Two-Way Radios, 1995

Field Use	Large Dailies[a]		Small Dailies[b]		Totals	
Yes	29	21.3%	25	19.4%	54	20.4%
No	107	78.7	104	80.6	211	79.6
Totals	136	51.3	129	48.7	265	100.0

Note. n = 287; missing observations = 22.
[a]Circulation over 52,800. [b]Circulation under 52,800.

TABLE 7.10
Field Use of Portable PCs with Cellular Links, 1995

Field Use	Large Dailies[a]		Small Dailies[b]		Totals	
Yes	10	7.4%	4	3.1%	14	5.3%
No	126	92.6	125	96.9	251	94.7
Totals	136	51.3	129	48.7	265	100.0

Note. n = 287; missing observations = 22.
[a]Circulation over 52,800. [b]Circulation under 52,800.

POTENTIAL APPLICATIONS AND USES OF PCAR

There seems to be a vast number of possibilities for use of PCAR in newsrooms and on the road for newsgathering and information processing. With speed and power comparable to desktops, there are few limits. As wireless communication connections and networks become less expensive and more reliable, the potential seems to grow in geometric proportions. Perhaps the only limit is cost, but if portable computing continues to drop in price per unit, its applications and uses will expand.

As the preceding tables have shown, the most obvious combination of new technology in newsgathering would be to take greater advantage of cellular telephone technology and portable computing, but this is only one example of bringing new concepts of communication and computing into the newsroom.

Online field research is another area not often used by journalists. The typical field research model used in most newsrooms calls for a reporter or editor to call a request into the news library, have a librarian search for the information online, then the librarian calls the reporter or faxes the information back to the reporter. But the tools are available for short-cutting the process. This process is also often used in remote bureaus across town or across the state. Reporters and editors in the field can do their own research with the right software and account access, but this has not yet caught on. It is likely that lack of sufficient cost controls is one reason.

Developments in portable computing technology may offer even newer and yet-unimagined applications for computer-based information gathering. In the fiercely competitive portable computing marketplace, innovative user-oriented features and improved computing capacities are the motivating factors of manufacturers to gain an edge in sales. This drive has brought portable computing to CAR in a serious manner and the potential for new uses is vast (Gillooly, 1995).

Lower unit weights, smaller box footprints, richer colors, bigger screens, faster processors, additional tiny peripherals, improved pointing devices, bigger and more usable keyboards, interchangeable parts, increased expandability, improved durability, and longer lasting batteries are some of the changes that have attracted journalists involved in CAR to portables.

It makes sense to consider taking a top-of-the-line portable into a government office to download large databases instead of dealing with tapes or other storage media. Portability of databases means greater flexibility in analysis. Data can be taken to experts, for example, or moved around to story sites for on-the-spot use.

Newsroom managers should also investigate wireless communications. This will ultimately lead to newsrooms without walls and give computer-equipped reporters and editors the needed links to do their work in the most effective manner. One of the hallmarks of the newsroom environment has been interaction and collegiality. But with enhanced connectivity of wireless networks and other communication links, this does not have to be lost. This, it seems, may be the direction of PCAR in the early part of the 21st century.

TYPICAL PORTABLE COMPUTING SET-UPS IN NEWSROOMS

The use of laptops at the *Waterbury Republican-American* is still not typical of most U.S. newspapers using portable computers in newsgathering. How do more typical daily newspapers use their portable computing and communication tools to enhance their reporting? The following six case studies show how several newspapers, from large dailies to smaller ones, configured and used their portable computers for CAR in 1995.

The Orlando Sentinel

- *Daily circulation*—300,000.
- *Portable computer configurations*—Laptops, built-in modems, communications software, word processors, America Online software and accounts. Additionally, some reporters and editors own and configure their own portable systems.
- *Other portable communication devices*—Cellular telephones, pagers and beepers.

- *Source*—John Huff, editor for new technology (personal communication, March 5, 1995).

Sacramento Bee

- *Daily circulation*—275,000.
- *Portable computer configuration*—Laptops, built-in modems, communications software, word processors, online services. Additionally, some reporters and editors own and configure their own portable systems.
- *Other portable communication devices*—Two-way radios, cellular telephones.
- *Source*—David Jensen, CAR editor (personal communication, March 30, 1995).

News Journal, New Castle, Delaware

- *Daily circulation*—125,000.
- *Portable computer configuration*—Laptops, built-in modems, communications software, word processors, spreadsheet program.
- *Other portable communication devices*—Two-way radios.
- *Source*—Merritt Wallick, assistant city/state editor (personal communication, March 3, 1995).

The Desert Sun, Palm Springs, California

- *Daily circulation*—55,000.
- *Portable computer configuration*—Laptops, built-in modems, communications software, word processors.
- *Other portable communication devices*—Two-way radios, cellular telephones.
- *Source*—Bette Miller, senior reporter/projects (personal communication, March 10, 1995).

Montgomery Advertiser

- *Daily circulation*—50,000.
- *Portable computer configuration*—Laptops, built-in modems, communications software, word processors, online service.
- *Other portable communication devices*—Pagers and beepers, cellular telephones, PC–cellular telephone links.

- *Source*—John Hasselwander, city editor (personal communication, March 6, 1995).

Press-Republican, Plattsburgh, New York

- *Daily circulation*—24,000.
- *Portable computer configuration*—Laptops, built-in modems, communications software, word processors, spreadsheets.
- *Other portable communication devices*—None.
- *Source*—Jim Dynko, editor (personal communication, March 20, 1995).

THE RISKS AND PROBLEMS WITH PORTABLE CAR

Portable computers have many advantages that have been described in the preceding discussion, but they also have some inherent problems. In addition to the higher general cost of smaller and more portable computing hardware, many businesses, such as news companies, fear them because of their vulnerability to theft and handling damage. A national study of laptop disasters by Contingency Planning Research (Anonymous, 1995c) revealed that the biggest problems are hardware damage while being transported (30%) and problems caused by errors made by the user (30%). Other problems include hardware and software malfunctions (20%), theft (10%), and other trouble causes by matters out of control of the company or the user such as fires or flooding (10%).

Most news organizations experience problems from wear and tear on their systems because of their extensive almost-daily use. Even the highest quality desktop monitors burn up, the toughest keyboards will break, and the strongest hard drives eventually wear out. Movement and exposure to elements can damage any sophisticated electronic devices, of course. But improper handling and care can lead to numerous difficulties and it makes sense for newsroom managers, especially those involved in systems management, to carefully train portable users in the proper care and maintenance of their systems.

One way to bring a bit more care to a portable system is to assign it to an individual rather than use a "check-out" approach. If this can be done, the portable is likely to be handled more responsibly because the individual has a longer term use investment in the unit. A second concern is the need for insurance. Most companies will want to invest in some coverage for their computer systems that leave the building. A third way to protect the investment is to provide proper carrying case protection for the PC. And finally, regular maintenance, the same as is routinely provided for in-house workstations, must be planned. However it is accomplished, a user program for portables is a necessity if PCAR is to work over the long term.

RULES FOR THE LAPTOP ON THE ROAD

For a successful road trip on assignment, there are a checklist of things to remember when using a laptop or notebook computer:

- *Check it out.* If this is the first time out of the office with a newly assigned portable, check it out completely before leaving the building. Check for the right software and run the programs. For example, make sure the word processor and communications programs are installed and work properly.
- *Test the connections.* Write something and test transmitting files from home or another local location to the newsroom system.
- *Check the hard drive.* If the laptop will be used for database work, make certain the right software is installed and that there is sufficient storage space on the hard drive to accommodate the files that will be created or copied onto the drive.
- *Plan ahead.* Check with the hotel about telephone lines and connections. For foreign trips, be prepared for things not to work at some hotels. Have contingency equipment, such as telephone connection adapters and a small tool kit, ready.
- *Anticipate modem trouble.* Bring a second external modem along in case the internal modem fails.
- *More power.* Carry a backup battery along.
- *Have an online option.* Install software and carry account information for a major international online service such as America Online, CompuServe, or a national Internet provider to access that system if all other connections fail. Text can be sent using e-mail in this manner, especially if there are problems connecting directly with the newsroom system or newsroom local area network.

8

Moving Toward
21st-Century CAR

Computers are not the miracle answer to the shortcomings of newsgathering, but they do go a long way toward solving some of the problems of information overload. Computing often creates the impression that it is the end-all solution to any and everything. This belief is often held by beginners who are dazzled by the speed, systematic nature, and comprehensiveness of computing. The popular media do not dampen this type of thinking, either. Microsoft Corporation's efforts to promote the new Windows 95 operating system and Compaq's advertising campaign to sell its line of Pentium-based computers in late 1995 and early 1996 are two highly visible examples. Microsoft's advertising and marketing efforts tried to create the impression that the new operating system would do everything for users—transform not only the way users interact with their computers, but pretty much the way a user lived. Compaq's series of television advertisements encouraged belief in that same message even more directly by posing the question about a given model in its new computer line, "Has it changed your life yet?"

Microsoft's OS and Compaq's PCs, separately or together, may be significant steps toward revolutionizing computing in the last part of this decade, but they can never be more than that. Computing does not substitute for basic life functions any more than CAR substitutes for basic reporting techniques. It is the users and how they take advantage of these tools that make the real difference in newsgathering. The most effective users of computing in newsrooms will use CAR to supplement their usual reporting or to serve as a foundation for a story or project that is enhanced with the more traditional approaches such as firsthand observation, personal interviews, and old-fashioned page-by-page document searching.

Nevertheless, computing is no less than the present and future of journalism. Each day that passes in the remaining years of this decade means another journalist is a little more computer literate and has learned another way to enhance his or her reporting or editing through computing. Computers remain at the heart of newsgathering and information processing, as they have been for nearly three decades.

"CAR presents both new challenges and opportunities. No daily news-gathering service can excel today without employing it," argued Michael Walsh (personal communication, February 20, 1995), a reporter for *The Muskegon Chronicle*, a 50,000-circulation daily in Michigan.

Some journalists feel the gee-whiz attitude about CAR that has dominated many reporting and journalism news organizations in this decade is old news. It is time to move forward and assume CAR is part of reporting, these critics argue. "We mustn't let the dazzling glare of what's possible with computers blind us to the fundamental concepts of journalism. CAR is just another tool; it does not automatically turn bad stories into good ones. That can be easy to forget when magically extracting a neat budget summary from a morass of numbers with a few mouse clicks," warned Paul McElroy, systems editor at the *Seattle Post-Intelligencer* (personal communication, October 13, 1995). "Cranking out a 20-inch story on those numbers serves no one if it doesn't include context and relevancy. Computers may bring volumes of data to our fingertips, but that data is not sacrosanct. A simple typographical error can look like a good story, so it behooves us to still double check the 'facts.' "

Jeff Browne (personal communication, January 31, 1995), a former CAR reporter for the *Milwaukee Journal-Sentinel*, argues that computers and reporting should be as natural in newsrooms as telephones and reporting or any other hardware used in information gathering. "I think it's time to stop thinking of CAR as a single entity or process. I've been using computers in my reporting since 1970, almost as long as I've used the phone in reporting. There are many ways computers can be used. Also, we need to distinguish between using computers for generating information and producing a product; 99 percent of newsroom technology goes into production functions such as word processing, graphics, type-setting, and so forth."

ARE THESE TOOLS CHANGING JOURNALISM?

The computer-based newsgathering tools of this decade are changing journalism and changing journalists. Journalism is changed because the depth and scope of journalism has been redefined. Journalists themselves are changed because of how they now do their jobs. New information-gathering technology in the newsroom means the potential for new thinking about how and what journalists do to gather and process information. It may eventually mean that news itself will be redefined. "It has become impossible to use any of our traditional news media without being told something about how those uses, as well as the media themselves, are being transformed. Information about information—the Information Age, the Information Superhighway, the Information Revolution—is inescapable and, inescapably, contributes to the ways in which those changes are perceived," wrote David Craig, Jane Singer, Chris Allen, Virginia Whitehouse, Anelia Dimitrova, and Keith Sanders (1995, p. 1), of University of Missouri researchers interested in how changing media technology is received by journalists.

"Journalists are part of an information industry that lies at the very center of sweeping changes, and the way they approach those

---

"A GREAT GIFT AND A STERN WARNING"

"CAR is a great gift and a stern warning to newspapers," advises Paul Overberg (personal communication, September 19, 1995), database editor for *USA Today* in Washington, DC:

CAR gives newspapers the tools to truly stand apart in the info glut, to cut past the paid phrase-meisters and institutional facades with a feisty, public-spirited agenda of their own local choice. CAR lets newspapers see and study the whole community, not just the middle-class circle that journalists travel in. CAR lets newspapers challenge the elites, the assumptions, the relativity of debates. CAR lets a newspaper become the voice of factual and moral authority on whatever local issue it chooses. This is a Promethean gift!

But CAR is not easy. It is not cheap. It is especially difficult and expensive compared to the standard in too many newsrooms: Cover local sports and local government by printing what happens, fill leftover space with whatever the flacks and the wires drop on the doorstep each day. Too many publishers and top editors encourage this: It's low-cost journalism, part of the recipe for propping up a handsome return to investors in a no-growth industry.

And CAR's power goes wherever there's a will and a PC. A local cable TV firm or phone company could slice into a local newspaper's franchise by adding a creditable print product to their current offerings. Or a political party or church could create something that looks like a newspaper, but shares none of the values of modern journalism: fairness, independence, honesty. Desktop publishing and CAR would make it easy.

changes will affect our entire society. Like it or not, journalists are, in many ways, in the driver's seat on this high-speed highway. It promises to be an interesting trip, indeed" (p. 25).

Journalists are adjusting to the new capabilities of computing in all parts of the newsgathering and distribution enterprise. Although computers have made work more efficient and journalists more productive, journalists have endured a classic love–hate relationship with their workstation computers for more than two decades (Garrison, 1995; Russial, 1995).

Robert Tiernan (personal communication, February 21, 1995), projects editor for *Newsday* on Long Island, believes CAR's strength is in specific needs and projects. "The projects work best with well-defined needs and projects. The idea for the story is paramount. The technology is just a means to nail it down." *Orange County Register* CAR specialist and reporter Ron Campbell (personal communication, March 4, 1995) strongly supports that position. "If CAR is going to make a lasting change in journalism, it must cease to be a specialty. It must become a routine tool of reporting."

The Virginian-Pilot Editor Cole C. Campbell feels computers have been an asset for newspapers beyond just reporting for a long time and will continue to be a major part of the entire newsgathering and news distribution enterprise. "Newspaper computers have reduced production costs, pushed back deadlines, given us new design tools, helped us tap new media and increased our access to experts, data bases and regular folks," Campbell (1995, p. A2) observed.

John Huff (personal communication, March 5, 1995), editor for new technology for *The Orlando Sentinel*, offers a different perspective. A manager and planner for editorial applications of technology including CAR, Huff feels news organizations will be looking for more new staff members that already know CAR:

> Reporters and editors have yet to take the personal responsibility for preparing themselves to professionally take advantage of the technology that is already available to them. In a period of increasingly strained resources, it is easier to provide a computer than to train (or motivate or baby sit) a user, particularly one who will not take his or her own initiative. Lack of computer knowledge, like lack of computer access, is becoming an outdated excuse for failing to apply the power of technology to the mission of journalism.

RAISING LEVELS OF CAR LITERACY

For journalists getting started in CAR, there are numerous options for on-the-job learning. First, look within the news organization. For journalists that can find in-house training available, the solution is simple. But for those in the majority of news organizations that do not offer in-house classes or other forms of training, the options begin to get expensive and time consuming.

There are a number of national organizations offering CAR training. NICAR and IRE top the list, of course. Often these programs require travel, but some of the NICAR programs can be offered at local sites. Other organizations offer less frequent training and exposure through annual or occasional special workshops. Figure 8.1 provides a list of publications useful to those interested in or working in CAR.

Still another way to learn about computing products and services useful to journalists and news organizations is to attend and participate in computer industry-oriented exhibitions and conferences. For example, the largest two conferences at a national level are the enormous Comdex/Windows exhibitions held for computer dealers and industry manufacturers, held in the spring in Atlanta and in the fall in Las Vegas each year. The spring meeting draws about 100,000 computer-oriented visitors and vendors. The fall meeting is even larger, drawing more than 200,000 participants. But these meetings offer first looks at what will be next in retail stores. The exhibitions are open to the public through sale of visitor passes and many vendors sell the newest hardware and software products on the spot at discounts.

For students or others close to college and university campuses, the options to learn CAR may be either easier or more difficult. There

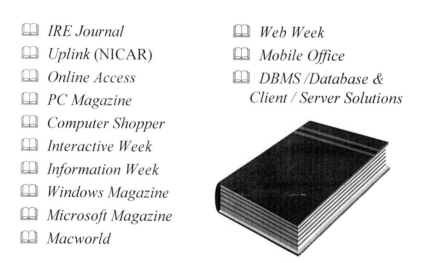

- *IRE Journal*
- *Uplink* (NICAR)
- *Online Access*
- *PC Magazine*
- *Computer Shopper*
- *Interactive Week*
- *Information Week*
- *Windows Magazine*
- *Microsoft Magazine*
- *Macworld*
- *Web Week*
- *Mobile Office*
- *DBMS /Database & Client / Server Solutions*

FIG. 8.1. A regular CAR reading list.

may be classes available in campus journalism and mass communication programs that focus generally on CAR. Or there may be more specific classes and seminars focusing on the Internet and online services, survey research, or databases and database analysis. For students in journalism programs that do not offer such courses, there may be other options on campus. There may be course offerings in the business school and in the computer and information systems programs. Business schools often offer business applications courses that cover such basics as word processing, spreadsheets, database programs, and may, in some cases, offer some focus on programming and statistical packages. Courses in computer and information systems departments are often programming oriented for majors and minors, but in some cases these programs will offer entry-level applications or computers in society classes for campus-wide service.

INTERNET GROWTH AND CAR STRATEGIES

Who really knows what will happen with the Internet in the next few years? And how will journalists use the Internet? The answers are certainly not going to be found in these pages.

Not many people know, and if they know, they're not talking about it. But it is intriguing to speculate. Numerous experts who have analyzed the future of world communication point to the information highway, whose foundation might be a television, cable, and telephone system linked together and carrying 500 channels of interactive content. Yet others believe the Internet is the electronic future of the United States and other electronically advanced nations entering the new century. *Newsweek* and *New York Times Magazine* columnist Steven Levy (1995) believes that the Internet and its World Wide Web subset have replaced the television and cable information highway with a computer network and telephone information highway. "[A] different vision of the media future has begun to form. . . . It moved from the academic and scientific communities, then to the business world, then to politics, As it grew and grew, it suddenly became clear that this new vision had the potential to pull the plug on the 500-channel dream," Levy wrote (p. 58). Levy argues that the Web and its variations has arrived and will be the real future. He suggests the day when public stock was initially offered by Netscape Communications Corporation as a benchmark. "Aug. 9 [1995] marked the moment when Wall Street finally realized what had been becoming increasingly apparent to computer users: a set of highly technical but reliably standardized communications protocols known as the Internet had established itself as the real key to the electronic future."

The Internet is expected to continue its extraordinary growth, most experts state. One study released in late 1995 predicted the consumer market for both the Internet and commercial online services will expand, perhaps by as much as 20% in 1996 (Beniger, 1995). But the growth, no matter how meteoric it has been in recent years, was not by any particular design. Development of the Internet into the mid-1990s, as well as its future, has been need driven rather than anything else (Tolhurst, Pike, Blanton, & Harris, 1994).

It is hard for some Internet enthusiasts to quell their excitement about the system. Harley Hahn, senior author of the voluminous *The Internet Complete Reference* (Hahn & Stout, 1994), is one of the preachers of the Internet gospel. His message is quite enticing, even if it may be a little overstated: "The Internet is, by far, the greatest and most significant achievement in the history of mankind. What? Am I saying that the Internet is more impressive than the pyramids? More beautiful than Michaelangelo's David? More important to mankind than the wondrous inventions of the industrial revolution? Yes, yes, and yes" (p. xix).

Hahn argues that the Internet is changing our civilization and has brought with it two "completely unexpected ideas." First, he explains that the Internet focused the efforts of tens of thousands of people into a single purpose—its construction. Second, when the parts of the Internet are connected, it is something much greater than the sum of the parts. "I sense that we are near the beginning of a great and important change in human affairs," he stated. "Personally, I don't understand this change. Indeed, I suspect it is beyond the capabilities of any of us to completely appreciate what is happening, and the best we can do right now is ride the wave" (p. xx).

At the levels of mass communication in society and the newsgathering process, the impact of the Internet and online communication is equally significant, some scholars believe. "Online access to information promises to be extraordinarily important for journalists," wrote *The Online Journalist* authors Randy Reddick and Elliot King (1995, p. 11). "Access will allow reporters to fulfill their roles better."

They added, "In the same way that telephones allowed reporters to interview people around the country, electronic communications networks allow people to locate and obtain information from locations around the world. In short, online information allows reporters to do their jobs better no matter where they are physically located" (p. 14).

A key application already zooming with popularity in some news markets is use of the Internet to disseminate information gathered by a news organization. Electronic newspapers, or variations of them, are common on the Internet and other online sources today (Brill & Cook, 1995, Cameron & Curtin, 1995). One of the early successes was the NandO Times from the Raleigh *News & Observer.* The parent newspaper company, McClatchy Newspapers, continues to expand this product to test its possibilities.

Another form of growth of the Internet will be internal newsroom applications to assist reporters in gathering information. Some newsrooms are beginning to implement these applications already. Users interested in successful starts of this approach should check the work of *The Evansville Courier.* Although originally designed for newsroom staff members as reference tools, this Internet World Wide Web site <http://evansville.net/courier/scoop> has gone public and has become widely used by other journalists as well. The site is updated regularly with new links that may be useful to news librarians, reporters, and copy editors. "For newsroom staff still new to the Internet and unsure about how and whether it is a useful reporting and research tool, a newsroom Web page such as the Evansville effort may be just the way to get everyone started," offers *The Database Files* editor and news research expert Kathleen Hansen (1995, p. 3). "The chaos of the Internet seems a bit tamed when quality information is organized into coherent categories that make sense to journalists working on deadline."

AN INTERNATIONAL HIGH-TECH FAD?

Experts such as Levy would never consider the Internet to be a fad. But will it succeed and grow to expectations as the national communications network of the next century? Or is it more appropriate to extol its benefits within the news business, among professional information gatherers who are part of the true core of users?

Longtime online services authority Alfred Glossbrenner (1995) believes one rapidly growing part of the Internet is not much more than a fad. Glossbrenner, author of several books about the online world for more than a decade, says he is fascinated by the number of computer-literate and "otherwise intelligent" people using the World Wide Web who have not discovered that "there's a lot less there than meets the eye" (p. 64). Glossbrenner concedes WWW pages are attractive, but argues that they take far too long to transmit even at 28.8-Kbps. But his major criticism is that most WWW pages have little or no useful information. The hypertext links, he says, provide an excuse for browsing, but not for much else. Information professionals, he says, will not find it useful because many of these sites are not well developed nor do they offer much useful information:

> Today, most Web sites are "free". But "free" information is likely to be worth exactly what you pay for it. No people in their right minds are going to give away truly valuable information—at least not for long. So, expect to pay for the good stuff on the Web—just as you've got to pay for the good stuff on Nexis, Dialog, Dow Jones, CompuServe, or any other commercial system. But the commercial systems give you powerful search engines, printed manuals, and customer support. They are far better suited to fast, efficient, information retrieval. (p. 64)

Glossbrenner also argues that the Web can be fun to use as any entertainment source might be used and that it is certainly visually appealing. But, he strongly noted, the Web "is largely a gigantic waste of time. Once that realization sinks in, the frenzy will abate—until the hype machines pick up on the next new fad" (p. 64).

Randy Reddick, coauthor of *The Online Journalist* (Reddick & King, 1995) and an Internet authority, feels the general publicity and widespread attention through movies and television programs given to the Internet in the past several years are the real fad. "The hype will fade out. But when the dust settles, the fact of life is that life will have changed. Network communications is going to permeate and is going to be a part of society every bit as much as the telephone is now," Reddick (personal communication, September 21, 1995) stated.

There has been much confusion and uncertainty surrounding the Internet in the past 2 or 3 years. Not even the experts know what will happen to this amazing network of computer systems. Perhaps the most recent attention may be focused on the World Wide Web and its future, but the entire system has left journalists and other professional communicators perplexed about its potential and its future—in a year or two, not to mention a decade or two ahead.

"The Internet is what's between the immediate past and the year 2000. Extraordinarily, it has survived colossal growth and hype," believes Whit Andrews, a free-lance journalist and former Internet trainer for *The Times* in Munster, Indiana:

> The way it works is the way that any future information technology will work, if it does. For American society, the Internet is currently a fad, but that doesn't mean it will stay that way. Roadsters were a fad of sorts, but cars were not. Internal combustion engine-driven vehicles were too expensive for everybody until someone figured out regular people wanted them for utilitarian purposes. Until then, all

cars were aimed at the same market. Computers are now aimed at the same market, upscale dilettantes and ambitious business people, with a small difference between Macs and PC-clone users, which is mostly manufactured by the marketers anyway. That's a long-winded way of saying that the Internet itself is the backbone of some heretofore impossible beast we can only imagine.

PC Week Senior Executive Editor/News John Dodge (1995) shares the consternation over the direction of the Internet: "If you don't intimately understand the World-Wide Web or the Internet, you've got lots of company. It's still forming like a young exploding galaxy. Very little about it has hardened. And no company or person has stepped forward with the killer application that can make the universal Internet business case. What you can do today on the Internet and on no other medium occurred quite by accident" (p. 3).

But use of the Internet and the World Wide Web may not be as trendy as Glossbrenner and others may believe, at least at some levels of use, other experts believe. "In terms of the Internet being a reporting tool at a general level, I think it is definitely not a fad," said William Casey (personal communication, September 22, 1995), CAR director at *The Washington Post*:

> This is fundamentally changing the way people get information and the way they relate to each other. Bad information and bad people signing on the wrong ideas, not withstanding, it's really changing, fundamentally, the way a lot of things happen the same way telephones changed our whole way of life. . . . I can just see there are sources of information for people and these sources are really growing. And there's a lot of day-to-day things that newspapers five years ago thought they would be providing electronically, in terms of hours and schedules and community-oriented kinds of things, it looks like right now that will be on free Web sites by all these organizations. You can imagine all of this bypassing the newspaper completely.

Ray Robinson (personal communication, September 7, 1995), who supervises special projects and CAR at *The Press of Atlantic City*, is like many newsgatherers who feel the Internet is here to stay in journalism:

> I think it's the prototype of something pretty important that will have a profound impact on society and journalists. But for now, it's just a prototype. The information that I've found on the Internet seems a mile wide, but only an inch deep. A lot of it is outdated and the stuff that's up to date usually doesn't have a great deal of detail to it. A lot of the stuff on the World Wide Web is nothing but advertising puffery, which really isn't fit for use in a news story. The other day, I was looking for a copy of the much-discussed White House report on

affirmative action in government. I went to the White House home page. I found pretty pictures of Bill and Hillary, information on tours, and—after drilling deep enough—found a few meaningless statements the president and his advisors had made about the report. But to get the actual information (i.e., the report itself) I had to pick up the telephone, call the White House press office, and ask for a copy—just like reporters have been doing for decades.

And as for the so-called "newsgroups" on Usenet, they're so full of misinformation posted by cranks and crackpots that I very seldom go there. Still, I have a lot of hope for the Internet. It's got incredible potential. The "Thomas" site run by the Library of Congress is an example. The "Edgar" project disseminating Securities and Exchange Commission documents is another.

Mary Kate Leming (personal communication, September 15, 1995), assistant managing editor at the *Palm Beach Post*, is a veteran online news researcher and believes the Internet is just in its infancy as a newsgathering and communication tool:

The idea of the Internet is not a fad. The ability that anybody in the world essentially can present information that the rest of the world can have access to is what the information revolution is all about. I don't think surfing the Internet is going to become part of people's lives. You do it for a while and it's fun. There are some people who are addicted to serendipity and I'm one of them. I think people who really enjoy newspapers are the same kind of people because that's what we get out of a newspaper—the ability to go from one thing to another, read what we want, not focus on one thing. The Internet provides that. There is a group of people that will be interested in the Internet just for that. For the ability to really exchange information, that is not so critical to the general public.

Kathleen Hansen, a former news librarian and information services expert at the University of Minnesota (personal communication, September 19, 1995), explains why she thinks the Internet is a major change in how people communicate and gather information:

I think the corporate world has discovered the Internet, and since it runs the universe, it will find a way to keep it going as long as it suits them. The other reason is that I really believe that we're seeing something of a revolution in the way that people think about information. Brian Eno said something during an interview with a reporter for Wired magazine—he said that the change from the idea of text as a line to the idea of text as a web is one of the most revolutionary things the human mind has conceived. Since I've already said that I think this is really about information rather than about computers and machines, I feel I'm being consistent in saying that the Internet is really about a new and revolutionary way to create, gather, communicate, modify, embellish, and store information. That doesn't seem like a fad to me. I think journalists had better try to understand what that means for their own role in society.

PORTABLES, NETWORKS, AND OTHER INFLUENCES

Portable hardware is making its move into worldwide computing. And with this, it will continue to make an impact on news companies and their newsrooms as well. As the proportion of all computers sold that are portables grows substantially each year, as each new generation of portable PC becomes more and more powerful, the need for desktop systems is reduced.

The old excuses for not substituting a portable such as a laptop or notebook PC for a desktop are disappearing. The standard arguments focusing on storage capacity, screen display color quality and size, processor speed, memory capacity, communications capability, keyboard size, peripherals, and even multimedia tools such as CDs and sound cards are all but gone. Only the industry's seeming inability to boost battery power and strength and lowering its unit price seem to remain as barriers to even wider use of portables in corporate America, at home, and in newsrooms.

Combined with this increasing portability power each year is the growth of wireless tools for communication. Wireless pointing devices, two-way wireless paging, wireless online communications through cellular systems, and other tools will only enhance newsroom computing and broaden and deepen the information-gathering potential of journalists.

Newsroom Network Strategies

Networks of computers share resources, and networks of personal computers are growing in popularity and use in newsrooms as older proprietary word processing systems wear out. Networks, whether they are local, such as in a newsroom, or wide, such as linking a number of distant sites, are important to news organizations today and will continue to grow in importance. With the advent of more reliable and less expensive wireless networking, the reach of networks will also continue to be extended. To fully draw the power of computing, wired and wireless linked personal computers are necessary.

A recent study by Workgroup Technologies forecast astronomical growth in the number of remote network users in the years ahead.

These are individuals who enter their company's computer systems with remote connections. There were about 3 million personal computer users in the United States networked in some form in 1994 and about 8 million in 1995, and that number was expected to double to about 17 million in 1996 and double again to almost 30 million in 1997 (Costa, 1995a).

Networks are one of the ways CAR has spread in the newsroom of the *Duluth News-Tribune* in Minnesota. A medium-size daily of 60,000 daily circulation, the newspaper has linked all newsroom PCs with a local area network. Research and Technology Editor Jody Cox (personal communication, March 15, 1995) explained how the newsroom staff benefits: "Our new PC-based front-end system offers us a leg up in CAR," Cox explained. "We've got Excel and Access up on our network. We plan to add Internet access and eventually go online with our paper."

Merging Technologies and Merging Media?

Rich Gordon (1995), director of online services at *The Miami Herald*, feels that print news organizations can be successful in the future, but it will require changes:

> If we are going to be successful in a multi-media future, we are going to need to use our content, our brand name, and our talented staff as a foundation and then build a completely different product or products on top of it. We are going to need to find, filter, and deliver information that is so valuable, so easy to use, so essential to people's lives, so customized to the individual, that it's worth a lot more than we now charge for it. If we achieve this, people, I think, will pay more or it will make more advertisers see more merit in subsidizing in what we do. To do this . . . newsrooms will have to look completely different.
>
> First off, reporters, editors, and news researchers are going to need the right tools. They are going to need up-to-date computers, networked together with access to the Internet, online databases, and all the hardware and software they need to find, analyze, and share information effectively. More broadly, newspapers are going to have to invest a lot more in technology. Reporters are going to need a lot of new skills. . . . Reporters and editors are going to have to learn to think about information in a fundamentally different way. They are going to need to think about databases, the kinds of information that people are going to find essential. They are going to need to think about the kind of information people are willing to pay for. The set of skills we have been calling computer-assisted journalism, I think, are going to become more important in that regard.

In 1994, the average cost of a year's subscription to a Knight-Ridder newspaper was $129, or a little over $10 a month. Gordon (1995) noted that this is about the same cost at that time as a month's use of a commercial online service such as CompuServe or America Online:

> Depending on how you look at it, that's either depressing or, maybe, a little bit encouraging. It is depressing because millions of Americans are willing to pay about what they pay for their newspaper to a company that does no original journalism. It just packages information from a variety of sources and delivers it to your home over the telephone line to your computer. It is encouraging because it suggests we might have an edge in a future where our companies deliver information in lots of different ways. On paper, to be sure, but also online, fax machines, over cable wires . . . Lord only knows what the possibilities are.

A number of news organizations are exploring alternative electronic distribution systems that include use of the Internet and commercial services. At the same time, some news organizations are using CAR-related databases as revenue sources, or, at least, there is discussion of the prospects. Some journalists oppose using public information in database form as revenue sources, fearing it will increase cost or difficulty of access to the original information. Selling data, whether it has been enhanced or "value added" by the newsroom, is a debatable issue. It dominated several weeks of discussion, for example, in 1995 on NICAR-L, the NICAR list server on the Internet. However, news organizations with electronic full-text, searchable archives have been generating revenue from those databases for more than a decade and there seems to be no objection to reselling those originally developed databases to help meet news library expenses.

There will be new services offered in the next decade that will offer new revenue prospects as well. One example is the looming digitalization of photograph archives. The prospect of selling access to these electronic images is just as real as the prospect of selling text archives a decade to two decades ago seemed. But the big interest in computers and distribution in the last half of this decade will be the form of that message. Will it contain text? Graphics? Photographs? Of course. Will it include audio and video clips? Perhaps. How will be it distributed? Subscription? Online services such as the ones already in use (e.g., *The Washington Post's* Digital Ink, Raleigh *News & Observer's* NandO Times, or the *San Jose Mercury News'* Mercury Center)? How will the final products look? Like a newspaper? A multimedia extravaganza? And, of course, there are questions about how subscribers or members—or whatever they wind up being called—will receive their products.

Microsoft Corporation Chairman Bill Gates, whose thinking about the future of computing carries considerable weight, recently looked into his crystal ball to think about the future of computing. Gates (1995) wrote:

> As we look further into the future, the personal computer itself will assume some new form. The portable will be like a tabloid paper you can carry around. You will commonly have a wireless connection. The server PC will scale up to beyond the largest computers we have now. And we will have two new form factors for which there is no current analogy: the large screen machine that you are far away from (which we call the TV PC) and a very small device you can put in your pocket that we call the Wallet PC. Finally, there will be a special form of what is almost a kiosk PC—but one that is publicly available where ever there's a pay phone, an Automated Teller Machine or a fax machine today. It will be a screen-based device in which you place your "smart card" and see your messages, browse information, initiate a video conference, get cash, and do anything you want to do with information on a very easy basis. (p. 62)

Suggestions of this type by Gates and his mammoth Microsoft Corporation have numerous implications for computer-based journalism for certain, and, perhaps, journalism in general. Miami's Gordon (1995) observed:

> I honestly believe that the future for journalists is bright. Journalists, if they are truly excellent at what they do, will be more important and more highly valued than they are today. That's the good news. The bad news is that we might all be working for Bell South, TCI Cable, or Microsoft. I think even today, maybe naively, that most newspapers retain some important values that Bell South or Microsoft don't have and never will. I prefer to keep working for a company with a newspaper's values, not a phone company's, not Bill Gates'. If we don't make the adjustments we need to make as fast as we need to make them, I think our future is very much at risk.

To meet the needs of the changing information needs and changing distribution system, *The Miami Herald's* Gordon believes journalists must further develop their skills with computers. "I think journalists are going to have to get a lot better at finding and analyzing information. They are going to need to know how to search the Web, how to track down information in government databases, and how to make sense out of numbers. I think the math-phobic and technophobic among us may have a place in our business in the future, but I think that place is definitely shrinking," Gordon (1995), a former assistant metro editor and CAR editor, believes.

CONCERNS, PROBLEMS, AND TAKING RISKS WITH COMPUTERS

Reporters and editors directly involved in CAR sense its problems better than outside observers or those who would like to use it but do not. One environmental reporter, Whit Andrews (personal communication, October 6, 1995), who specializes in using the Internet in his work and trains other reporters and editors in his Indiana newsroom, sees two major difficulties with CAR:

> As with any new technology that costs any money or time, there are two problems: The first is that there are people who fail to fit the innovation into already successful patterns of work, but instead embrace it utterly as a universal cure for all ills. *The Bartlett's Familiar Quotations* available at the Bartleby Project is profoundly out of date, for instance, and valuable mainly for Victorian-era homilies. The paper (up-to-date) *Bartlett's* could very easily be more useful. But there are people who will shrug at quotes that can't be found in the Internet version and surrender. Internet research is a tile in a mosaic. Take out the tile and the image is less comprehensible; look only at the one tile and the image is invisible.

> The second problem is access. Poorer newspapers and freelance reporters are more likely to lack access to expensive computers and Internet links. This is improving. You could set up a starter CAR program for $300 now and maintain a commercial online service Internet link for $20 monthly. One problem is that some papers and plenty of freelancers don't have that. Everybody's got a pad and pencil.

Surviving the Period of Change

Philip Meyer (personal communication, September 23, 1995), one of the first journalists to use computer tools regularly in his reporting for the *Detroit Free Press* and *The Miami Herald*, feels journalism and newsgathering are in a period of change:

> Right now, the whole field is evolving and the stage it is in right now is that all the easy projects have been done. These are the ones where you use the computer as a searching device or a sorting device. The next layer of problems involves statistical analysis, drawing conclusions, asking questions of the data in a way that you are not fooled by the answer. And that takes some training in scientific method and requires some statistical tools. And I think a lot of computer-assisted

reporters are just now beginning to realize that they need to go to that next level.

Neill Borowski, director of CAR for *The Philadelphia Inquirer,* agrees:

> To a degree now, the CAR record is skipping. Everybody is using the same databases to do the same stories—which is fine, there are good stories in each market—but what's the next big story? What's the next big database we'll discover and do a big story on? I think a lot of it will be grow-your-own. You have to go out and build your own databases. . . . I think we have to figure out a way to do it efficiently and cheaply. (personal communication, November 17, 1995)

More Original Programming?

Another direction for CAR in the future will be programming. At some newspapers, programming has already become a part of the CAR process. In most cases, this does not mean developing software to fill voids where products do not exist on the business software market. Instead, it means using programming tools such as Visual Basic or Delphi to develop programs to execute analytical tasks and solve data entry problems. These programs are often called "front ends" because they are placed "on top" of an existing database and are used in conjunction with a powerful relational database program or other database management system.

Tom Torok, a member of the CAR team at *The Philadelphia Inquirer,* specializes in preparing "front ends," or programs, for his newsroom databases. Torok's Windows programs are an example of how a sometimes difficult to use database program can be made easier to use for less computer-literate reporters and editors. Torok, a former columnist and reporter for his newspaper, began preparing these tools for the newsroom in conjunction with databases the newspaper acquired in 1994. One example is a voter registration database. All registered voters in Philadelphia are included in a database on a network server in the newsroom. Torok's front-end program, written in Visual Basic to work in Windows, makes searching for information about voters much simpler for the casual user. Reporters can search by address, name, or other characteristics of a voter registration record.

"With these front ends available, even if people know databases, they don't have to get in there and massage it, get familiar with it, and find out what it is," Torok (personal communication, November 17, 1995) stated. "By having these things, you are going to start seeing . . . a scope, depth, and context that is unmatched. Even if you are not hitting the ball out of the park every day in day-to-day reporting, you are going to see a significant increase in quality that nobody else will have. That's the future."

Torok also sees greater integration of databases at two levels. First, he feels public databases will be combined or be able to be merged more easily that at present. Instead of a state or federal agency having a half dozen or more distinct databases, there will be fewer, perhaps even one. Second, Torok also sees this convergence of databases occurring in newsrooms as well:

> Perhaps with this latest generation of databases and computers, newsrooms will become more integrated in their data. Things won't be in so many separate compartments. If you need to link one piece of data to another, you are going to be able to do it rather quickly and not in such a cumbersome way. You can make more complex relationships known that you couldn't before. I think you are going to be able to get into a lot of factor analysis, even though we won't be reporting it, we will be able to identify issues just by them being there, in relationships that are not readily apparent. (personal communication, November 17, 1995)

Need for More Knowledge of Statistics

The addition of statistics skills as part of the CAR tool kit may be another important stage of growth and level of success for journalists using computers in their work. Basic bivariate analysis—using two variables at the same time for analysis—is the limit of many journalists' statistical skills. Most commonly, this means running contingency tables, or cross tabulations with a spreadsheet or statistical package. Philip Meyer (personal communication, September 23, 1995) feels an example of moving to the next level is analyzing the relationship of two variables with a third variable or even more variables. One such approach is regression analysis.

> The way that diffuses is somebody finds an application for one kind of story and then other newspapers copy it. One place I've seen regression used is in evaluating schools. They used "percent on school lunch" as one of the variables. It is a very strong predictor of the average test score in a school. And then you can use that to produce an adjusted ranking of schools based on their test scores. You can equalize the playing field so that we statistically adjust for the number of poor kids in the school, then we can re-rank the schools and see which schools produce the best results with the kinds of kids that they get. And that's been done in at least three places.

Meyer feels journalists may be becoming instant social scientists. "That's legitimate. We've always been instant historians. We can write history in a hurry, we might as well write social science in a hurry," Meyer stated.

With this comes potential risks and problems. Randy Reddick, a journalism professor at Texas Tech University, summarized the main concern:

> We may be letting the Genie out of the bottle. We're putting a loaded automatic weapon in the hands of a bunch of kids. We're teaching journalists how to push the buttons, but not how to understand. They don't have the background to really understand necessarily what we are dealing with. Maybe we need a way of thinking and a way of approaching data. If we're arming people with these Uzies, or SPSS, or whatever we're arming them with, then we need to run them through a different type of boot camp. We need to get big time into data analysis. (personal communication, September 21, 1995)

Daniel Browning (personal communication, October 16, 1995), CAR specialist for the *Saint Paul Pioneer Press,* feels original analysis is a soft spot for many journalists involved in CAR. "Editors and reporters alike have a hard time getting around the concept that our analysis is our analysis. They're more comfortable quoting some academic or government official and are fearful of relying on our own assessment of the data. This is problematic," Browning stated. "All CAR stories are generated out of the muck of data by the inquisition of the reporter/analyst. In that sense, we are creating the news we seek to cover. That makes many people nervous, as well it should."

Reddick warned of the dangers of giving such tools to unprepared persons. "Problems can occur when you misread, misinterpret data, and so forth, and go running with it. It now gets repeated to the point that error becomes truth and we act upon false assumptions," Reddick stated.

"Folks still don't get what CAR's good for and what it's not good for. That folks—editors in particular—think of computers as some sort of magic boxes on which you type a few keys and PRESTO! an investigation into government corruption pops out. Until news managers and reporters understand that CAR generally takes more time but permits deeper journalism, database journalism will never move to the next step and become truly widespread," stated Neil Reisner (personal communication, October 30, 1995), NICAR training director. "The problem is this: We are used to collecting anecdotes and from them reducing situations into black-and-white, good-and-bad, or otherwise binary views. Computers make that a lot harder. In general, the truth is usually a lot more gray and that's what computers let us understand. But that often doesn't make happy the folks who have to get the paper out every day and want nothing more than a good gotcha! story with which to lead the front page."

PERCEPTIONS OF CAR'S PROBLEMS AND FAILURES

Respondents to the 1995 national CAR survey were asked what they thought were the major failings in their newsrooms involving CAR. As shown in Table 8.1, there were three major areas of concern. The leading issue is related training. A total of 18% of the editors and reporters replying to this question stated there was slowness in learning CAR in their newsrooms. The second most common prob-

TABLE 8.1
Perceived Biggest CAR Failures, 1995

Type of Failure	Frequency	Percentage	Adjusted Percentage
Slow to learn to use	21	7.3%	18.3%
Not taking advantage of CAR	20	7.0	17.4
Can take too long	16	5.6	13.9
Not using it	9	3.1	7.8
Lack of access	7	2.4	6.1
Not enough time to learn it	7	2.4	6.1
Need expertise	6	2.1	5.2
Lack of support	4	1.4	3.5
Not having it	4	1.4	3.5
Trouble with government data	3	1.0	2.6
Need to control cost	3	1.0	2.6
We're lost so far	2	0.7	1.7
No story ideas	2	0.7	1.7
Not enough training	2	0.7	1.7
Can't find information we want	2	0.7	1.7
Editors don't understand it	1	0.3	0.9
Seduced by high-tech	1	0.3	0.9
Getting bad information	1	0.3	0.9
No comprehensive approach	1	0.3	0.9
Don't share resources	1	0.3	0.9
Information lost, cut stories	1	0.3	0.9
Not reusing data	1	0.3	0.9
Missing	172	59.9	Missing
Totals	287	100.0	100.0

Note. n = 287; missing observations = 172.

lem, cited by 17%, was a perception that not enough people were taking enough advantage of these tools that did exist in their newsrooms. The third most cited concern reflected some impatience. CAR was perceived to take too long by about 14% of the responding newspapers. Other concerns included: not using it (8%), not enough access to CAR resources (6%), not enough time to learn it (6%), and need for expertise in the newsroom (5%). It should be noted that 60% of the newspapers in the 1995 survey did not reply to the question.

Editors and reporters working in CAR were also given the chance to make other general comments about the state of CAR in the United States in 1995. These open-ended comments are quite revealing when content is analyzed and quantified. Table 8.2 reveals that the most frequently made comment (15%) was that the newspaper staff was just beginning to learn CAR techniques, reflecting the still-new status of using computer tools for newsgathering in many U.S. newspaper newsrooms. Second on this list was expression that reporters must learn CAR (7%), that CAR is not a separate entity and cannot be treated that way (7%), and that the responding news organization wanted results of the survey when they were made available (7%).

A second layer of concerns place focus on the financial side of CAR. Additional comments said the newspaper was not budgeted for CAR (6%), that there was a need for inexpensive CAR methods (6%), and the new organization's editors do not support CAR (6%). The complete list reveals a wide range of many concerns that suggest the newspaper industry needs to place its attention on training and support, strategies and uses, and on annual budgeting on resources for CAR. It should be noted that only 24% of the responding newspapers in the survey chose to respond to this optional item.

THE BASE OF CAR PROBLEMS MAY BE WIDENING

In addition to the concerns and issues raised in the preceding pages, there are still other concerns about CAR expressed by those who use it the most. As more and more individuals begin to use computers in information gathering, the number of daily problems grows as well. Some of these are explained in the following.

Simply Too Much E-Information

How many e-mail messages do online journalists receive in a single day? Some journalists are light e-mail users and receive only one

TABLE 8.2
Miscellaneous Comments About CAR, 1995

Type of Comment	Frequency	Percentage	Adjusted Percentage
Just starting, learning	10	3.5%	14.5%
Wants study results	5	1.7	7.2
Reporters must learn CAR	5	1.7	7.2
CAR is not a separate entity	5	1.7	7.2
Need cheap CAR methods	4	1.4	5.8
Not budgeted for CAR	4	1.4	5.8
Editors don't support CAR	4	1.4	5.8
Look forward to beginning	3	1.0	4.3
Feel overwhelmed	2	0.7	2.9
Hope to begin within a year	2	0.7	2.9
Hope to begin in 1995	2	0.7	2.9
Need to get many involved	2	0.7	2.9
Local news oriented, no CAR	2	0.7	2.9
Staff not yet motivated	2	0.7	2.9
Teaching CAR is tough	2	0.7	2.9
Training for CAR is essential	2	0.7	2.9
We're behind at this	2	0.7	2.9
Some disappointments so far	1	0.3	1.4
Use it for quick backgrounding	1	0.3	1.4
We're committed to CAR	1	0.3	1.4
CAR is in danger of overhype	1	0.3	1.4
Papers slow to adopt technology	1	0.3	1.4
Investigating online uses	1	0.3	1.4
Moving to more frequent use	1	0.3	1.4
Many changes in year	1	0.3	1.4
Online is most popular CAR tool	1	0.3	1.4
New newsroom system helps	1	0.3	1.4
Government agencies resistant	1	0.3	1.4
Missing	218	76.0	Missing
Total	287	100.0	100.0

Note. n = 287; missing cases = 218.

or two, perhaps even no messages in a single day. Journalists on a newsroom network might get a few more. Those on the Internet may have busier electronic mailboxes. And those on electronic conferences and distribution lists may be drowning in e-mail. These individuals are already victims of an information overload, a glut, of the transmissions that are the result of easy-to-transfer and mass-distribution messages. Unfortunately, many of them are a waste of time of the sender and the receiver.

Even in a normal newsroom environment, there is a lot of e-mail traffic on the local network: messages relating to stories, projects, meetings, scheduling, office politics, gossip, and company policy. But there is a decent supply of e-mail that is not necessary, even counterproductive to the cause. Some companies, but no newsrooms that have made the policy public yet, have actually stopped e-mail access during certain times in the business day to enhance employee productivity. Some individuals who consider themselves to be heavy e-mail users check their mail at "quiet" times during the early morning or late evening and use screening software to filter out unwanted junk e-mail (Foley, 1995).

Information overflow is coming in other forms as well and these have been well documented. Editors often have complained of too much copy from news services, for example, that must be reviewed for potential use. Public relations firms have discovered fax machines and are now discovering e-mail and other electronic transmission forms to get their messages to news organizations. Many of these organizations have recently found the Internet to be a good medium for this purpose, creating World Wide Web sites, for example, for spreading the gospel of their clients.

E-mail is one example of overflow of electronic information. The valueless information that seems to dominate more and more of the World Wide Web and other systems that are part of the Internet is another. With computers and their speed and comparative ease in locating information comes some heavy baggage: Some of that information is not the type most journalists want to gather.

The High Expectations Syndrome

There are numerous other things troubling journalists about computers and newsgathering. The high-tech nature of the tools give users and beneficiaries such as editors sometimes unrealistic hope for all projects regardless of their nature. This might be labeled the "high expectations" syndrome.

Atlantic City's Ray Robinson points to high expectations that many journalists, especially editors, now hold about CAR, and he feels the perception can be troublesome: "Expectations are too high. People don't understand the limitations. I've had staffers come to me and ask if I can get on the Internet and get them copies of all the expense vouchers that some obscure government official has put in for the past five years. All I can say is, 'Sorry. No.' When we're working on stories involving record analysis, people are always disappointed that there's still work to be done after the computer work is finished. They seem to think the computer will make the calls and write their story for them too," Robinson (personal communication, September 5, 1995) stated.

Isolated Number Crunchers

The growing philosophy to integrate CAR into all areas of the newsroom and to train all reporters to use it has led to a relatively new problem: isolating the number crunchers. Too many times, CAR editors and reporters are given their own corner of the newsroom and told to work on their projects on their own, not being a part of the news flow or newsroom activities on a regular basis. Several years ago, when CAR was very new, this was not considered a problem. It is becoming one in the minds of some CAR experts.

"CAR has been cordoned off in many newsrooms as an exotic skill accessible only to wizards. These barriers prevent editors from doing their jobs: Asking tough questions to keep headstrong reporters from getting the newspaper into trouble," observed Dan Browning (personal communication, October 16, 1995), a CAR specialist for the *Saint Paul Pioneer Press.* "Related to this is the fact that there's some bad CAR projects being done. It's easy to make mistakes and even easier for the mistakes to get buried under pages and pages of code. So far, the readers seem cowed by CAR projects. Someday, someone is going to get a CAR reporter on a witness stand and grill him or her about his methods and whether this or that statistical test was considered, and so on."

Giving Credit for Work Well Done

As more and more news stories involving computer-based information gathering are published or broadcast, the issue of providing proper credit has arisen. For both electronic and printed forms of journalism, it can become a sticky issue. Some news organizations, for example, are beginning to give "trailer" credit for online or other forms of valuable background research conducted by news librarians. And some news organizations are readily giving credit for individuals handling analysis or data processing for database-oriented stories. But there is still a problem looming over this issue.

"CAR is still struggling for respect in newsrooms—evidenced by problems over by-lines. Is CAR reporting worthy of a byline? I say yes. Yet, this is a topic that is debated since by-lines are handled differently across the board," stated Rose Ciotta (personal communication, November 22, 1995), CAR editor at *The Buffalo News.* "I am leaning toward this model: When the CAR person does the analysis and hands off info, use a 'nerd box.' Use a tagline when the contribution is less. Use a double byline when the data person also shares in writing and interviewing. Don't ever let anyone in newsroom put the CAR person in a gopher role or something less than reporting."

Recycling Mistakes and Errors

One of the problems with online full-text archives is their easy access and frequent use. A problem? It is when these databases contain errors that are researched and repeated in new stories. Another problem with errors that comes with computing is in production as well. When the two types of errors are combined, it makes for mistakes with a long shelf life.

"The considerable ease with which text can be moved around contributes to more stranded words and typographical errors, which in turn are harder to detect on a screen than on paper. Factual errors can live a long time in an electronic data base," observed *The Virginian-Pilot* Editor Cole C. Campbell (1995, p. A2).

A similar problem exists with databases. Any journalist experienced with public records databases knows there are countless ways errors can enter the database and many are hard, if at all possible, to detect. These mistakes are often also recycled when analysis occurs and, unfortunately, often published in the form of mistaken identity or other troubling inaccuracies.

Improper Attribution and Plagiarism

Another burden that online archives and other database information carry is that of unattributed use of material. Some of it is wanton—to the extent that it is plagiarism at an ethical level and copyright law violation at a legal level. Most of these errors are made by careless journalists using database sources without proper attribution in their stories. The attribution problem occurs at several levels, but the most significant ones are complete lack of attribution or incomplete and inadequate attribution in the text of the story in which it is used.

"I have to go back to one of my pet peeves about online information searching. Journalists are finding all sorts of wonderful ways to make use of their expanded information universe in their stories. Sadly, some of them are also finding all sorts of ways to plagiarize, steal, copy, and put new tops on old bottoms of someone else's work. That is a downside of the online revolution," states Minnesota's Hansen (personal communication, September 19, 1995). "The way that a 'frame' gets put on a story, especially an ongoing and complicated one, and then gets repeated and repeated and repeated by every journalist with a laptop and a modem is really scandalous."

A large majority of plagiarism problems come from misuse by the journalist. Some, however, are caused by incomplete information provided by the source. Numerous sites on the Internet, for example, often offer information without clear acknowledgment of its author or its origins. Some commercial archives have similar problems, but are generally much better in providing the original source of information contained in its libraries and databases.

This is actually an easy problem to solve. Simply put, newsroom managers as well as their database and online trainers need to place more emphasis on forms of credit and attribution. Instead of emphasizing brevity, often at the expense of proper credit, newsroom leaders must place more value on proper forms of attribution and insist that reporters and editors use it.

Verification of Information Sources

Related to attribution and plagiarism problems is the trouble caused by journalists who use information from online and database sources with limited or no attempt to verify the information. Most journalists involved with any form of CAR have a commonsense rule of thumb: Check the information obtained online or in a database the same way a reporter would check the information obtained on the street or in a written report. Verify it from a second or, if needed, a third independent source.

The danger of many inexperienced journalists is to believe that information obtained from a public records database, an online service, or from a site on the Internet is correct. Experienced users know this is not always the case. Some databases, some services, and some Internet sites are more reliable than others. Experience will reveal which is reliable and which is not. If there is any doubt, double check database information, no matter its source or the level of sophistication of the information. Too often databases contain errors in basic fact that could be caused by transmission error, keypunching carelessness, the dated nature of the information, and other technical or human causes. It pays to be careful and take the time to verify.

Misuse of Statistics

Stephen Doig, associate editor for research at *The Miami Herald*, has built a reputation for his expertise in CAR in the past decade. Among his projects are a remarkable study of damage caused by Hurricane Andrew that his newspaper published only a few months after the storm. It was an important part of the package of coverage that helped win a Pulitzer Prize for the newspaper in 1993. Doig is acutely concerned about the use and misuse of statistics in CAR as journalists begin to move into the area of social science in terms of issues, problems, research tools, and methodologies.

"Is this something journalists ought to be doing without heavy social science training?" Doig (personal communication, September 21, 1995) asked. "I'm on the middle ground. I'm doing it. In the beginning, I was an enthusiastic committer of it because I figured it was easy. And, as I learned more of the power of statistics, as I have discovered more of the things that can be done, and those that shouldn't be done, I've become at least more cautious about what I'm doing with it. I'm not saying don't do it, but I'm saying it's relatively easy to make horribly embarrassing mistakes doing this stuff if you're not careful."

Some experienced CAR journalists believe that database analysis software offers so many tools that they can become dangerous in the wrong hands. "In an odd way, these programs may offer too much to too many of us," wrote Bill Casey (1995, p. F13), *Washington Post* director of CAR, in his computing column Cybertalk. "Misuse a grammar checker and the worst that happens is worser English. But dabble in data analysis and you can end up with wrong results—you think your company is making money when actually it's losing it. And the results that may not appear to be wrong at all."

Casey added:

> I know the answer for me. I've been using electronic spreadsheets since 1982—but a mortgage schedule I calculated for a private loan was inaccurate for the whole of year of 1993. Why? I set it up wrong, incorrectly linking two "cells" in the spreadsheet. Don't attempt this one at home!
>
> No computer program, no matter how good, substitutes for a strong, resilient background of mathematical understanding—ideally one that starts in our earliest school years and never stops developing. Regression analysis is a good case in point. As with other branches of a field known as inferential statistics, regression has undergone rapid growth in use in the past forty years. It is fundamental to work in myriad fields because it enables the influence of multiple factors to be measured and compared.

Ed Perkins (personal communication, March 23, 1995), managing editor of the 89,000-circulation *South Bend Tribune* in Indiana, is also concerned about reporters and editors misusing CAR tools, one of the major problems in the field. "We need to get more people involved. I am very concerned that reporters are analyzing data with no knowledge of statistics," Perkins explained. "What they see as trends may be just normal variance in the data sample."

Jack Lail (personal communication, September 30, 1995), assistant managing editor/technology for the *Knoxville News-Sentinel*, thinks the problem with statistics in journalism is a matter of drawing meaning from the numbers. "One of the easiest things to do is interpret the data wrong. Just because the computer produces some numbers doesn't mean the reporters or editors know what they mean. Since most of us have not had the grounding in this type of analysis in college, professional organizations are crucial to helping us get the skills to do this correctly."

Information "Surfing" and Data Crunching

Minnesota's Kathleen Hansen describes one big problem with CAR as "information surfing." Hansen (personal communication, September 19, 1995) explained:

I really see CAR as comprised of two facets—what Jean [Ward] and I call "information surfing" and "data crunching" in the next edition of our *Search Strategies* book [Ward & Hansen, 1996]. Information surfing is the information-gathering part of CAR. Data crunching is the data analysis part. I see two main problems: One is with information surfing—quality concerns are not as high as they need to be. Just because you found something in a database doesn't mean it is worth diddly. I'm not yet convinced that reporters, editors, and even some librarians, are as wary as they should be about the quality of information they find when information surfing.

The other major problem is with the data crunching aspect of CAR. It is not yet clear to me that reporters and editors have the requisite data analysis skills to confidently and accurately analyze much of the information they pour into their spreadsheets and DB management programs. Beyond that, and at an even more esoteric level, it is not clear that reporters and editors even know how to pose appropriate and interesting questions to ask of their data. Just because you've got this machine-readable file of data doesn't automatically lead to the conclusion that there are interesting and important questions that file can answer. And if they pose an interesting question, I am concerned that many CAR enthusiasts don't have the skills to structure their data analysis to generate reliable and valid results.

Changing Government Data Access Policies

Access to public information is a daily matter in the mid-1990s. Because technology has far outpaced law at the federal, state, and local levels, there remains a large amount of uncertainty about access of electronic public records. Most state open records laws have not yet been amended to consider electronic records. In some cases, access has been permitted for several years, but agency officials have reassessed the access issue and changed their minds. This has occurred at the executive level in most cases, but sometimes it has occurred at the legislative level, resulting in modified state statutes about access to some categories of records.

Another problem area is cost of the information. Most database-oriented reporters and editors have their "war stories" to tell about high-priced data. Although negotiations and repeated requests have usually resulted in compromises satisfactory to both sides, there remain problems in some states and local governments that put electronic records—analyzable data—out of reach of journalists. There are several possible reasons for this, says Hal Straus (personal communication, April 10, 1995), veteran database editor for the *Atlanta Constitution:* "Agencies are becoming more resistant to releasing electronic information, except on their own terms. Reasons? Financial—they want the money. Political—they've figured out that data are quite convincing and need to be controlled/spun."

CAR Hardware and Software Expense

Despite the fact that prices for computer hardware and software are slowly dropping, some editors and reporters feel CAR requires too much effort or too many resources to justify using it. For these resource-scarce news organizations, especially small daily and weekly newspapers, small-market television stations, small and specialized magazines and newsletters, any expenses for computers not related to production may be too much.

This problem is a considerable one because it often prohibits a news organization from beginning CAR at any level. Solutions to this problem have been widely publicized and discussed—ones such as using inexpensive shareware or last year's software, using hand-me-down hardware, or borrowing and sharing resources (Garrison, 1995). Despite the entry-level approaches that have been promoted by those already involved in CAR, the problem of getting started remains at many news organizations because of cost. Some optimism should exist, perhaps, if only because there is more computer to be had and more computing power to be used in today's systems for a lot less money. Little more than a decade ago, a dual disk drive system, running without a hard drive, using a monochrome monitor and 48K of memory, cost more than $2,000. And there was little to do with that system other than writing and primitive spreadsheet analysis.

The point is that there is much to be done with little or no investment in hardware and software. If a journalist wants to begin CAR, it can be done for little more than most newsrooms spend on stamps or fax machine paper.

Time Consumption

Numerous critics of CAR claim that it takes too much time and offers, often, little rewards in terms of the news story that is produced from the effort. This criticism has much more validity when the process is beginning because any sort of computer education process has a steep learning curve in the beginning. And with the perception of wasted or misused time comes skepticism about the potential success of CAR.

"Newspapers are very production driven. We get a product out the door every day. And if you are talking about taking a couple of people, letting them off, not putting a byline in the paper for a couple of months, that's where managers have a problem with CAR," believes Mary Kate Leming (personal communication, September 15, 1995), assistant managing editor at the *Palm Beach Post.* "It's not whether or not they are using a computer, it's how they are spending their time and whether it is the most productive use of the newspaper's time."

David Brooks, a copy editor who oversees Internet access and use for the 30,000-circulation *Telegraph* in Nashua, New Hampshire, offers that point of view. "The return, in terms of stories, is too small to justify time for small newspapers," he said.

Computer Dependency

Some journalists have become computer dependent. This simply means that they blindly believe their computers, with the new bells and whistles, will do everything. There is a major flaw in this reasoning. Computers don't do everything, of course. They cannot draw meaning from the data that have been processed or the information gathered from a remote site.

Christopher Feola, who manages the systems, new media, and CAR for the *Waterbury Republican-American* in Connecticut, strongly feels this is dangerous for reporters and editors. "Here's the tricky part about computer-assisted reporting. The computer doesn't have a brain. You do. The computer gives you questions, not answers. The computer arms you with the data you need to go in and ask intelligent questions," Feola (1995, p. 16) stated. "If the mayor of Big City says the jump in spending or taxes or whatever was caused by the feds, run the numbers. But don't leap to conclusions. Lots of things can cause a big jump in spending. Bad storms can cause road repair spending to jump, for example."

CAR as Social Science

Journalists have always had their academic roots in the social sciences. Most journalism programs at major universities and colleges had origins in a social–psychological tradition. There is no doubt that journalists and social sciences have much in common—both study human behavior, both seek the truth, both are analytical in nature and seek understanding of the behavior they study. The similarities of journalists and social scientists in their methods of inquiry have long been noted by individuals such as Philip Meyer in his original edition of *Precision Journalism* (1973) and Maxwell McCombs, Donald L. Shaw, and David Grey in their ground-breaking *Handbook of Reporting Methods* (1976).

Some CAR specialists would like to advance their analytical and methodological skills to approximate the levels of practicing social scientists. Is this possible without formal advanced or graduate-level education? Do journalists, even a few in each newsroom, need to have this level of expertise? These questions are becoming more and more a concern of those interested in CAR and those whose skills have advanced beyond the basic levels.

"When I discovered that, in fact, that sociologists disagreed about a measurement, then I figured, 'Why can't I do it too?' If we're down to opinion about how it ought to be done, then my opinion, given a certain amount of background and so on, is as reasonable as theirs," *The Miami Herald*'s Doig (personal communication, September 21, 1995) reasoned. "If the newspaper ideal is to print the truth, what I've learned is the truth is actually pretty fuzzy about some things. You can take the same set of data and produce different versions of truth. If you try to be honest with what you are doing and, in fact, you can do it well, you can produce something that is defensible."

KNOWING COMPUTER ABILITIES AND LIMITATIONS

Perhaps the long list of potential problems and dangers of using computers in journalism contained in the preceding section raises proper caution flags for most journalists. This does not mean journalists should avoid using computers. In fact, the opposite is the desired position. However, in using computers, journalists must know their abilities and limitations of those abilities when it comes to using computers to gather information or analyze and interpret information to be used in a news story. Assuming that a computer is the end-all solution is a very precarious attitude to take when it comes to reporting and editing news. Thus, the most experienced computer users in newsrooms know their capabilities and know when to go to for additional assistance. Pride is often a factor in any journalistic effort, but veteran CAR supervisors are not afraid to go to others within the company, such as management information systems people, or experts on the outside, such as academic specialists, software experts, or even professional statisticians. They have no ego problems. They want to do the job right.

William Casey is a veteran computer user. Casey, director of CAR for *The Washington Post,* strongly believes that knowing your limitations with a computer is critical to overall success with CAR:

> It's real important for people to have enough skills to do some things, but to be aware of them enough to come to ask others with more experience about how to proceed or set it up if it gets complex because a lot of this does. It's frustrating for anybody in the business to see someone repeating the same errors that he made ten years ago. I'm not saying this happens a lot, but it happens everywhere. There should be a process that allows people to do the work themselves, but also to draw on the expertise that's around them. (personal communication, September 22, 1995)

Casey feels this is an even larger problem than simply making mistakes:

> These are more conceptual errors that people make. If I have these data and I put these numbers in and if I look at these numbers in the output, it will make this result and I can make this statement. Well, there are a lot of steps in that process and we are pretty careful about being orderly and make sure that it comes out fairly and it comes out accurately. But with more people in the newsroom doing more things and having more of those kinds of tools, it is a conceptual problem: Is every story getting the full benefit of balance, modeling, or whatever other issues are going into it? Most computer stories don't involve a lot of social science or modeling. They involve using a computer in a primitive way, which is perfectly okay. . . . But there is still the problem of errors. I just don't do anything without knowing I'm going to have to go back and reproduce it. I document it as I go along so I remember what I did and why. I have to have these cross-checks all the time to make sure everything adds up and I am not double-counting things. These are things that are natural to someone like me. I have a math background generally and I am very quantitative and very logical in terms of analysis.

The second concern is the actual mechanics of doing CAR. Some people don't have the same premium on fastidious and totally thorough cross-checked results the way that some do. That's a danger. The third thing is getting bad data and people not being as sensitive to bad data as someone who has worked with a lot of data. I can look at a dataset and know sooner that it's lousy data than someone who is new at this.

GROWTH AND CHANGE IN NEWSROOM COMPUTING

Philip Meyer, "father" of CAR's predecessor, precision journalism, thinks the fundamentals of journalism may change so much that we may not have traditional journalism much longer:

> Is journalism here to stay? It may be so different that we won't call it journalism any more. It depends, I guess, on what you mean by journalism. I define it as something that mediates between information creators and information users. The editing function will become much more important than the reporting function. The mediating function will become more intense, simply to help people cope with the overload of information. For a while, when the Internet first started to become popular, there was a theory that everybody would become his own editor because so much was available. But nobody has the time or the resources for that. We need editors more than ever now. (personal communication, September 25, 1995)

Many experts agree that CAR is not going to fade from newsrooms. In fact, it will become so well integrated into newsrooms of the future, it will no longer be unique. "It's going to disappear as a specialty, I think. After a while, you're just not going to think about it anymore," stated *The Miami Herald's* Doig (personal communication, September 21, 1995). "People now talk about projects that are not computer-assisted reporting, but are being done with a spreadsheet. Ten years ago, when I started doing this stuff, using a spreadsheet was computer-assisted reporting. That was high-end stuff! Now it should be a tool that everybody is using."

USA Today's Paul Overberg (personal communication, September 19, 1995) says CAR will grow more and more into the fabric of newsgathering. "CAR will spread, slowly but surely. It's not a fad. Some of it's already becoming part of the tool kit for beat reporters. The proliferation of easy-to-use info tools will force reporters to embrace them or lose out, especially to aggressive new competitors from TV, cable, phone companies, weeklies, and so forth."

Much CAR in the mid-1990s was still project oriented, *The Washington Post's* Casey observed. This will be changing, he hopes, toward more daily reporting with CAR elements:

> It's different today than it was two years ago, but there's still a lot of project orientation about computer-assisted reporting. I'm less interested in that than I'm interested in everybody using these tools all the time and having projects become an outgrowth of that kind of competence. So, I think there is no leveling off of CAR at all. I think reporters and editors will become more and more knowledgeable of these tools and how they work. Then a proportion of these projects might actually be supplemented by serious computer analysis. But a much larger percentage of projects would just use it as part of doing a story about city hall or transportation or whatever it is. (personal communication, September 22, 1995)

FUTURE STRATEGIES AND TOOLS FOR CAR

More and more, CAR is becoming a daily news reporting tool. And, perhaps, less and less, CAR is a special- or large-projects strategy. News organizations that believe CAR is an important reporting tool want it integrated into daily efforts.

"From the publisher and managing editor on down, the *Post-Dispatch* is strongly convinced of the value of CAR," explained *St. Louis Post-Dispatch* Information Technology Manager George Landau (personal communication, April 5, 1995). "Huge projects, however, that take many, many months, are viewed skeptically by many editors, with good reason. We do them, but not on a lark."

The gradual transition from paper record-keeping to electronic records by governments gives Rose Ciotta, director of CAR for the 300,000-circulation *Buffalo News,* hope for the future of CAR as well as its successful use as a newsgathering tool:

> I'm sold—and, of course, many others are, too—that CAR has found a firm place in the future of journalism. Why? More and more government data can only be obtained electronically, our readers and viewers expect us, or someone, to cut through all of the information noise out there and tell them something definitive. Journalists, as Phil Meyer says, are the only honest information brokers out there. Software is becoming easier to use and more sophisticated. The skills that a journalist needs to be successful are now increasingly available including being able not only to use a computer to write a story but to get information and analyze information.

At the same time, I believe J-schools not only must include CAR into their curricula, but must also emphasize the more traditional skills of interviewing, critical thinking, evaluating records, and so forth. I'm worried by what I see on the listservs that too many students are being lulled into thinking that the computer will tell them everything. They risk getting lazy. "I need to know a phone number for an editor at the *New York Times?* I just get on the listserv and someone out there will answer me." That's an abuse of the tool.

Also, with the crunch on circulation and loss of readers, CAR has become one way for us to come up with the kind of compelling stories that our readers will not only read, but tell their neighbors about. We can't forget what sells newspapers. It's the "oh-shit" story, the story that people didn't know, the information we are telling them. In the past, it was the specialty of investigative reporters. We now must teach all reporters to feel comfortable writing a story with original information.

CAR can look like magic but it isn't. Yes, it's a wonderful tool, but so is a saw if you know how to use it. *Patience* is an important word, yet paradoxically we seem to all be running right now to keep up with technology. The best I can offer is that both patience and impatience are critical words. Patience so the tools can be learned. Patience by editors in what their staffs can produce. Patience that you can't do all of the stories that you may want to do either because of time and staff limitations or because they are more complicated than you can handle. In this case, it's important to be wise, to evaluate what you or anyone around you can do. If the task is more complicated reach out for the statistical expert. By impatience I mean that we can't be satisfied with the status quo. Technology is changing too fast around us to think that the skills we learned in college five, ten, twenty, or more years ago are still adequate. They aren't. As professionals, we need to drive home the notion that we need to sharpen our skills to keep up with changes around us. That was easy when we had to keep reading to keep up with political changes or go for an economics masters to be able to understand what's happening in the world around us. But now, with computers, the needs are greater for journalism professionals to educate themselves to keep up with the changes. Yes, newspaper companies have a responsibility to offer training, but individuals have a role to play too and they can't wait for their company to teach them all they will need to know in the next millennium. It's going to be a wild ride, I think. While I usually don't like roller coasters, I'm getting my seat belt on and hope it will be fun. It's great to be involved in CAR at this point in our business. (personal communication, November 22, 1995)

Brett Blackledge (personal communication, April 5, 1995), a CAR projects reporter for the *Mobile Press Register* in Alabama, agrees with Ciotta. "It is a necessary tool for newsrooms today, but reporters and editors aren't taking enough time to learn it. PATIENCE!"

David Jensen (personal communication, March 30, 1995), CAR editor for the *Sacramento Bee* in California, feels CAR attitudes must change for ultimate success:

> The key to successful computer-assisted reporting is making it useful every day to every reporter and editor at the paper. Computer assisted reporting is not necessarily a story about big projects and megafindings. It is a story about how these tools improve the paper and benefit the reader daily. It helps a reporter find an unlisted phone number and conduct an interview that adds an extra dimension to a story. CAR helps to understand a neighborhood and why certain events may happen there (through the use of demographics off a census CD). And it can lead to sources and information that otherwise might be overlooked through older methods of reporting.

North Carolina's Philip Meyer believes there is no limit to CAR and how it can be used successfully. "Don't ever make the mistake of saying a CAR project is too sophisticated or so sophisticated it is not journalism. I had people telling me that way back when I was doing three-way crosstabs," Meyer (personal communication, September 25, 1995) recalled. "One person told me I was going to fall between the two stools of journalism and social science and wouldn't be anything. And it is not true. It is really good that journalism is a field that can develop, it can improve its technology."

Appendix A:
1994–1995 Research
Questionnaires

COMPUTERS AND REPORTING
1994 RESEARCH QUESTIONNAIRE

Completion of this questionnaire will require only a few minutes, but it will make an important contribution to a new book, *Computer-Assisted Reporting,* to be published by Lawrence Erlbaum Associates in 1995. Answer as completely and accurately as possible. Prompt return of the questionnaire by mail or fax is appreciated, but should be completed by February 14, 1994.

PART 1: INSTITUTIONAL AND PERSONAL
INFORMATION

1. NEWSPAPER NAME _____

2. DAILY CIRCULATION _____

3. YOUR NAME _____

4. YOUR POSITION _____

5. YOUR TELEPHONE _____

6. YOUR ROLE INVOLVING COMPUTERS IN THE NEWSROOM

_____

_____

Dr. Bruce Garrison, research project director
Journalism and Photography Program
P.O. Box 248127
Coral Gables, Florida 33124-2030
(305) 284-2265 and (305) 284-3648 (fax)
Internet: 73507.160@compuserve.com; CompuServe: 73507,160

PART 2: COMPUTER-ASSISTED REPORTING

1. Does your newspaper currently use computers for newsgathering in addition to writing and word processing? (Check or mark an "x" in only one box).
- ❑ Yes
- ❑ No
- ❑ Don't know

2. Does your newspaper currently have a computer-assisted reporting desk or an individual who supervises such projects?
- ❑ Yes (if yes, go on to question #4)
- ❑ No
- ❑ Don't know

3. If you said no, does your newspaper plan to begin any computer-assisted reporting (CAR) projects or create a CAR desk within the next year?
- ❑ Yes
- ❑ No
- ❑ Don't know

4. How many reporters, editors, librarians, or other news personnel are involved in CAR work on a regular basis at your newspaper?

_____

5. Do you have any type of training or educational program for CAR at your newspaper? If yes, briefly describe it. _____

_____

6. Describe two or three of the most recent CAR projects conducted by your newspaper (or, better, send a photocopy, reprint, or tearsheet of your favorite projects). Use space on the back of this page if necessary. _____

_____

_____

_____

_____

_____

7. Briefly describe your computer hardware configuration (by name of product if possible) which is used for most of your CAR work in the past year:

A. Mainframe computer? _____

B. Mini computer? _____

C. Personal computer(s)? _____

D. Operating platform(s)? _____

E. CD-ROM? _____

F. Hard-drive capacities? _____

8. Briefly describe your software usage for the past year. List the most commonly used by product name, if possible:

A. Word processors? _____

B. Spreadsheets? _____

C. Relational database managers? _____

D. Mapping software? _____

E. Statistical packages? _____

F. Personal information managers? _____

G. Software development/programming package? _____

9. In terms of growth and advancement in your own CAR work, what will be the next new computer tool (e.g., hardware or software) you plan to add or learn? _____

_____

_____

_____

_____

10. What sort of support do you get from your editors for CAR projects? _____

_____

_____

_____

PART 3: ONLINE RESEARCH AND REPORTING

1. Does your newspaper currently use online resources for reporting?
- ❑ Yes (if yes, go on to question #3)
- ❑ No
- ❑ Don't know

2. If no, why not? _____

_____

3. How often does your newspaper use online research to supplement reporting? _____

_____

4. Briefly describe two or three of the most recent uses of online research to assist in reporting a news story (enclose a photocopy, clipping, or tearsheet if you prefer): _____

_____

_____

5. Please indicate which of the following online services your newspaper regularly uses:
- ❑ America Online
- ❑ Burrelle's Broadcast Database
- ❑ CompuServe
- ❑ DataTimes
- ❑ Dialog/Knowledge Index
- ❑ Dow Jones News/Retrieval
- ❑ Delphi
- ❑ GEnie
- ❑ Internet
- ❑ Lexis/Nexis
- ❑ NewsNet
- ❑ Prodigy
- ❑ TRW, CBI-Equifax, or Trans Union Credit Information services
- ❑ U.S. Datalink
- ❑ Westlaw
- ❑ Commercial bulletin board systems
- ❑ Government bulletin board systems
- ❑ Private bulletin board systems
- ❑ Other: _____

6. List, in order, your three most often used online databases or services which you or your newsroom staff uses for reporting:

A. _____

B. _____

C. _____

7. Who most often completes the online research at your newspaper?
❑ Reporter working on the assignment
❑ A librarian or news researcher
❑ Anyone in the newsroom who knows how to use the database
❑ Other: _____

_____

8. Approximately how much money does your newspaper plan to spend in 1994 to use online services? How much was spent in 1993?

1994 _____ 1993_____

9. Which communications software package is the one most commonly used in your newsroom? _____

_____

_____

10. What do you feel are your newspaper's biggest <u>successes</u> with online research? _____

_____

_____

_____

11. What do you feel are your newspaper's biggest <u>failures</u> with online research? _____

_____

_____

_____

PART 4: FIELD REPORTING AND COMPUTERS

1. Do your reporters and editors use online research capacities when reporting from the field?
- ❑ Yes
- ❑ No
- ❑ Don't know

2. Typically, when a reporter or editor goes into the field on assignment, how is he or she equipped with hardware? _____

_____

_____

3. Typically, when a reporter or editor goes into the field on assignment, how is his or her PC equipped with software? _____

_____

_____

4. What other tools are used (e.g., modems, fax cards, cellular telephones, beepers, and so forth)? _____

_____

PART 5: OTHER COMMENTS

If you have any other comments on this subject, please include them below:

_____

_____

_____

_____

_____

Thank you very much!
Please place this questionnaire in the self-addressed return envelope to be mailed or fax it to 305-284-3648 today.

COMPUTER-ASSISTED REPORTING STUDY
1995 RESEARCH QUESTIONNAIRE

Completion of this annual study questionnaire will require only a few minutes. Answer as completely and accurately as possible. Prompt return of the questionnaire by mail or fax is appreciated, but should be completed by April 22, 1995.

PART 1: INSTITUTIONAL AND PERSONAL
INFORMATION

1. NEWSPAPER NAME _____

2. DAILY CIRCULATION _____

3. NAME _____

4. NEWSPAPER ADDRESS _____

5. YOUR POSITION/TITLE _____

6. TELEPHONE (_____)_____

7. E-MAIL ADDRESS _____

8. YOUR PRIMARY ROLE INVOLVING COMPUTERS IN THE NEWSROOM _____

_____

_____

_____

_____

_____

_____

_____

Dr. Bruce Garrison, research project director
Journalism and Photography Program
P.O. Box 248127
Coral Gables, Florida 33124-2030
(305) 284-2846 and (305) 284-3648 (fax)
BGARRISO@UMIAMIVM.IR.MIAMI.EDU

PART 2: COMPUTER-ASSISTED REPORTING

1. Does your newspaper currently use computers for newsgathering—in addition to writing and word processing? (Check or mark an "x" in only one box).
- ❏ Yes
- ❏ No
- ❏ Don't know

2. Does your newspaper currently have a computer-assisted reporting desk or an individual who supervises such projects?
- ❏ Yes (if yes, go on to question #4)
- ❏ No
- ❏ Don't know

3. If you said no, does your newspaper plan to begin any computer-assisted reporting (CAR) projects or create a CAR desk within the next year?
- ❏ Yes
- ❏ No
- ❏ Don't know

4. How many reporters, editors, librarians, or other news personnel are involved in CAR work on a regular basis at your newspaper?

_____

5. Do you have any type of training or educational program for CAR at your newspaper? If yes, briefly describe it.
- ❏ Yes
- ❏ No
- ❏ Don't know

If yes, describe: _____

6. Describe up to three of the most recent CAR projects conducted by your newspaper (or, better, send a photocopy, reprint, or tearsheet of your favorite projects). Use an additional page if necessary.

a. _____

_____

b. _____

_____

c. _____

_____

7. For the following items, briefly indicate your *primary* CAR computer hardware configuration (by name of product if possible) that is used for *most* of your CAR work in the past year:

a. Do you use what is known as a "mainframe" computer for any CAR work?
- ❏ Yes
- ❏ No
- ❏ Don't know

b. Do you use what is known as a "mini" computer for any of your CAR work?
- ❏ Yes
- ❏ No
- ❏ Don't know

c. Personal computer(s)?
- ❏ Pentium-type (80586)
- ❏ 80386-type
- ❏ Macintosh
- ❏ Don't know
- ❏ None
- ❏ Other_____

- ❏ 80486-type
- ❏ 80286- or 8088-type
- ❏ Unix

d. Operating platform(s)?
- ❏ DOS only
- ❏ OS/2
- ❏ Macintosh system
- ❏ None
- ❏ Other_____

- ❏ DOS/Windows (any version 3.xx)
- ❏ Unix
- ❏ Don't know

e. CD-ROM drive?
- ❏ One in newsroom, any speed ❏ More than one in newsroom
- ❏ None
- ❏ Other_____

f. Hard-drive capacities?
Megabyte capacity (write-in) _____
- ❏ None
- ❏ Don't know

g. Modem speed?
- ❏ 300 baud
- ❏ 2400 baud
- ❏ 14400 baud
- ❏ 57600 baud
- ❏ None
- ❏ Other_____

- ❏ 1200 baud
- ❏ 9600 baud
- ❏ 28800 baud
- ❏ Don't know

h. Other storage medium?
❑ Digital tape   ❑ Optical disk
❑ Don't know
❑ None
❑ Other_____

8. Briefly indicate your *primary* software usage in each category for the past year:

a. Word processors?
❑ Lotus AmiPro   ❑ Microsoft Word
❑ WordPerfect   ❑ XyWrite
❑ None
❑ Other_____

b. Spreadsheets?
❑ Borland/Novell Quattro Pro   ❑ Lotus 1-2-3
❑ Microsoft Excel   ❑ None
❑ Other_____

c. Relational database managers?
❑ Borland dBase   ❑ Borland Paradox
❑ Lotus Approach   ❑ Microsoft Access
❑ Microsoft FoxPro   ❑ None
❑ Other_____

d. Mapping software?
❑ Atlas GIS   ❑ MapInfo
❑ None
❑ Other_____

e. Statistical packages?
❑ SAS   ❑ SPSS
❑ None
❑ Other_____

f. Personal information managers and text database managers?
❑ askSam   ❑ Lotus Organizer
❑ Lotus Smartext   ❑ None
❑ Other_____

g. Software development/programming package?
❑ Borland C++   ❑ Borland Turbo Pascal
❑ Microsoft Basic   ❑ Microsoft Visual Basic
❑ None
❑ Other_____

9. In terms of growth and advancement in your own CAR work, what will be the next new computer tools (e.g., hardware or software) you plan to add or learn?

a. _____

_____

b. _____

_____

c. _____

_____

10. What sort of support do you get from your editors for CAR projects? _____

_____

_____

_____

PART 3: ONLINE RESEARCH AND REPORTING

1. Does your newspaper currently use online resources for reporting?
- ❑ Yes (if yes, go on to question #3)
- ❑ No
- ❑ Don't know

2. If no, why not? _____

3. How often does your newspaper use online research to supplement reporting?
- ❑ Daily or more often
- ❑ Once a week or more often
- ❑ Once a month or more often
- ❑ Less than monthly
- ❑ Never used

4. Briefly describe two or three of the most recent uses of online research to assist in reporting a news story (enclose a photocopy, clipping, or tearsheet if you prefer): _____

_____

5. Please indicate which of the following online services your newspaper regularly uses (check all that apply):

❏ America Online
❏ CompuServe
❏ Dialog/Knowledge Index
❏ Delphi
❏ Genie
❏ Interchange (Ziff-Davis)
❏ Lexis/Nexis
❏ PACER (federal courts)
❏ TRW, CBI-Equifax, or Trans Union Credit Information Services
❏ Commercial bulletin board services
❏ Government bulletin board services
❏ Private bulletin board services
❏ Local government online services
❏ Other: _____
❏ Other: _____
❏ Other: _____
❏ None

❏ Burrelle's Broadcast Database
❏ DataTimes
❏ Dow Jones News/Retrieval
❏ FedWorld
❏ Information America
❏ Internet
❏ NewsNet
❏ Prodigy
❏ U.S. Datalink
❏ Westlaw

6. List, in order, your three *most frequently used* online databases or services which you or your newsroom staff uses for reporting:

a. _____

b. _____

c. _____

7. Who most often completes the online research at your newspaper?

❏ The reporter working on the assignment
❏ A librarian or news researcher
❏ The editor overseeing the assignment
❏ Anyone in the newsroom who knows how to use the online service
❏ Other: _____
❏ None

8. Approximately how much money has your newspaper budgeted in 1995 to use online services? How much was spent in 1994?

1995 _____   1994 _____

9. Which communications software package is the one most commonly used in your newsroom?

❏ Crosstalk   ❏ Procomm Plus
❏ SmartCom   ❏ Windows Terminal
❏ Other: _____
❏ None

10. What do you feel are your newspaper's biggest <u>successes</u> with online research? _____

_____

_____

11. What do you feel are your newspaper's biggest <u>failures</u> with online research? _____

_____

_____

PART 4: FIELD REPORTING AND COMPUTERS

1. Do your newspaper's reporters and editors use online research capacities when reporting from the field?

❏ Yes
❏ No
❏ Don't know

2. Typically, when a reporter or editor goes into the field on assignment, how is he or she equipped with hardware (check all that apply)?

❏ Portable computer   ❏ Cellular telephone
❏ Internal (built-in) modem ❏ Fax card
❏ Beeper   ❏ PC-cellular telephone link
❏ Two-way radio   ❏ Don't know
❏ Other: _____

3. Typically, when a reporter or editor goes into the field on assignment, how is his or her PC equipped with software (check all that apply)?

❏ Word processor   ❏ Communications package (any type)
❏ Spreadsheet   ❏ Database management system
❏ Online service   ❏ Don't know
❏ Other: _____

PART 5: GENERAL COMMENTS

If you have any other comments or observations about CAR, please include them below:

_____

_____

_____

_____

_____

_____

Thank you very much!
Please place questionnaire in the self-addressed return envelope to be returned by
April 22, 1995 . . . or fax to 305-284-3648 today.

Appendix B: Muskegon Chronicle Jail Crowding Case Study

Sunday, October 2, 1994, Final edition, p. 1A.
"Jail crowding lets criminals evade the law: Police must hunt down criminals who should have been in jail anyway, but were released early"

By Michael G. Walsh

Chronicle staff writer

Jamie Allen Belka didn't like jail and apparently liked the idea of going to prison even less.

Belka, 22, in March allegedly broke into Muskegon's Betten Chevrolet, stole a pickup truck, then led police on a dangerous high-speed chase.

Police arrested him March 14 after the stolen truck he was driving crashed into another vehicle. Officers then booked Belka into the Muskegon County jail, but jailers released him the same day because of jail overcrowding.

Belka fled, abandoning a $3,000 bond and leaving behind a string of charges that that could have netted him a prison term.

Police today are still searching for Belka, one of dozens who flee justice each year after they are kicked out of jail because their crimes weren't heinous enough or too many people were behind on a certain day.

In fact, almost half the bench warrants issued by Muskegon County judges seek people released from custody under a court-ordered measure to ease jail overcrowding, a computer study of jail and court records show.

Bench warrants are ordered by judges to arrest someone.

That means area police now must hunt down felons and individuals charged with a variety of crimes who should have been in jail anyway, but were released early.

Catch-and-release

A *Chronicle* study of Muskegon County Jail and 14th Circuit Court records shows 44 percent of bench warrants issued here seek people released from custody early under a 1990 ruling by Kent County Circuit Judge Dennis Kolenda.

That ruling, modified over the last four years, orders the Muskegon County Sheriff to limit jail population to 244 inmates. When more people are taken in, jailers then must begin releasing inmates.

Over the last four years, 3,906 people arrested on a variety of charges have been released from jail early. Of those, 891 failed to show up for trial or sentencing and bench warrants were issued for their arrests.

This year, authorities project 1,216 people arrested on a variety of crimes will walk out of jail—usually before the arresting officer completes the paperwork on the case.

Of those, 120, like Belka, will fail to show up for court dates, trials or sentences and police will pursue them—again. So far this year, about 10 percent of bench warrants have been issued against people released early from the Muskegon County Jail.

Capt. Robert Baker, jail administrator, said the releases make little fiscal sense and jeopardize the community's safety.

"It doesn't make any common sense whatsoever to pay all these police officers and use court time and hundreds of thousands of taxpayer dollars to take these people to court and then release them," Baker said.

However, from that point the issue becomes political.

"Somebody has to be responsible in this county, and county commissioners have to be held responsible," said Baker, "No one has taken any responsibility yet."

County board Chairman Kenneth J. Hulka said the sheriff's department has made little use of other alternatives—including a contract allowing Muskegon County to divert prison-eligible inmates to Oceana County Jail.

Hulka also urged the sheriff's department and local judges to support the county board's position that early releases should be based on a "first in, first out" policy, which Hulka said would ensure that more inmates sentenced to jail would serve at least some time.

Alternatives

Jail expansion plans are "on hold" following state rejection of a grant application that would have combined an expansion of the jail, the county building and the county library system, Hulka said. "We're exploring some other opportunities now."

Kolenda in 1990 ruled that overcrowded conditions at the jail violated inmates' constitutional rights. The judge then threw the issue at Muskegon County officials.

"Muskegon County does not seem able or willing to resolve these matters," Kolenda said in May 1990. "I have been appointed to do so, and I will do so."

County officials responded by modifying the layout of the jail, creating room for several more beds. But they balked at enlarging the jail or building a new facility.

Instead, local leaders initiated several jail diversion programs such as use of electronic tethers to keep low-risk people at home and out of custody.

Judges said such methods can safely be employed with only a handful of people, and those resources are overtaxed as well.

"(Alternative programs) haven't done a damn thing for us, not a thing," Baker said. "These are people who would be released under 'Kolenda' (the judge's order) anyhow and most are not a threat to society. Why are we spending any money on them?"

Handcuffing judges

Kolenda's catch-and-release policy not only frustrates jailers, but judges who often find lack of jail space erodes their power.

As a result, Muskegon's circuit judges have begun ordering some people to state prison who in other years would have gone to county jail.

"As far as I'm concerned, the (state) Department of Corrections will become my jail because our jail is not available," said 14th Circuit Judge Ronald Pannucci.

Prisons generally are reserved for sentences of one year or longer; jails are used for terms of less than one year. That, however, is no longer true, at least in Muskegon County.

Judges are reacting to lack of local jail space by tabbing state prisons. Last year, for example, the county's four circuit judges sentenced 31 people to prison rather than jail for an average term of six months.

So far this year, Pannucci alone has sentenced 48 convicted felons to prison who otherwise would have received jail terms, records show. Terms averaged four months.

He has few other options, Pannucci said. If sentenced to jail, "they do not stay one day. That is unfair."

Getting away with crime

Because of chronic jail overcrowding and resulting releases, certain crimes essentially have few penalties, Pannucci said.

"Basically, we've removed (jail as a penalty for) property offenses. Those people can't go to jail," said Pannucci, who still orders convicted property offenders to pay fines and costs. However, Pannucci finds himself with no jail option when they balk at paying up.

People who violate probation also often avoid penalties, Pannucci said.

For example, Debra Paggett, 30, wore an electronic tether following conviction for property theft, but violated curfew at will, Pannucci said.

Records show Paggett was booked into the jail Nov. 23, 1993, and released the same day.

"Once she was brought in, she said 'you can't do anything to me,'—and she was right," Pannucci said. "(Those like Paggett) know no punishment in the system."

However, Pannucci sentenced Paggett to serve between one month and two years in prison, meaning she had to serve her time in a state facility.

"There are too many injustices occurring every sentencing day," Pannucci said. "For me, this is a conscience problem."

Reprinted with permission of *The Muskegon Chronicle.*

Appendix C
Miami Herald Crime and No Punishment Case Study

Sunday, Aug. 28, 1994, final edition, p. 1A
"Dade justice puts felons on the street"
First in the series "Crime and No Punishment"

By Don Van Natta and Jeff Leen
Miami Herald Staff Writers

Miami has more crime and less punishment than any other big city in America.

Besieged by 36,000 felony cases a year, Dade County's court system survives by giving breaks to thousands of hardened criminals.

An eight-month *Miami Herald* study of millions of court records uncovered a startling pattern:

A Dade criminal has less risk of going to prison than other U.S. felons, but a Dade resident has a greater risk of being a victim than anyone else in America. The only people who think the system works are the criminals and their attorneys.

"Miami is the best place to be in Florida," defense lawyer Simon Steckel said. "They try to work things out. It's easier to get a plea deal here than anywhere else."

The Herald study found:

• Dade County, with the highest crime rate in the nation, sends only 15 of every 100 convicted felons to state prison— the national average is 46 of 100. Miami is more lenient than New York, Los Angeles, Washington, D.C., and 20 other large, crime-plagued American cities.

• The odds of a Dade robber getting arrested and going to prison, for instance, are 1 in 40. Elsewhere in the United States, they are 1 in 20.

250

• When Dade felons are sent to state prison, they get substantially less time. In Miami, robbers sentenced to prison receive an average of seven years, three months. The national average: nearly 10 years.

• 22 percent of Florida's serious crime occurred in Dade in 1992. But Dade criminals made up only 10.9 percent of the felons sentenced to Florida's prisons. That's the smallest share of state prison beds used by any of the 24 most crime-ridden U.S. cities.

All metro areas have crime problems, but none surpass Dade's. For example, the crime rate countywide is worse than the rates for the most crime-ridden portions of Detroit, Washington, St. Louis and Dallas.

Yet all those cities punish their felons more severely. Seen through criminal justice statistics, Dade exists in a world of its own, a zone of low punishment.

Just across the border in Broward County, which has less than half of Dade's crime, felons have it much tougher. A robber convicted in Broward is three times more likely to go to prison than one in Dade.

Kurt Van Bryant, for example, was arrested nine times in Dade County, including five times on robbery charges. Each time, prosecutors dropped the charges.

Then he crossed the line: He went into Broward and attacked an 86-year-old woman. Van Bryant knocked the woman's glass eye out of its socket and stole $260 from her purse. He was convicted of strong-arm robbery and aggravated battery.

A Broward judge sentenced him to 50 years in state prison.

The implications of Dade's failure reach far beyond South Florida.

U.S. Attorney General Janet Reno helped shape Miami's court system for 15 years as Dade state attorney.

"I have long felt that the level of punishment for many convicted felons was too lenient," Reno said, "and that both their sentences and the proportion of the sentence actually served were inadequate."

She blamed the system's woes on heavy caseloads, a lack of resources and an inability to make dangerous criminals serve their sentences.

Faced with spiraling crime in the 1980s, Reno and others pushed a policy of "diversion"—giving felons drug treatment and counseling instead of locking them up.

The Clinton administration made diversion measures—such as Drug Court and domestic violence programs—a big part of its $30 billion crime bill, which President Clinton will soon sign into law.

Miami's diversion experiment, however, has failed to put a dent in Dade's crime rate, which has remained No. 1 in the country for 15 consecutive years.

To be sure, Dade has a very difficult crime problem. It is aggravated by rampant drug smuggling, a volatile disparity between races and classes and constant infusions of immigrants, transients and tourists.

Each factor has helped make Miami synonymous with crime, and overwhelmed those whose job it is to punish the guilty. The people in the system say the criminals know they have all the advantages.

"They thumb their noses at us," said Dade State Attorney Katherine Fernandez Rundle, 44, who succeeded Reno in March 1993. "That's what's wrong with the whole system: the punishment. Nothing's swift, nothing's severe. They know it. And we know it."

Long before Rundle became state attorney, Dade sent inmates to state prison at a slower rate than other Florida cities with smaller populations and lower crime rates.

The trend began in 1983, and by 1992 Tampa/St. Petersburg—with just 63 percent of Dade's crime—was sending twice as many criminals to prison as Dade.

If Dade had sent twice as many criminals to prison over the last decade, it could have prevented roughly 18,000 robberies and 54,000 burglaries.

Criminologists call this the "incapacitation effect," an estimate of the crimes eliminated when criminals are locked up.

"If you put people in prison who commit robberies and burglaries, you'll get fewer robberies and burglaries," said Patrick Langan, senior statistician with the Bureau of Justice Statistics in Washington. "It doesn't take a degree in physics to figure this out."

The cost of leniency is tallied on the streets: Two stark murders of German tourists on Miami highways, the killing of a young Metro-Dade police officer on a friend's doorstep and the home-invasion robbery of then-Miami Mayor Xavier Suarez.

Each time, repeat offenders, given breaks by the courts, preyed on the victims. Before long, Miami became known around the world as the most dangerous city in America.

How did Miami's $400-million-a-year criminal justice system go so wrong?

The story begins at the Metro Justice Building, a drab, nine-story urban courthouse where defendants and their defense attorneys hold the upper hand.

The wheels of justice don't turn slowly there. They spin with blinding speed, driven by the engine of compromise. Everyone who works there—judges, prosecutors and even defense attorneys—shares the same goal: Dispose of the crush of cases as quickly as possible.

With so many felony defendants, Dade's criminal courts have evolved into a plea-bargain bazaar. By making deals on 98 percent of the cases, judges, prosecutors and public defenders dispose of their cases; the criminals get lighter sentences.

Dade judges labor under one of the heaviest caseloads in the nation, with each judge responsible for more than 1,200 new felony cases a year. By comparison, each Los Angeles criminal court judge gets 470 new felony cases a year and each Chicago judge handles 700.

"Heavy caseloads mean too little time to try cases," one circuit judge complained in an anonymous poll conducted by *The Herald*. "Consequently, I accept pleas which may not be appropriate."

Miami also has a severe shortage of prosecutors, who must juggle as many as 300 cases. To be as well-staffed as New York, Dade would have to increase its number of prosecutors from 239 to 750 at a cost of millions of dollars a year.

On some Monday mornings, Dade prosecutors must be ready to go to trial on any one of 100 pending cases.

"It's sweetheart-deal time," assistant state attorney Averill Dorsett said. "Time for the Blue-Light Special."

Buckling under the weight, prosecutors—and in many cases the judges themselves—make generous offers that the defendants cannot refuse.

Most of the time, it means probation or a sentence of 364 days in the Dade County Jail— the maximum sentence someone can receive in a local jail—instead of years in the Florida state prison system, where the minimum sentence is a year and a day.

Prosecutors and judges wish it didn't have to be this way, but they feel they have no choice. If they tried to get tougher, defense attorneys could refuse to plea bargain and the courthouse would be clogged with thousands of pending trials.

"Many of us are appalled at the cases we have to plea to probation," Dade Circuit Judge Rodolfo Sorondo Jr. said. "The alternative, however, is a complete gridlock of the court system."

For prosecutors, the heavy caseload is aggravated by Florida's uniquely burdensome court procedures.

Under pre-trial "discovery" rules, defense attorneys can call victims and witnesses repeatedly for depositions. A judge is never present and, often times, neither is a prosecutor. In addition to learning the state's case, the defense gets the opportunity to impeach and, sometimes, bully witnesses and victims.

"The way these people mistreat you when you come there, it's just inconceivable," said Jose Martinez, the victim of an armed robbery in North Dade whose deposition was taken by public defenders in 1992. "You have no rights. This system is a disaster. After what I went through, it doesn't pay to go over there."

Only three other states have such liberal discovery systems: North Dakota, Vermont and New Hampshire—all rural, with very low crime rates.

Caseload and discovery demands make prosecutors feel outgunned, overwhelmed and ready to negotiate justice.

But to make the deals that make the system run, the prosecutors and judges must have the cooperation of the defendants and their attorneys.

To get it, often times, prosecutors and judges hand out a little-known legal gift to defendants that keeps crimes off their permanent records, even when they agree to plead to the charges against them.

It is called a "withhold of adjudication," and it is the oil in the Dade court's engine of compromise.

In Dade County, nearly one-third of the people sentenced for the crimes that touch most people's lives, such as robberies and burglaries, get a withhold—6,600 in 1992 and 1993 alone. Said former state prosecutor Richard Gregorie: "A guy comes in, the courtroom is crowded, the judge has got four or five people just sitting there. The judge thinks, 'I want to get him out of here, I want to get him off my calendar, I want to get him out of my courtroom' . . . He says, 'I tell you what: I'll give you a withhold.'"

A withhold may not count as a conviction against a defendant's record, but Dade prosecutors count it as a conviction in their statistics.

"Withhold is considered a successful prosecution," said Barry Lynch, the lead statistician for the Dade State Attorney's Office.

When Reno appeared before the Senate Judiciary Committee last year, she said her office had a "successful prosecution" rate of 89 percent. She was only able to claim such a high rate by counting diversions and withholds in her favor.

In Dade, a successful prosecution doesn't usually end in prison.

"The emphasis here has been to come up with ways to divert people from prison or jail," Lynch said. "That's never been seen as a problem."

It has never been seen as a problem because Dade residents have always assumed that the problem is not at the Dade courthouse but in an overcrowded state prison system that releases inmates early.

Rundle, the state attorney, says her office does not try to send many criminals to prison because of the overcrowding problem.

She believes many inmates sentenced to one year in jail will serve more time than inmates sent to state prison.

"Prison admissions don't mean anything to me," Rundle said. "I don't think that is the appropriate measure. The question for me is how long an inmate serves somewhere."

In a report directed by Rundle's prosecutors, the Dade County Grand Jury announced last May that felons sentenced to one year in the Dade County Jail actually serve more time than those sent to state prison for four years.

Thus, in many cases, judges could better protect the public by sending criminals to jail rather than prison, according to the grand jury.

"We were amazed by this," said the grand jury, citing unidentified "witnesses" as the sole source of the information.

The grand jury's finding is contradicted by the state of Florida: A Dade burglar sentenced to four years in state prison will serve an average of about 19 months, according to statistics from the Florida Department of Corrections' Bureau of Planning Research and Statistics.

Prison officials point out that Florida's prisons are less crowded now. The number of inmate admissions has dropped steeply—from 44,701 in 1990 to 26,623 this year. And each year since 1990, inmates have served a higher percentage of their sentences, up from 33.1 percent to 44.2 percent today.

While prosecutors and most judges are skeptical of the state prison statistics, they willingly believe courthouse lore that felons sentenced to 364 days in jail will spend 10 months behind bars.

But the average length of stay in local jails for inmates serving a sentence of 364 days is actually six to seven months, said Charles Felton, Metro-Dade corrections director.

The fact that Miami's justice system punishes criminals less severely cannot be attributed simply to caseload, prison overcrowding or Florida's discovery system. Other Florida metropolitan areas—like Fort Lauderdale and Tampa/St. Petersburg—punish more severely, even though they too have burdensome caseloads and prison and discovery pressures.

The difference is one of philosophy, shaped by a complex calculus of fears and expectations among Dade judges, prosecutors, defense attorneys, defendants, victims and the public.

The people who work in the system feel that they themselves are the victims of it.

"We're drowning here," said Circuit Judge Leonard Glick, a prosecutor for 19 years before taking the bench in 1991. "You just can't try these cases. There's a lot of pressure on just to move cases."

And many of them believe the system has lost its ability to protect the public.

"There's absolutely no punishment, there's absolutely no deterrent, and that's why we are facing the numbers we are today," said Tommy Moran, a Miami Beach detective for 25 years. "We're not teaching anybody not to commit crimes. We're teaching them that crime pays."

The criminals have known it for a long time.

"I don't intend on being here very long," said Everett Forbes, a serial robber known as the Gentleman Bandit, from his jail cell. "Your judicial system is great."

Herald staff writer Ronnie Greene also contributed to this report.

Reprinted with permission of *The Miami Herald.*

Appendix D
CAR Software Publishers' Technical Support Hotlines

For help with software commonly used in computer-assisted reporting, contact the product publishers, use their technical support or customer service hotlines. Most of these support lines will require a product registration number or other ownership proof before assistance is rendered. Note that there may be fees assessed as well and callers should inquire at the beginning of the call to determine if additional costs beyond the call will be incurred.

These are the telephone numbers, as of January 1996:

Product	Company	Telephone Number
1-2-3	Lotus Development Corp.	617-693-1377
Access	Microsoft Corp.	206-635-7050
America Online	America Online	800-827-6364
Approach	Lotus Development Corp.	617-693-1377
askSam	askSam Systems	904-584-6590
Claris Works	Claris Corp.	408-727-9004
		800-735-7593 (recorded)
CompuServe	CompuServe	800-848-8199
dBase	Borland International	408-461-9110
Excel	Microsoft Corp.	206-635-7070
FoxPro	Microsoft Corp.	206-635-7191
NetManage	NetManage	408-973-8181
Notes	Lotus Development Corp.	617-693-1377
		800-437-6391
Paradox	Borland International	408-461-9166

Product	Company	Telephone Number
pcAnywhere	Symantec Corp.	503-465-8430
Procomm Plus	Datastorm Technologies	314-875-0530
Q & A	Symantec Corp.	503-465-8600
SPSS	SPSS Inc.	312-329-3410
Visual Basic	Microsoft Corp.	206-646-5105
Windows 95	Microsoft Corp.	800-936-4200
Works	Microsoft Corp.	206-635-7130

Appendix E
Internet Distribution
Lists for CAR
Journalists

For journalists interested in monitoring computer-assisted reporting subjects and issues, there are a number of special topic distribution lists that are available on the Internet. These lists offer ideas, discussion, comments, problem solving, and other advantages to journalists interested in advancing their CAR skills.

There are differing ways to sign on and sign off distribution lists and the protocol depends on the software used. For many, however, the procedure is simple:

1. Prepare to send an e-mail message to the list server computer by typing the address of the list serve home computer in the e-mail "TO" field.
2. Leave the subject and any other header fields blank.
3. In the message field, type a message in this format:
   subscribe "listname" "username" or
   subscribe NICAR-L Joan Smith
4. Send the message as you would normally send e-mail.
5. An automated e-mail response confirming the subscription should be sent from the list server, not from a person, to indicate receipt of the message. The list server may also send another standardized e-mail message containing instructions and policies of the list as well as instructions for leaving the list.

Some of the leading CAR distribution lists include:

List Title	List Address	List Summary
ASKSAM-L	listserv@vtvm1.cc.vt.edu	For users of askSam free-form text database management software.
CARR-L	listserv@ulkyvm.louisville.edu	Devoted to computer-assisted reporting and research issues.
CRTNET	listserv@psuvm.psu.edu	Devoted to communication research methods and theory issues.
EXCEL-G	listserv@peach.ease.lsoft.com	For users of Microsoft Excel spreadsheet software. Level: novice to professional.
EXCEL-L	listserv@peach.ease.lsoft.com	For advanced users of Microsoft Excel spreadsheet software interested in developing spreadsheet applications.
FOXPRO-D	foxpro-d-request@dswi.com	For users of Microsoft FoxPro relational database software (digest edition of FoxPro-L below).
FOXPRO-L	foxpro-l-request@dswi.com	For users of Microsoft FoxPro relational database software.
IRE-L	listserv@mizzou1.missouri.edu	Investigative Reporters and Editors (IRE) organizational list.
NEWSLIB	listserv@gibbs.oit.unc.edu	News researchers, news librarians, online issues and services list.
NICAR-L	listserv@mizzou1.missouri.edu	National Institute for Computer-Assisted Reporting organizational list.
NIT	nit-request@chron.com	List for discussion of Internet resources for journalists.
ON-LINE NEWS	majordomo@marketplace.com	Online newspapers and news magazines list.
SPSSX-L	listserv@uga.cc.uga.edu	Computer, statistical, and other operational issues related to SPSS.

Appendix F
Internet World Wide Web
Sites for CAR Journalists

For journalists interested in CAR methods and issues, there are a number of World Wide Web sites available on the Internet. These sites are offered by organizations, businesses, institutions, and individuals interested in CAR. The sites often offer ideas, resources, discussion, comments, problem solving, and other advantages to journalists interested in advancing their CAR skills.

The following list provides the sponsor or source of the site, its uniform resource locator (URL), and a brief summary of the content of the site.

Web Site	URL (Address)	Site Summary
askSam Systems	http://www.asksam.com	News and product information about askSam, the text database program and related products.
Borland International	http://www.borland.com	News and product information about Paradox, dBase, and other related database and development tools.
Claris	http://www.claris.com	News and product information about Claris News and products such as Claris Works and FileMaker Pro.
Computer Associates	http://www.cai.com	News and product information about Computer Associates database products.

Web Site	URL (Address)	Site Summary
IRE	http://www.reporter.org	Information about the organization and programs.
Lotus Development	http://www.lotus.com	News and product information about Lotus products such as Notes, 1-2-3, and Approach.
MapInfo Corp.	http://web1.digital. net/~mapinfo/	News and product information about MapInfo, MapInfo databases, and related products.
Microsoft Corp.	http://www.microsoft. com	News and product information about Microsoft software such as Windows 95, Excel, Access, FoxPro, Visual FoxPro, and peripherals products.
NICAR	http://www.nicar.org	Information about the organization and its programs.
Novell	http://www.novell.com	News and product information about Novell's software such as QuattroPro.
Poynter Institute	http://www.nando.net/ prof/poynter/home. html	General journalism information includes special section devoted to CAR and online news research.
Pulitzer Prizes	http://www.crj.org	An online collection of the full-texts of major reporting prize winners, including those projects that used CAR techniques.
Reporting groups	http://www.reporter.org	A gateway to information about several national reporting organizations, including IRE and NICAR.

Web Site	URL (Address)	Site Summary
SAS Institute	http://www.sas.com	News and product information about SAS System software such as the SAS statistical program and related database tools.
SPSS, Inc.	http://www.spss.com	News and product information about SPSS programs and related products.
Strategic Mapping	http://www.stratmap. com	News and product information about Atlas GIS and other mapping tools products.
Symantec	http://www.symantec. com	News and product information about pcAnywhere, Norton Utilities, and other related products.

Appendix G
Cleveland Plain Dealer
"FAA's Unreliable Air
Records" Case Study

Sunday, January 8, 1995, Final/All, Section: National; p. 11A
"Poor records set back air safety effort"

By ELIZABETH A. MARCHAK and KEITH C. EPSTEIN
Plain Dealer Reporters

It's doubtful that any passengers on MidWest Express Flight 180 from Milwaukee to Cleveland on the morning of Dec. 8 knew of the aircraft's extensive service record—more than 144 repairs, according to the government's maintenance records.

Tail number 500ME's records show the DC-9 has had a variety of service problems—from emergency lights that wouldn't shut off to cracks in the cargo door to nose gear wheels rubbing against the skin of the aircraft.

But dangerous? Probably not.

Now consider the record of a USAir Boeing 737, tail number 513AU: Only 37 reports of problems—corrosion and rusting, common in older planes; fuel improperly flowing between tanks, some low-frequency vibrations—nothing that would alarm safety experts.

"Trivial," said aviation consultant Richard Williams.

Yet 513AU was Flight 427—the jetliner that crashed in Pittsburgh last September, killing 132 people, for reasons still unknown.

The two planes' histories illustrate the perils—for regulators, inspectors, reporters and the public—of drawing conclusions about relative safety from information in federal government computers. Even though that's why the computerized information exists in the first place.

So many discrepancies abound as to render questionable any conclusions drawn from them, critics say.

The number of records submitted by airlines operating similar aircraft itself varies greatly. Among major airlines operating Boeing 727s in 1988, the average per plane ranged from only one service difficulty report (SDR) by one airline to more than six for another, according to the General Accounting Office.

A one-day sampling of records for flights in and out of Cleveland Hopkins International Airport last month shows similar disparities. And an examination of maintenance records of Great Lakes region aircraft shows maintenance reports vary by fleet even within the same airline.

For instance, ComAir, a Delta Airlines commuter line, has filed numerous reports, as recently as June, for repairs to its 30-passenger Brasilias—but only one report since 1991 appears in government files for its fleet of the 33-passenger Saab 340s. The analysis was based on tail and serial numbers provided by the airline.

"That is absolutely incorrect," said Charles Chrest, chief inspector for ComAir. "Literally hundreds of reports must be missing." Chrest estimated that he files two to three reports each week on the Saabs. The reports are there but under different versions of the serial number, making them almost impossible to find.

Besides entire records, what else is missing from the backbone of the Federal Aviation Administration's daily effort to keep the skies safe?

The basics, say critics.

"The FAA isn't doing a good job on this and they'd be the first or second to admit it," said Steve Erickson, director of maintenance materials for the Air Transport Association, which represents major airlines.

Among items missing from the information:

Many reports, perhaps as many as nine out of 10. "The operators are very sensitive about reporting," said Keith Hagy, manager of engineering and investigations at the Air Line Pilots Association. "We are told possibly one in 10 are reported." The GAO report also noted that the FAA's system is so inadequate the aviation industry uses information from Boeing and McDonnell Douglas rather than the FAA.

Numbers of hours flown. Nowhere do the reports give a clear indication of how often problems crop up, per number of flight-hours, or numbers of takeoffs and landings, or similar measures. Such information is particularly critical for what it indicates about wear and tear on the plane.

A reliable assessment of the seriousness of each repair. The FAA's system is still widely open to interpretation of individual mechanics and is often mislabeled.

Accuracy and consistency. Records are sloppy and inconsistent. Records in more than 200 cases during the past six years didn't identify the plane, either by tail number or serial number, rendering the records virtually useless.

January 8, 1995 Sunday, Final/All, Section: National; p. 1A
"FAA data on flight hazards unreliable; poor records could risk lives, experts say"

By ELIZABETH A. MARCHAK and KEITH EPSTEIN
Plain Dealer Washington Bureau
WASHINGTON—Which airplanes are safest? Which airlines? What models need the most repairs?

Sometimes inspectors, manufacturers or the airlines do not know. Computerized information meant to help the government spot hazards—before people get killed—is flawed and unreliable.

Thousands of mechanical breakdowns, perhaps nine of every 10 affecting the nation's 294,000 aircraft, never are reported to the Federal Aviation Administration the way regulations require, a study of records shows.

Among unreported breakdowns are instances in which mechanics for commuter airlines, to avoid costly delays, placed bad parts in other planes rather than fix them. Those planes then took off.

"That happens in the industry—taking bad parts off one plane and putting them on a plane elsewhere so you can clear it," said Don Brigham, a Chicago-based FAA inspector of commuter airlines.

Interviews, documents and an analysis of FAA records suggest serious flaws in public perceptions about airplanes, airlines and aviation hazards.

Just because a particular airline or aircraft model suffers from what appears to be a high number of reported defects, for instance, doesn't mean it is more dangerous than others.

It is more likely that the airline or manufacturer simply has been more conscientious about notifying the government.

More than airline reputations are at stake. People in the aviation community say crashes could be prevented and lives saved if the government did a better job of collecting and analyzing the data.

In July 1992, for instance, a TWA L-1011 veered off a runway at takeoff and erupted into flames at Kennedy International Airport in New York. The pilot later said he aborted the flight, in which 51 people suffered minor injuries, when a warning system indicated engines were stalling. Investigators later could find only two reports on the government's database of stall warning system failures on L-1011s.

But when they checked out records at Lockheed, the manufacturer, investigators found another 14 instances in which the warning system had failed. TWA had another 10 in its files. None of those 24 appeared in the FAA's database.

In another case, when a cracked engine mount and failed landing gear sent a Cessna 208 hurtling to the ground in a non-fatal crash in Orlando, Fla., investigators found only two reports of engine-mount cracking in the FAA's database. But the manufacturer had records of 17 such cracks, and 250 incidents of landing gear failure.

A big 'black hole'

The FAA is required to promptly sift through maintenance records known as service difficulty reports, or SDRs, to "detect trends which may indicate future safety problems."

Regulations require airlines to file such reports on 17 types of potentially dangerous in-flight problems. In reality, "no formal system exists to ensure aircraft problems do not fall into a black hole," FAA inspector general A. Mary Schiavo concluded in a recent report.

A 1991 General Accounting Office study of the SDR system noted that the FAA fails to analyze data "as required by FAA policy" because of "insufficient staff and unreliable data."

Such official complaints have resulted in few improvements. Only seven people are assigned to the FAA's Safety Data Analysis Section, the Oklahoma City, Okla., office responsible for the analysis. None is assigned the task full time.

"We all do it now and then," Phil Lomax, an aviation safety inspector in the analysis office, said of SDR analysis. "If we had the budget we need, we could do a lot more things."

Schiavo's report noted only slight improvements since the 1991 GAO study, which concluded that the information "is of little value" to aviation engineers and government inspectors.

"Unreliable, incomplete and outdated," is how Schiavo describes the information.

Those remarks are echoed in the field.

"I don't find it useful," said John Michelli, the FAA's safety inspector for Piedmont Airlines. "It's a bad place to go to reach conclusions."

"There's either not enough information," said Norm Wilkins, an FAA inspector for California-based Westair, "or there's erroneous information."

Many FAA inspectors told the GAO they rarely used the information. Eleven of 12 airlines said it never helped them identify a problem. Two-thirds of FAA engineers said eliminating it would have no effect on safety. All this despite an annual tab to taxpayers of at least $2.5 million for the SDR system, and a cost to airlines of $1.6 million.

Cutting corners

Airlines and their mechanics are reluctant to submit malfunction reports to the FAA partly because doing so costs time and money, and partly for fear of public reaction.

Numerous investigations by the advisory National Transportation Safety Board, citing industry sources, have noted that management pressures on mechanics to shortcut procedures and failure to follow proper procedures remain big problems for both commuter and long-haul airlines.

Keith Hagy, accident investigation manager for the Air Line Pilots Association, said "A lot of operators don't make the required reports because they know the media gets access to the information, and it shows up quite a bit in litigation."

Whatever the reason, many carriers don't report breakdowns as required.

One government analysis showed that, for a two-year period, Northwest Airlines averaged more than 15 reports of breakdown per aircraft, while United had only two. UPS had more than 60.

"Who is the safer airline? Beats me," said California aviation consultant Paul Kolbenschlah. "I would ride on any of the three."

An examination of the maintenance records of the planes that made more than 400 takeoffs and landings at Cleveland Hopkins International Airport during the daylight hours of Dec. 8, for instance, turned up no maintenance records since mid-1993 for many of the aircraft. Some did have records on file.

In other words, the federal government's database doesn't show a record of even a single instance in which maintenance was done on these planes which carried the Continental, U.S. Express and ComAir insignia, for more than a year, a period during which the planes are certain to have had repairs performed.

Recent news accounts have focused on problems with aircraft models that crashed, and raised questions about specific airlines and commuter safety, but the accounts were all based on incomplete records.

One such account, in the Seattle Times, involved two decades of problems with rudders on Boeing 737s like the USAir jet that crashed in Pittsburgh last September, killing all 132 on board.

The implication of the story, which suggested 2,200 jetliners were flying with a bad part, was that the manufacturer should have known and solved the flaw.

"We got roasted but we didn't know about all the SDRs in the SDR database," said Boeing spokesman Randy Harrison. "All we know are those the FAA chooses to tell us about."

Gauging safety a hard task

Airlines, too, are acutely aware of the system's shortcomings.

After the Pittsburgh crash, Patricia Goldman, a former NTSB chairman who was then USAir's spokeswoman, said she wished she could change the appearance of an airline with safety problems—five crashes in five years.

But safety's a hard thing to prove.

"I wish I could tell you there were a way to gauge safety, a set of data you could look at to get an answer, to show we're among the safest," Goldman said, "but I just can't."

Since 1987, consumer activist Ralph Nader has urged the government to publish an annual report card assessing airlines' relative safety, using maintenance records and training programs among other factors.

Critics complain that the Transportation Department publishes little besides baggage liability and flight delay issues.

It isn't that the necessary data are missing, but what's there is almost impenetrable, critics say.

Burt Blosser, a consultant for the Worthington, Ohio-based watchdog Aviation Safety Institute, is trying to adapt the SDR system for consumer use on the CompuServe computer network.

"But people will have to be careful about what conclusions they draw," he cautioned. "There's always a chance of misinterpreting data like this."

Investigators complain

The FAA says it faces more important issues than upgrading the SDR system and doing more analysis.

"There is no value to researching each and every record," an FAA assistant administrator, Nicholas S. Stoer, responded to the agency's inspector general report earlier last year. "Ninety-nine percent are not significant, do not constitute an unsafe condition, are not a design issue, or have been identified elsewhere," he said of the records.

Government watchdog agencies that study safety issues disagree.

During the past five years several reports have singled out the reporting system—including the NTSB, which said the system was inadequate.

Documents show that the NTSB struggled for more than a decade to get the FAA to set up and improve the system to collect and spot service problems.

After the 1979 crash of an American Airlines DC-10 in Chicago, the NTSB urged the FAA to make sure "all . . . service problems are properly analyzed and disseminated to aircraft users."

The FAA promised to do so, but its other mission—energizing the aviation business—got in the way.

In 1982, the FAA argued that improving the system "would cause an economic burden without yielding a corresponding increase in safety benefits."

The issue came up repeatedly over the years, culminating in complaints by NTSB accident investigators in 1993 that they had been unable to "effectively" use the information to uncover aircraft failures, malfunctions and defects in similar aircraft.

Meanwhile, FAA critics say, the agency has spent more than a decade exchanging letters with the NTSB, while unexplained crashes killed people.

An especially troubling case involved the TWA L-1011 accident in 1992. Checking the FAA information for previous instances in which a stall warning system had failed on L-1011s, investigators found only two reports.

But stall warning systems had failed at least 24 times—incidents that the airline and manufacturer, Lockheed, had known about. None of these additional incidents were found in the SDR information.

"The current program is incomplete and of limited value . . . because many reportable service difficulties are not reported to the FAA," the NTSB told the FAA at the time.

System 'needs reworking'

Now, with attention focused on the agency and airline safety with the recent spate of commuter airline tragedies, some FAA officials seem inclined to agree.

"Suffice it to say that we all have agreed that the SDR database is a file cabinet," said Tony Broderick, the FAA's associate administrator for regulation and certification. "It needs reworking, and within resources available is getting that attention."

Some argue that it needs more attention.

Follow-up studies with a broader scope should be done, said Charles Barchok, assistant director of the GAO, noting he hopes to have the ear of incoming Republican House and Senate committee chairmen and subcommittee chairmen. In the electronic age, he'd like to see all the FAA computerized data usage re-evaluated.

Even the FAA's own people have trouble using the SDR system, they say.

Norm Wilkins is among inspectors who prefer to call another bureaucrat to get maintenance records, rather than use the expensive computers. "I can't get information out of the system when I need it," he complains.

John Eakin, a consultant who customizes the aviation data for a variety of uses, now counts the FAA itself among his biggest customers.

The FAA employees find his version of their data is easier to read.

"My biggest customer is the FAA," he said.

Reprinted with permission of the *Cleveland Plain Dealer*

References

Ablondi, W. F. (1995a). The E-mail explosion: E-mail is becoming an essential tool for mobile professionals. *Mobile Office, 6*(4), 45–46.

Ablondi, W. F. (1995b). Research from the road: Drop that desktop, pick a portable. *Mobile Office, 6*(10), 40–42.

Adrian, P. (1995, September 21–24). *Jailhouse rock: Computers, crime, and television.* Unpublished presentation at the CARROCK 95 National Conference, Investigative Reporters and Editors and National Institute for Computer-Assisted Reporting, Cleveland, OH.

Albers, R. R. (1994a). Reporters tap data power. *Presstime, 16*(10), 34–39.

Albers, R. R. (1994b). Wanted: Information coaches. *Presstime, 16*(11), 21.

Anderson, I. E. (1994). *Editor & Publisher international year book 1994.* New York: Editor & Publisher.

Anderson, I. E. (1995). *Editor & Publisher international year book 1995.* New York: Editor & Publisher.

Angell, D., & Heslop, B. (1994). *The elements of e-mail style: Communicate effectively via electronic mail.* Reading, MA: Addison-Wesley.

Anonymous. (1995a, September 25). Lapping up laptops. *Newsweek, 126*(13), 14.

Anonymous. (1995b, September). Purses vs. pockets. *Mobile Office, 6*(9), 16.

Anonymous. (1995c, June). Top laptop disasters. *Mobile Office, 6*(6), 15.

Anonymous. (1995d, September 23). *Transactional Records Access Clearinghouse.* Unpublished brochure, Syracuse, NY: TRAC.

Anonymous. (1995e, November). Two-way data revolution. *Mobile Office, 6*(11), 14.

Armao, R., & Houston, B. (1995). Introduction. In T. L. Barnett (Ed.), *Investigative Reporters and Editors: 100 selected computer-assisted investigations, Book II* (pp. v–vi). Columbia, MO: Investigative Reporters and Editors, Inc., and The National Institute for Computer-Assisted Reporting.

Ayer, R., & Raskin, R. (1995, February 21). On-line services: The changing face of on-line. *PC Magazine, 14*(4), 109–175.

Bartlett, D. (1995, May 1). Broadcast journalism undergoing fundamental reconfiguration. *PR News, 51*(18), n.p.

Barnett, T. L. (Ed.). (1995). *Investigative Reporters and Editors: 100 selected computer-assisted investigations, Book II.* Columbia, MO: Investigative Reporters and Editors, Inc., and The National Institute for Computer-Assisted Reporting.

Beniger, J. (1995, September 26). New Response Analysis Corp Net survey. AAPOR-NET list serve (aapornet@usc.edu), American Association for Public Opinion Research.

Bloom, D. (1994, March–April). Analyzing data on the beat. *The IRE Journal, 17*(2), 10–11.

Brill, A. M. & Cook, S. (1995, August). *Online newsrooms and traditional print newsrooms: Developing models of integration.* Unpublished paper presented to the annual meeting of the Association for Education in Journalism and Mass Communication, Washington, DC.

Brooks, B. S., & Yang, T. (1993, August). *Patterns of computer use in newspaper newsrooms: A national study of U.S. dailies.* Unpublished paper presented to the annual meeting of the Association for Education in Journalism and Mass Communication, Kansas City, MO.

Cahners Publishing Research Department. (1995, September 4). News directors survey '95. *Broadcasting and Cable, 32*–33.

Callahan, C. (1995, October 14). *Reporting from cyberspace.* Presentation at the national Society of Professional Journalists convention, St. Paul, MN.

Cameron, G. T., & Curtin, A. (1995, August). *Electronic newspapers: Toward a research agenda.* Unpublished paper presented to the annual meeting of the Association for Education in Journalism and Mass Communication, Washington, DC.

Campbell, C. C. (1995, June 11). In 20 years, computers have shaped newsrooms as well as communities. *The Virginian-Pilot* (Norfolk), A2.

Carleton, G. (1994a, September). Internet robust but unreliable. *Uplink, 6*(7), 8.

Carleton, G. (1994b, July). Why Internet is (mostly) cool. *Uplink, 6*(5), 2.

Carleton, G. (1995, March). Doing time in Miami. *Uplink, 7*(3), 5.

Casey, W. (1995, July 3). Cybertalk: Data in, statistics out—Maybe; a number of factors can affect statistics. *The Washington Post*, F13.

Costa, D. (1995a, May). Milestones: Remote LAN Users. *Mobile Office, 6*(5), 18.

Costa, D. (1995b, October). Subnotespeak: A glossary of terms. *Mobile Office, 6*(10), 84.

Coy, P., & Hof, R. D. (1995, September 4). 3-D computing: From medicine to war games, it's a whole new dimension, *Business Week, 3440*, 70–77.

Craig, D., Singer, J. B., Allen, C. W., Whitehouse, V., Dimitrova, A., & Sanders, K. P. (1995, August). *Facing the future: Attitudes of journalism educators and students about new media technology.* Unpublished paper presented to the annual meeting of the Association for Education in Journalism and Mass Communication, Washington, DC.

Craig, J. (1995, October 13). *Computer-assisted reporting success stories.* Presentation at the national Society of Professional Journalists convention, St. Paul, MN.

Crim, J. (1995, September 22). *Care and feeding of a computer-assisted reporting program: Management tips for making it work.* Unpublished presentation at the CARROCK 95 National Conference, Investigative Reporters and Editors and National Institute for Computer-Assisted Reporting, Cleveland, OH.

Davenport, L., Fico, F., & Weinstock, D. (1995, August). *Seven electronic information sources in the newsroom: A census of Michigan daily newspapers.* Unpublished paper presented to the annual meeting of the Association for Education in Journalism and Mass Communication, Washington, DC.

DeJesus, E. X. (1995, July). More powerful and sophisticated ways to create and display 3-D computer graphics are appearing right before your eyes. *Byte, 20*(7), 101.

Dodge, J. (1995, October 2). What a tangled Web we've weaved. *PC Week, 12*(39), 3.

Dvorak, J. C. (1995, October 24). Inside track. *PC Magazine, 14*(18), 91.

Eng, P. M. (Ed.). (1995, September 4). A bigger—and cheaper—online universe? *Business Week, 3440*, 100E.

Feola, C. J. (1993, November). Small paper, big project. *American Journalism Review, 15*(9), 25–28.

Feola, C. J. (1994, July–August). The Nexis nightmare. *American Journalism Review, 16*(6), 39–41.

Feola, C. J. (1995, January). By the numbers: spreadsheets in journalism. *Quill, 83*(1), 16.

Feola, C. J., & Johnson, J. T. (1995, March). Making the cut: Enhance your job opportunities by developing your computer skills. *Quill, 83*(2), 24–25.

Foley, J. (1995, October 30). Infoglut: New tools can help tame an ocean of data. *InformationWeek, 551*, 30–40.

Friend, C. (1994, Winter). Daily newspaper use of computers to analyze data. *Newspaper Research Journal, 15*(1), 63–72.

Garrison, B. (1979). *The video display terminal and the copy editor: A case study of electronic editing at the* Milwaukee Journal. Unpublished doctoral dissertation, Southern Illinois University at Carbondale.

Garrison, B. (1982, January). Electronic editing systems and their impact on news decision making. *Newspaper Research Journal, 3*(2), 43–53.

Garrison, B. (1983, Spring). Impact of computers on the total newspaper. *Newspaper Research Journal, 4*(3), 41–63.

Garrison, B. (1995). *Computer-assisted reporting.* Hillsdale, NJ: Lawrence Erlbaum Associates.

Gates, B. (1995, September–October). Windows 95—Gateway to the future. *Microsoft Magazine, 2*(3), 62.

Gerber, B. (1995, November 15). CD-ROM recordable drives: Managing your data. *Network Computing, 6*(15), 130–134.

Gillooly, B. (1995, October 16). The future of notebook computing. *InformationWeek, 549*, 34–44.

Glossbrenner, A. (1995, October–November). The terrible truth about the World-Wide Web. *Online User, 1*(1), 64.

Gordon, R. (1995, September 15). *How does the newsroom evolve into a multi-media future?* Unpublished presentation at the Florida News Librarians Association annual meeting, West Palm Beach, FL.

Greene, R., Leen, J., & Van Natta, D. (1995, May–June). Court system in turmoil. *The IRE Journal, 18*(3), 5.

Grossman, J. (1994, July–August). Locating experts via computer. *The IRE Journal, 17*(4), 10–11.

Hahn, H., & Stout, R. (1994). *The Internet complete reference.* Berkeley, CA: Osborne McGraw-Hill.

Hall, A. (1995, September 23). *My hometown, your hometown.* Unpublished presentation at the CARROCK 95 National Conference, Investigative Reporters and Editors and National Institute for Computer-Assisted Reporting, Cleveland, OH.

Hansen, K. A. (1995, May–June). Look to *The Evansville Courier* for a model newsroom Web page. *The Database Files, 3*(3), 1–5.

Houston, B. (1994, June 11). *Computer-assisted reporting.* Presentation to Florida Press Association and Florida Society of Newspaper Editors, St. Petersburg Beach, FL.

Houston, B. (1995a, July). From the NICAR library. *Uplink, 7*(7), 3.

Houston, B. (1995b, September 21). *What's CAR got to do with it?* Unpublished presentation at the CARROCK 95 National Conference, Investigative Reporters and Editors and National Institute for Computer-Assisted Reporting, Cleveland, OH.

Hunt, D. (1995, May 14). Ticket to trouble: Wheels of injustice? *Houston Chronicle,* 2 Star ed., A-1, A-20.

Johnson, J. T. (1995, September). Newspapers slow to embrace advances in computer world: Even so, on-line services first step in electronic reporting. *Quill, 83*(7), 20.

Kalman, D. M. (1995, December). Predictions '96. *DBMS, 8*(13), 8.

King, M. (1995, November 13). *Computer-assisted reporting.* Unpublished presentation, Knight-Ridder Editors meeting. Coral Gables, FL.

Kohlstrand, J. (1995, September 21–24). *You can make it if you try.* Unpublished presentation at the CARROCK 95 National Conference, Investigative Reporters and Editors and National Institute for Computer-Assisted Reporting, Cleveland, OH.

Kriss, E. (1995, October 13). *Computer-assisted reporting success stories.* Unpublished presentation at the national Society of Professional Journalists convention, St. Paul, MN.

Lee, T. (1995, September 22). *Bringing it all back home.* Unpublished presentation at the CARROCK 95 National Conference, Investigative Reporters and Editors and National Institute for Computer-Assisted Reporting, Cleveland, OH.

Leen, J., & Van Natta, D., Jr. (1994, September). Crime and no punishment: A *Miami Herald* series reprint.

Leen, J., Doig, S. K., & Van Natta, D., Jr. (1994). Crime and no punishment: A *Miami Herald* series (unpublished technical guide).

Leslie, J. (1994, July–August). Morgues no more. *American Journalism Review, 16*(6), 41.

Levy, S. (1995, September 24). How the propeller heads stole the electronic future. *The New York Times Magazine, 145*(50194), 58–59.

Loeb, P. (1995, October 13). *Computer-assisted reporting success stories.* Unpublished presentation at the national Society of Professional Journalists convention, St. Paul, MN.

Loving, B. (1995, October 14). *Reporting from cyberspace.* Unpublished presentation at the national Society of Professional Journalists convention, St. Paul, MN.

McCombs, M., Shaw, D. L., & Grey, D. (1976). *Handbook of reporting methods.* Boston: Houghton Mifflin.

McIntosh, S., Pearson, B., & Schmitt, C. H. (1995, September 21–24). *Building your own database.* Unpublished presentation at the CARROCK 95 National Conference, Investigative Reporters and Editors and National Institute for Computer-Assisted Reporting, Cleveland, OH.

McKercher, C. (1995). Computers and reporters: Newsroom practices at two Canadian daily newspapers. *Canadian Journal of Communication, 20,* 213–229.

Meyer, P. (1973). *Precision journalism.* Bloomington: Indiana University Press.

Meyer, P. (1991). *The new precision journalism.* Bloomington: Indiana University Press.

Microsoft Corporation (1995). *Microsoft Visual FoxPro user's guide. Version 3.0.* Microsoft Corporation, Redmond, WA: Author.

Migoya, D. (1995, January–February). The business of poverty: Tips on databases/spreadsheets. *The IRE Journal, 18*(1), 10–11.

Miller, M. J. (1995, October 10). Inside. *PC Magazine, 14*(17), 4.

Miller, S. C. (1995, September 21). *Personal information management for journalists.* Unpublished presentation at the CARROCK 95 National Conference, Investigative Reporters and Editors and National Institute for Computer-Assisted Reporting, Cleveland, OH.

Moeller, P. (1995, January–February). The digitized newsroom. *American Journalism Review, 17*(1), 42–47.

Napolitano, C. (1995, September 21–24). *50 C.A.R. ideas for your beat.* Unpublished presentation at the CARROCK 95 National Conference, Investigative Reporters and Editors and National Institute for Computer-Assisted Reporting, Cleveland, OH.

Neuzil, M. (1994, Winter). Gambling with databases: A comparison of electronic searches and printed indices. *Newspaper Research Journal, 15*(1), 44–54.

Newman, H. (1995, January 29). *How the* Tucson Citizen *used CAR techniques to produce "Who runs Tucson?"* Unpublished report, IRE Library, Journalism Forum, CompuServe Information Service.

Newspaper Association of America. (1995). *Newspapers lead all other media in electronic and online services.* NAA Home Page, World Wide Web ttp://www.infinet/naa/filetwo.html.

Norusis, M. J. (1995). *SPSS for Windows base system user's guide, release 6.1.* Chicago: SPSS, Inc.

Paul, N. (1993). A primer in computer-assisted research. In B. P. Semonche (Ed.), *News media libraries: A management book* (pp. 317–338). Westport: CT: Greenwood.

Paul, N. (1994). *Computer assisted research: A guide to tapping online information.* (2nd ed.) St. Petersburg, FL.: The Poynter Institute.

Peyser, M., & Rhodes, S. (1995, October 16). When E-mail is ooops-mail. *Newsweek, 126*(16), 82.

Podolsky, D. (1995, October 13). *Computer-assisted reporting success stories.* Unpublished presentation at the national Society of Professional Journalists convention, St. Paul, MN.

Reddick, R., & King, E. (1995). *The online journalist: Using the Internet and other electronic resources.* Fort Worth, TX: Harcourt Brace.

Ricciuti, M. (1995, October 9). New breed of visualization tools improves data analysis. *InfoWorld,* 25.

Rigney, S. (1995, October 10). The one for the road. *PC Magazine, 14*(17), 375–385.

Robertson, R. (1995, September 21). *Start me up (Version 2).* Unpublished presentation at the CARROCK 95 National Conference, Investigative Reporters and Editors and National Institute for Computer-Assisted Reporting, Cleveland, OH.

Russial, J. T. (1995, August). *Computers, ambivalence and the transformation of journalistic work.* Unpublished paper presented to the annual meeting of the Association for Education in Journalism and Mass Communication, Washington, DC.

Schroeder, E. (1995, September 4). 3-D gives business new view. *PC Week, 12*(35), 33.

Seese, D. (1995, September 21–24). *The* News & Observer *Wake schools reassignments lookup.* Unpublished presentation at the CARROCK 95 National Conference, Investigative Reporters and Editors and National Institute for Computer-Assisted Reporting, Cleveland, OH.

Semonche, B. P. (1993). Computer-assisted journalism. In B. P. Semonche (Ed.), *News media libraries: A management book* (pp. 265–316). Westport, CT: Greenwood.

Sidlo, S. (1995a, September 22). *Care and feeding of a computer-assisted reporting program: Management tips for making it work.* Unpublished presentation at the CARROCK 95 National Conference, Investigative Reporters and Editors and National Institute for Computer-Assisted Reporting, Cleveland, OH.

Sidlo, S. (1995b, September 22). *The Data Pages: InfoPLUS.* Unpublished presentation at the CARROCK 95 National Conference, Investigative Reporters and Editors and National Institute for Computer-Assisted Reporting, Cleveland, OH.

Stith, P. (1995, September 21). *Best database hits of the 80s and 90s.* Unpublished presentation at the CARROCK 95 National Conference, Investigative Reporters and Editors and National Institute for Computer-Assisted Reporting, Cleveland, OH.

Sullivan, D. (1995, March). Portables can do big jobs. *Uplink, 7*(3), 6.

Sylvester, E. (1995, September 22). *Bringing it all back home.* Unpublished presentation at the CARROCK 95 National Conference, Investigative Reporters and Editors and National Institute for Computer-Assisted Reporting, Cleveland, OH.

Tolhurst, W. A., Pike, M. A., Blanton, K. A., & Harris, J. R. (1994). *Using the Internet.* Indianapolis, IN: Que.

Walsh, M. (1995, September 22). *Computer-assisted reporting in smaller newsrooms.* Unpublished presentation at the CARROCK 95 National Conference, Investigative Reporters and Editors and National Institute for Computer-Assisted Reporting, Cleveland, OH.

Ward, J., & Hansen, K. A. (1996). *Search strategies in mass communication* (3rd ed.). New York: Longman.

Wendland, M. (1995a, October 26). *Rolodex program.* Unpublished posting, CARR-L <listserv@ulkyvm.louisville.edu>.

Wendland, M. (1995b, September 21). *Start me up (Version 2).* Unpublished presentation at the CARROCK 95 National Conference, Investigative Reporters and Editors and National Institute for Computer-Assisted Reporting, Cleveland, OH.

Wolfe, D. (1995, September 21–24). *Newsroom training at the* St. Petersburg Times: *A model: Empowering journalists for the worldwide electronic neighborhood.* Unpublished paper presented at the CARROCK 95 National Conference, Investigative Reporters and Editors and National Institute for Computer-Assisted Reporting, Cleveland, OH.

Index